P9-BZQ-485

Dynamics of
Intercultural
Communication

Dynamics of Intercultural Communication
Fifth Edition

Carley H. Dodd
Abilene Christian University

Boston, Massachusetts   Burr Ridge, Illinois   Dubuque, Iowa
Madison, Wisconsin   New York, New York   San Francisco, California   St. Louis, Missouri

McGraw-Hill

A Division of The McGraw·Hill Companies

DYNAMICS OF INTERCULTURAL COMMUNICATION

Copyright © 1998 by The McGraw-Hill Companies, Inc. All rights reserved. Previous editions 1982, 1987, 1991, and 1995 by Wm. C. Brown Communications, Inc. Printed in the United States of America. Except as permitted under the United States Copyright Act of 1976, no part of this publication may be reproduced or distributed in any form or by any means, or stored in a data base or retrieval system, without the prior written permission of the publisher.

♻ This book is printed on recycled paper containing 10% postconsumer waste.

6 7 8 9 10 QPF/QPF 0 5 4 3

ISBN 0-697-32725-6

Editorial director: *Phil Butcher*
Sponsoring editor: *Marge Byers*
Developmental editor: *Valerie Raymond*
Marketing manager: *Carl Leonard*
Project manager: *Ann Fuerste*
Production supervisor: *Sandra Hahn*
Designer: *Jeanne Calabrese*
Cover image: © *Susan Giamllombardo/SIS*
Photo research coordinator: *Carrie K. Burger*
Compositor: *Carlisle Communications, Ltd.*
Typeface: *10/12 Times Roman*
Printer: *Quebecor Printing Book Group/Fairfield*

Library of Congress Catalog Card Number: 97-70817

www.mhhe.com

Brief Contents

Contents

Chapter 7
Intercultural Communication and Nonverbal Messages   133

Part Four
Cultural Adaptation and Communication Effectiveness: Applying Intercultural Competencies   155

Chapter 8
Adapting to Culture   156

Chapter 9
Intercultural Communication Competencies Associated with Intercultural Effectiveness   172

Chapter 10
Intercultural Communication and Conflict   187

Preface

Intercultural communication is an exciting field of study in the many ways it explores cultural and group influence on communication. From the letters I have received and the meetings I have attended over the years inquiring about the earlier editions of this text, I have learned how experts from a variety of places and backgrounds use the intercultural communication principles contained in this text. It is rewarding to know of the contributions readers in turn are making to many people. Now in its fifth edition, this text represents an ongoing story of how people from diverse cultures communicate. In this edition you will find the usual updates on research and new concepts from the multiple areas associated with intercultural communication. We hope you like the changes in format, particularly the boxes within the text illustrating concepts discussed. We are also using endnotes for data references to aid in the flow of reading.

The examples and user-friendliness of the text continue to be positively evaluated by reviewers, students, and colleagues. They point to the communication concepts across cocultures along with the theories, principles, and skills needed for intercultural communication in macrocultures. When readers think of outcomes related to competency, preparation, and effectiveness, we hope they continue to turn to this text for those insights for themselves and their friends. To provide further insight into intercultural communication competencies, a number of models and self-evaluation scales are retained in relevant places in the chapters, in some cases, and in the appendix.

Finally, the central model for the book is employed throughout the text. The perception of difference or diversity motivates a drive toward intercultural competencies designed to create effectiveness in functional, intercultural communication. In dysfunctional, intercultural communication, the drive to deal with difference leads to distortion, withdrawal, hostility, alienation, and poor relationships. All this is explored in the text, but I think you will like the way the theme is carried in every chapter from the central, updated model in chapter 1.

Overall, this book explores cultural variability's influence in the communication process. This influence ranges widely. Consequently, this text covers a wide range of issues. The text attempts to blend faithfulness to research and insights from many other authors in a way that you can understand and use.

An instructor's manual is available, providing professors with a computer test bank, semester and quarterly daily syllabi, overviews, and numerous skills exercises. In this edition, like the last four editions, I have not hesitated to bring analogies, illustrations, and examples from my students as well as from research and consulting work that spans twenty-five years. This work has included field work in numerous countries and consultations with small and large groups including Fortune 500 organizations and private organizations. The data and experiences are broad and have taught me many lessons in my growth in attempting successful intercultural outcomes. Fortunately, I am still learning and look forward to exploring together these questions raised in the book. I hope you will observe a desire for cultural sensitivity, awakening, and empathy so badly needed when communicating in a culturally diverse world.

A number of people have been very helpful in developing various aspects of the book. Cecile Garmon, Richard Paine, Peggy Kirby, Diane Schwalm, and Gary Hughes uncovered a great deal of primary research for me in the first edition for which I am truly grateful. Reviewers of the first edition of the book in 1982 include Bill Gudykunst, Young Kim, Nemi Jain, and Jess Yoder. Second edition manuscript reviews were provided by Mara Adelman, Don Boggs, Carolyn Wilkins Fountenberry, Wallace Schmidt, and Andrew Wolvin. The reviewers for the third edition include Roger Conaway, Paul Lakey, Michael Prosser, and Curt Seimers. Thank you for the very helpful insights you provided and the specific suggestions you offered. The fourth edition reviewers and people with helpful comments include: Val Clark, Spokane Community College; Scherrie Foster, Minneapolis Community College; Janie Fritz, Duquesne University; Paul Frye, Trenton State College; and Sue Pendell, Colorado State University.

The fifth edition reviewers are Janie Harden Fritz, Duquesne University; Alan C. Harris, California State University, Northridge; Madeline M. Keaveney, California State University, Chico; Sara B. Pfaffenroth, County College of Morris; Carol S. Tan, State University of New York College at Brockport; and Fathi S. Yousef, California State University, Long Beach. Special thanks also goes to John Baldwin, Illinois State University for several contributions and points of feedback.

The staff at Brown and Benchmark have been fantastic. I appreciate their many hours of work and give special credit to Kassi Radomski and Michelle Kelley. I am sure there are others about whom I do not know whose tireless efforts contributed greatly. Also, I owe thanks to the staff and faculty at Abilene Christian University for their support and encouragement. Rachel Welborn has been a remarkable help in the last few days of detail work on the manuscript as well as for her computer graphics skills that she applied toward the model in chapter one.

I want to thank my parents, Carlysle (now deceased) and Leota Dodd, for the encouragement they have provided me all these years.

Most of all, I dedicate the book to my wife, Ada, who is my best friend and counselor, and to our children Jeremy, Matthew, Philip, and Jennifer. They sacrificed family time for me to complete this project and were noncomplaining cheerleaders throughout this project.

Carley H. Dodd
November, 1996

Part One

Introduction and Background to Intercultural Communication

Chapter 1

Overview to Intercultural Communication

OBJECTIVES   *After completing this chapter, you should be able to*

1. Define intercultural communication

2. Describe crucial elements within the intercultural communication process

3. Diagram and explain a model of intercultural communication

4. Identify the major variables involved as two persons or a group from differing cultural backgrounds communicate

5. Discuss conditions of intercultural communication among groups, identifying types of cultural differences engaging intercultural communication

6. Identify intercultural communication effectiveness outcomes

A U.S. government official in a conversation with the Minister of Education from a Latin American country offers aid to assist what the former calls "backward" regions of the nation. The Latin American smiles wistfully and continues to talk in a friendly and positive manner. Upon returning to her office in Washington, D.C., the U.S. official finds a scathing letter from the Latin American condemning her for her paternalistic attitudes. How did this communication fail?

The wife of a new foreign service officer in Sierra Leone, a country in West Africa, is just learning to buy in the local marketplaces. She returns from an afternoon of shopping, her feelings hurt, because owners of market booths shouted at her during their bargaining transaction. She considers this behavior insulting. Was there a misunderstanding?

An African American third-grade student from an inner-city school lowers his head and casts his eyes downward when his teacher looks at him. The teacher is insulted since the young man "refuses" to look at his teacher. What nonverbal communication aspect has been overlooked?

A top manager from Amoco in Houston goes to work for a branch office in Saudi Arabia. After spending two years of successful work, she returns to Houston but no one seems to listen to her ideas for improvements. She also has the feeling she is being passed over for a promotion. What has occurred in this case of cultural reentry?

Samuel is joining a management team for a Japanese car company doing business in his native Nigeria. After six months he becomes discouraged with what he considers lack of friendliness and concern among his Japanese supervisors. His management training in the United States encouraged quicker decisions and more rapid policy movement than he feels he is receiving from the Japanese organization. What cultural differences would you consider if Samuel called you for an intercultural communication consultation?

Yuko came to the United States one summer from her native Japan to attend graduate seminars. She liked the courses and decided to stay for a complete graduate degree. What troubled her was classroom informality and a sense of personal inadequacy as she frequently was asked to speak in class. What cultural adjustments would be proactive for Yuko or the classroom environment?

A Vietnam veteran seems withdrawn and distant to his family and old high school friends. They try to talk with him but consistently avoid the subject of the war. One by one, the veteran loses contact with these individuals. What dynamics are occurring?

These examples open this chapter to demonstrate the need for intercultural communication. The U.S. government official failed to recognize bias and arrogance exhibited toward other groups, for in this case, ethnocentrism was manifested in subtle messages and silent actions. The foreign service officer's wife has not learned her host culture's expectation and enjoyment over intensive bargaining. Rather than intending animosity toward her, that culture was practicing a form of social interaction. The third-grade teacher had not recognized important cultural reasons for the student's lack of eye contact. The student learned that looking away signifies respect for authority, but the teacher's culture emphasized respect by direct eye contact. The Japanese student's actions can be explained by cultural emphasis on proper behaviors, roles, and rules. The Vietnam veteran faces a prolonged cultural reentry adjustment. Sadly, his family and friends lacked the knowledge or skills to intervene effectively regarding his condition.

Intercultural communication involves building a common culture in order to be effective in tasks, relationships, and adaptation to a new culture.
© MCMXCI Charles Gupton/Tony Stone Worldwide, Ltd.

These examples of multiple cultural encounters highlight our theme of this intercultural communication book: culture influences communication. The study of intercultural communication recognizes how culture pervades what we are, how we act, how we think, and how we talk and listen. Richard Brislin indicates how not only are we *socialized* into a cultural context, but how culture influences our interaction along with many other areas such as work, gender expectations, and health.[1]

The field of human communication is rich in its many principles and theories concerning relationships and their connection to messages. Over time, communication theorists recognized the vast influence of culture as a primary variable in the communication process. This emphasis has led to theories and principles which now trace culture's socializing patterns and imprints related to intercultural encounters. Of course, this book's theme is to introduce the many cultural elements that influence communication where intercultural conditions develop.

In this book the term *intercultural communication* refers to the influence of cultural variability and diversity on interpersonally oriented communication outcomes. Differences in communication and social style, world view, customs, expectations, rules, roles, and myths illustrate a few of the elements that explain how culture shapes the communication process. Outcomes in this definition can refer to friendship, negotiation, information clarification, adjustment to a new culture, successful task completion, and developing positive interpersonal relationships in a new culture. Using this general definition as a framework, we would want to point out how encountering group or cultural differences initiates a communication pattern that can turn out to be constructive, or functional, and lead to positive outcomes, as we will indicate later. Sadly, some individuals encounter cultural differences and engage a dysfunctional experience that draws from negative attitudes and fails to structure positive relationship-building communication.

What are some foundational presuppositions that can help us understand this area of communication studies? Most intercultural researchers point to negative outcomes which draw attention to why we need intercultural knowledge and skills. Some of these negative outcomes include poor relationships, unclear message outcomes, lack of adjustment during cultural transitions, and poor task performance. What captures our imaginations to consider intercultural relations? What dynamic influences interaction when people from diverse cultures talk and listen? Is there a central point of theory or basic ground where we must first start our understanding of this process involving communication?

When we dig below the surface of what initiates the process in the first place, most intercultural scholars discuss an experience of "contrast." That is, you may interact with a person who in some ways seems contrasted to you. This idea of contrast has evoked a number of metaphors in the intercultural literature that describe a sense of chasm between people. Some of these over time have been applied: "cultural bridge," "intergroup relations," "intercultural encounters," "interracial communication," "intergroup conflict," "acculturation," "socialization," "social encounters," and so on. William Gudykunst and Young Kim and others apply the metaphor of *stranger* to these encounters with people perceived as "different from me."[2]

What many of these descriptions have in common is the term we will use for this book, *perceived cultural differences*. The phrase is not all that exotic, but the term *perceived cultural difference* (or PCD) underscores diversity in features illustrated by differences in world view, values, thought process, customs, appearance, expectations, communicator style, verbal behavior, and nonverbal communication. These are qualities we often encounter. In turn, they galvanize our inquiry if not deeper human drives to resolve uncertainty, sometimes anxiety, experienced when facing diversity. Interaction with someone from a contrasting group background is inescapable in today's world. Such encounters initiate a person into a state of some degree of needing knowledge and skills. How do I manage myself in the presence of diversity? Do I know what to say or how to behave in a new environment? Effective intercultural communication occurs when the PCD motivates or involves some form of accommodation to engage the resulting uncertainty and anxiety. Adjusting, appealing to commonality, and exercising cultural sensitivity represent few functional, intercultural coping skills. Reinforcing bigotry, negative stereotyping, denial, and withdrawal illustrate dysfunctional pathways to intercultural communication.

All this may become more familiar to you, if you take a moment and consider the many encounters you find in college, at work, at places of worship, in neighborhoods. Is there a perceived difference with a person from another region of the country where accent and values might seem dissimilar? Is a person of color perceived to be "different" from a white anglo? How comfortable is their initial and later communication? Are physically challenged individuals usually included in group activities of people who are not physically challenged? When a Generation X teen meets a 45-year-old Baby Boomer, what perception of difference might erupt? Is their nonverbal manner the same? In the presence of significant similarity, we can share common experiences, perhaps use jargon that we both understand, talk freely, and feel relatively comfortable. When faced with dissimilarity, we must listen and speak with a cultural consciousness. That is why

Presuppositions and Theory: The Genesis of Intercultural Encounters

The Story of Strangers Meeting

I offer a personal illustration to make the point of how we deal with uncertainty. I was out jogging on a half-moonlit, half-cloudy night and thought the sometimes deserted road was all mine. When two dark figures seemed to come out of nowhere, I confess I felt a slight uncertainty. (Who were these people? I've never seen them before.) An accompanying moderate anxiety developed. (What are they doing out here? Should I be worried?) I quickly moved to the other side of the road, but as I got closer I realized they were husband and wife joggers. When they spoke with an enthusiastic "Good evening," my anxiety disappeared. The uncertainty was reduced, and, smiling, I chugged down my beaten neighborhood path. The dissimilarity I felt (maybe they were muggers) gave way to similarity (I don't know where they are from but who cares—they are fellow joggers into the culture of lowered heart rates and improved HDL ratios. It's okay. They are like me.).

Source: C. Dodd, "Reflections on cultural encounters," 1997

---

at first conversing interculturally is awkward. Why? Culture differences obscure "certainty" and produce a form of psychological discomfort from this ambiguity.

Therefore, if we have to choose a single, precipitating factor resting in the realm of presupposition and theory to explain why intercultural communication even happens in the first place, we choose the phrase "perceived cultural difference." Not only does this concept appear to capture a common thread in many intercultural descriptions, but the phrase is easy and useful. It should serve our purpose throughout the book as we explore a rich set of concepts carefully selected to provide readers with knowledge and skill to use in intercultural relations situations.

A Model of Intercultural Communication

The model of intercultural communication presented here extends the definition and presupposition of PCD indicated above. In preview, the model (figure 1.1) and the text to follow (1) indicate that culture is only one source explaining why people perceive differences, (2) describe the dynamics of PCDs as they motivate drives to reduce uncertainty and anxiety, (3) illustrate how we can develop functional or dysfunctional approaches to resolving the presence of diversity, (4) show that originating a third culture C provides a common ground for developing relationship-building strategies, (5) underscore how we can utilize several simple but powerful intercultural insights and skills, and (6) reveal desired positive intercultural outcomes. In sum, the model is an adaptive model, calling for participants to suspend judgment and bias while they engage in a third culture created by the intercultural participants to explore mutual goals and common concerns. In other words, out of a perception of dissimilarity, participants A and B can carve out a third culture between them, a culture of similarity.[3]

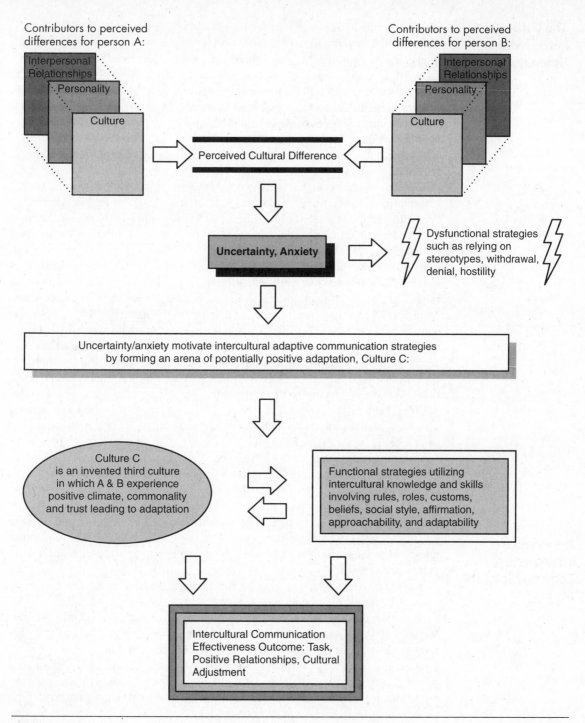

Contributors to perceived differences for person A:

Interpersonal Relationships

Personality

Culture

Contributors to perceived differences for person B:

Interpersonal Relationships

Personality

Culture

Perceived Cultural Difference

Uncertainty, Anxiety

Dysfunctional strategies such as relying on stereotypes, withdrawal, denial, hostility

Uncertainty/anxiety motivate intercultural adaptive communication strategies by forming an arena of potentially positive adaptation, Culture C:

Culture C is an invented third culture in which A & B experience positive climate, commonality and trust leading to adaptation

Functional strategies utilizing intercultural knowledge and skills involving rules, roles, customs, beliefs, social style, affirmation, approachability, and adaptability

Intercultural Communication Effectiveness Outcome: Task, Positive Relationships, Cultural Adjustment

Figure 1.1

Model of intercultural communication.

The Causes of Perceived Difference

Obviously, this book isolates on the major cause of perceived differences as indicated above. As you will read later in this chapter, numerous large and small cultural contexts illuminate the many times you might experience PCDs. Also, we acknowledge many factors within a person's culture that are actively influencing the communication. Intercultural communication indicates what to do when we encounter these differences, not just their existence. However, our model acknowledges two other sources of perceived differences that are not always directly related to culture.

A second cause of perceived differences emerging in a relationship can be attributed to personality differences. There are many ways to describe these differences captured in phrase such as "communicator style," "social style," "interaction expectation," "interpersonal differences," "rules perspectives," "coordinated management of meaning," and many others.[4] Of course, personality and communicator style sometimes interlock with culture. Consider the reserved nonverbal manner of a Japanese individual who prefers to go unnoticed in a crowd believing "the nail that sticks up gets hit." Contrast this personal style with an assertive North American who believes public recognition relates to success. In this interaction, acceptable and perhaps expected communication behaviors can be perceived as mutually offensive. The U.S. dominant cultural person who insists on handshaking and backslapping within a nontouching culture, such as the Laotian culture, may find that his or her personality type is repugnant to Laotians. Each student of intercultural communication must learn as much as possible about ideal roles and cultural expectations. We are not trying to argue here for why personality emerges, for that debate is beyond the scope of this book. We recognize that culture and personality may interact jointly or that personality may stand alone uniquely leading to people liking or disliking each other. In any case, culture cannot be said to be a single cause of perceived difference.

A third cause of perceived difference is relationship attraction. All of us have "yardsticks" by which we evaluate an interactant in communication. This perception of another person falls into several domains. Is this relationship of potential worth? Does this person present risk for me? Power over me? Is there believability? Have I been hurt by this person? Attraction? These and other questions point out how we can perceive difference in relationships apart from cultural differences.

In other words, what social or personal attributions do I make about my relationship? Perhaps my history with a person affects my feelings of difference. For most people, these personal histories of relationships color our perceptions of difference. Typically, previously unsatisfactory relationship signals significant difference, divergence not necessarily related to culture. If another person seems to hold little importance or attraction for you, how likely is your motivation to approach, bridge the gap, accommodate, and engage in the process of communicating? Common relationship orientation revolves around interpersonal attraction, group attraction, social network potential, similarity, credibility, opinion leading relationships, and the perception of an interpersonal relationship on communication outcomes. Again, a point here is that we can account for perceived differences in ways besides culture.

We turn again to the question of the nature of culture as a cause of perceived differences, or PCDs. To preview the idea, we will see how PCD creates "blind spots," which filter our potential relationships. Rather than seeing another person from a "different" culture in terms of similarity, many people are trapped in biases, misunderstanding, arrogance, labels, and negative stereotypes. In the presence of cultural difference, the human system beckons communicators into some form of action.

The experience of interfacing with cultural difference motivates many individuals to close the dissimilarity gap and connect with the encounter. Two reasons account for the onset of this motivational tendency for many people. One response is *uncertainty,* that is, a belief or opinion leaving us primarily with a sense of being unsure of what to think, do, or feel. Often, information alone is needed to fill in the gaps. Sometimes, knowledge and skills assist this sense of not being sure. A second response is *anxiety* which is an emotional response based in fear. That is, a person experiences some degree of fright in an intercultural encounter. As you might have thought already, uncertainty or anxiety can be experienced in combination as well as uniquely.

Thus, the questions and emotions we experience in the presence of cultural "difference" ignite the intercultural communication process by fueling a drive to know another person and do something. In turn, we draw from our cultural and personal identities to estimate something about this new person. In the perceived difference "scanning," we may forecast ahead and call on highly functional, adaptive skills in our communication, without which relationships remain indifferent, warped, or hostile.

We would divert too far from our purpose to address fully the theoretical reasons underlying this motive or drive. We could discuss our coming to grips with diversity because of dissonance and consistency theories, or a version of drive theory. These are no doubt important explanations, but whatever the theoretical reason, one simple fact remains. Perceiving cultural difference inherently implies that we assess others internally, as if to measure according to a scale of similarity or dissimilarity. Scholars call this process *social categorization.* It stimulates individuals to attribute names, labels, and consequent positive or negative communication toward another person. When social categorization turns negative, it becomes a source of racism, bigotry, intolerance, ethnocentrism, and prejudice.

One way of solving the uncertainty or anxiety leads to *dysfunctional* strategies, as for instance when the drive leads toward ignoring another person, pretending to like someone, avoiding communication responsibility, or outright hostility. A goal of this text is to lead readers toward *functional* strategies. The necessary knowledge and skill is developed in each chapter throughout the book. Taken holistically, these concepts and skills are based on desired outcomes scholars typically associate with effective intercultural communication. We might call these competency-based intercultural communication outcomes. Competent intercultural communication users apply their awareness of cultural variability and rules, an adaptive style, and a motivation for positive relationships to facilitate their reaching goals of effective outcomes.

To arrive at those outcomes, successful intercultural practitioners instructed by research in this area agree on a crucial step illustrated in the model.

Macrocultural differences refer to national and regional cultural factors, illustrated by this Masai tribal man. Photo by Mike Moore, Kenya.

An *adaptive culture,* culture C, is invented by each participant A and B whereby they put aside their A and B culture in order to emphasize common ground. At the moment of encounter, they focus on the construction of this new culture shared between them. They do not necessarily merge their identities from A into B or B into A, but create an arena of commonality at least for the time they need to communicate. In this way, each can maintain identity with A or B but operate in C as demands dictate.

The idea of a third culture is not new; researchers for some time have viewed some form of merging, commonality, or coalescing as an important strategy.[5] In the model developed for this text, we build on the new culture concept and associate it with antecedent drives and motivation leading to the creation of culture C and we explore the consequent and associated knowledge and skills occurring within the interaction of C's promise to lead ultimately to outcome success. Almost everyone develops an adaptive style or set of procedures when faced with uncertainty or anxiety. We recognize maladaptive or dysfunctional behaviors in culture C, but we identify other adaptive or functional cultural behaviors and their association with intercultural effectiveness outcomes.

To make the new culture a functional adaptive arena is not automatic. Several concepts and skills help us understand how to make culture C successful. Three principles are important in developing a successful interaction in culture C between A and B.

First, there must be a positive *feeling* toward the other person or group (referred to as the affective level), such as trust, comfort, safety, affirmation, or lowered anxiety. Without this feeling—that one is regarded as worthy and can experience mistakes without being ridiculed or ignored—a person is less likely to communicate well with another who is different. Moreover, adjustment and effectiveness in a new culture may be lessened or prolonged or may never occur at all.

The second area needed to make a successful third culture climate involves recognizing the *beliefs* we bring to intercultural encounters (frequently called the cognitive level). These include expectations, uncertainties (because of things we do not yet know about a person or a lack of accurate observation), misunderstanding of rules or procedures, lacking appropriate strategy to exercise communication competency, and activation of cues that trigger negative or positive social cognitions (such as stereotypes and attributions). Without accurate understanding a person is less likely to communicate well with another who is different.

A final area needed to build the third culture is intercultural communication *actions.* This means developing actions and skills (called the behavioral level), such as verbal and nonverbal communication performance, survival skills, and interfacing with systems and institutions in a new culture. When Marie, an American student spending a semester in Jerusalem, asked the hotel clerk to change a broken light in her room, she was surprised when he smiled and handed her the replacement bulb. She said later, "I guess I expected the Holiday Inn, where they would fix it for you. I didn't even know where to get a ladder." The light bulb went unchanged. Her expectations and failure to perform to their expectations led to ineffectiveness.

In sum, taken together, these three principles constitute intercultural competence. That is, using the right affective, cognitive, and behavioral patterns are essential qualities leading to effectiveness. These occur in the nonthreatening climate established in culture C.

Moving Toward Intercultural Effectiveness

From the adaptive culture C positive and effective intercultural outcomes can result. These do not happen by accident, but normally results from serious attempts to apply intercultural knowledge and skills. Positive feelings, beliefs, and actions set the stage for acceptance and significant groundwork in culture C. But specific skills and application of knowledge moves us directly from the third culture C to experience outcomes defined by scholars as "intercultural effectiveness." At the core of intercultural effectiveness is task effectiveness, relationship effectiveness, and adaptation effectiveness. These are developed in detail in a later chapter in the text, but suffice it for this discussion of the model to note these fundamental outcomes.

The Failure to Engage Culture C

The affective, cognitive, and behavior process in building a successful third culture C is well illustrated in the case of Kaoru (not her real name), a Japanese woman who at twenty-two married an American serviceman. At the time, she felt a need to disengage from her traditional roots. However, she now sees that her marriage was symbolic of her need for autonomy, although she loved her husband. Her parents, steeped in tradition, not only rejected the marriage, they rejected Kaoru. At first, the consequences seemed mild—after all, she was with the man she loved and would find a new life in America. Over time, the consequences were severe.

After some twenty years, Kaoru still knows very little English, engages little with non-Japanese and with only a handful of Japanese, is frequently depressed, and remains secluded from the U.S. culture. At first, it appears that the loss of parental support accounts for her trouble, but deeper examination reveals that she never felt safe in her new culture. Despite efforts by many people, she never developed positive feelings interacting with anyone. Her insecurity was only worsened by negative attitudes she held toward Americans in general. What is more, no one encouraged her development of language skills or of basic survival skills, despite numerous opportunities by Japanese and non-Japanese acquaintances. She never embraced friends, group members, and institutions that would have welcomed her.

Source: Case study from interview, name withheld, 1995.

Contexts for Intercultural Communication

As we will discuss in chapter 3, culture is the "summation and interrelationship of an identifiable group's beliefs, norms, activities, institutions, and communication patterns." Every culture has world view, themes, thought process, expectations, values, modalities, procedures, rules, roles, appearance and material, language and interaction principles, and nonverbal behaviors. With its kaleidoscopic shapes and colors, culture lies at the root of communication impact. When we think of culture, we must not be restricted by narrow cultural definitions. Rather, it is more helpful to observe many group contexts where the metaphor "culture" aptly describes the system under consideration.

Macrocultural systems. Obviously, there are large global regions and national cultures that are structurally and organically bound together into a social system where people have developed a cultural network. Examples include what might be globally described as North American culture, Latin American culture, African culture, Middle Eastern culture, European culture, and Asian culture. These global differences, marked by geopolitical factors and national identity, fit into the study of cultural influence on communication.

Microcultures and cocultures.   The term microculture, used interchangeably with coculture and diversity culture in this text, is a collectivity with conscious identity and grouping coexisting within a larger culture. Microcultures, or cocultures, often experience common themes regarding image, bonding, and association.

Microcultures of social and ethnic identification.   Most people belong to a number of groups, some voluntary, some by birth, adoption, or selection into those groups. Salient groups—the ones we consciously value—provide a source of identity. Structurally, these are microcultures or cocultures within a macroculture. A person might identify an elderly microculture, a cowboy microculture, an Appalachian microculture, or a volunteer association microculture. Each group exhibits some similarities to the large culture, but also some differences. Microcultures of identification are often defined by class, education, age, religion, wealth, residence, work, family, and gender. The significance of social identity groups lies in their saliency for any one individual. For instance, your friend might not find much use for a civic club that you enjoy.

Heritage cultures involve common origins, race, or family ties. Ethnic groups are identifiable bodies of people noted for their common heritage and cultural tradition, which are often national. *Interethnic communication* is communication between two or more persons from different ethnic backgrounds. Although any listing of ethnic heritage is certain to omit some significant group, the following exemplify ethnic groups in the United States: Native American, Polish American, Italian American, Irish American, African American, Asian American, Mexican American, and Puerto Rican American. *Interracial communication* is communication between two or more persons of differing racial backgrounds. Whether or not you agree with the current debate about the usefulness or harm of the construct "race," the important conflicts involving racial differences are real. At one university, an administrator in the office of student affairs argued in a meeting with an African American fraternity leader. Only after a cooling-off period did both men realize and freely admit that their racial differences had produced an immediate and mutually negative response in each, even before either had spoken a word.

The conceptual baggage we often carry with us, such as stereotypes of other racial groups, can easily blind us to the fact that, in many instances, few significant differences exist between two people. Real cultural differences do not always exist beyond ethnicity and race—we simply magnify the immediate through stereotypes.

Countercultures.   Countercultural communication involves persons of cocultures who in some form oppose a dominant host culture. Prosser defines it as "interaction between members of a subcultural or cultural group whose members largely are alienated from the dominant culture. Members of the group not only reject the values of the dominant culture or society, but may actively work against these values. Conflict is often the result."[6]

Prosser also cites an example of the Amish, a coculture whose members have reacted passively, withdrawing from the dominant culture. Several years ago before the fall of the Russian Empire, Polish laborers, without historical precedent and risking retribution from the Soviet Union's anti-strike policies, went on a well-publicized strike to seek to free labor unions from government control. Many of the communication encounters that followed could be considered countercultural types of intercultural communication, at least in terms of rejecting establishment values existing up to that time.

Communication between social classes.   Some of the differences between people are based on status inferred from income, occupation, and education. Communication between these classes is appropriately labeled social class communication. There is a large gap in many parts of the world between the elite and the masses as well as between the rich and the poor. Often accompanying this gap are significant differences in outlook, customs, and other features. Although these social classes share some aspects of a common culture, their differences become a cultural concern.

Rural-urban communication.   Rural and urban lifestyles are noted for differences in pace of life, world view, values, philosophy, and interpersonal relationship formation among other qualities. These differences represent communication styles and functional differences in communication when rural and urban individuals interact.

Regional communication.   People from one region of the United States sometimes encounter communication differences with people from another region. A reserved New Englander is sometimes put off by a syrupy-sweet southern style of communication because he takes it to be a sign of insincerity. On the other hand, a southerner may interpret the reserved style of her northern friend as a sign of rudeness.

Gender communication.   Evidence confirms how communication patterns markedly differ between men and women. From examples in management to cases in families, data bases and scholarly literature remind us of male and female cocultures. The different communication styles of males and females can be a source of enormous interpersonal misunderstanding. An understanding of the cultural differences involved can improve intercultural skills.

Organizational cultural communication.   Another kind of cultural communication context in which most of us interact is called organizational culture. Most organizations can be described by many of the same elements of macrocultures. Such systems incorporate accompanying norms, procedures, customs, rules, communication patterns, and other elements which profoundly influence interaction among organizational members. The culture influences how they interact with people from other organizational cultures. For instance, an organization that emphasizes task and performance above other factors will likely experience some frustration in communication with an organization that has a more laid-back approach emphasizing personal relationships. One of the discoveries in the field of intercultural relations is that individuals who adhere to organizational cultural norms are vastly influenced by their systems.

Family cultures.   Families are cultural systems also. Researchers like Galvan and Brommel have adapted family systems models and expanded them to identify unique communication patterns resulting primarily from the family system. Other scholars explain a number of communication and relationship outcomes developing in concert with family culture.[7]

The text is organized around the model presented in this chapter. By nature of its topic, the book elevates cultural variability by introducing intercultural communication in part 1 (chapters 1–2), by underscoring the many elements of culture in part 2 (chapters 3–5); by indicating linguistic and nonverbal aspects of intercul- ture communication in part 3 (chapters 6–7), by pointing out the numerous ways to adapt to intercultural differences and relationships through intercultural com- petency skills and strategies in part 4 (chapters 8–10), and by focusing on factors influencing social change in part 5 (chapters 11–13). The multiple topics presented in this text are intended to help the reader account for the dysfunctional and func- tional adaptive qualities of intercultural communication and to discover what works well in practicing competent intercultural communication.

One reason for explaining the philosophy, theory, model, and contexts for in- tercultural communication early in your reading is that each chapter to follow pre- sents material that explores some aspect of the central model presented in this chapter. We hope readers can visualize where sections and chapter topics fit by re- ferring back to the "big picture" once in a while.

The scholarly resources for each chapter are conveniently listed as endnotes at the end of each chapter. The end of each chapter also has insights and skill building suggestions as a method of encouraging intercultural communication preparation.

Developing Skills in Preparing for Intercultural Communication

1. *Try to be a facilitator with people.* Another skill that can be helpful in inter- cultural relations is the ability to link persons. By simple introductions, by em- phasis on their commonalities, and by staying with people long enough, we can serve an important liaison role. Sometimes, just knowing the right questions to ask can spotlight others in a positive way. You do not have to be glib or effer- vescent, just sincere and willing to invest time and energy in others.

2. *Own the first steps of your responsibility.* Many people simply avoid the sometimes difficult task of communicating with someone from a culture dif- ferent from their own. Assuming the burden for making this attempt is an im- portant first step in improving intercultural communication.

3. *Work on developing a theory-oriented mind-set.* Part of a theory-oriented mind- set includes looking for single and multiple causes and effects, ascertaining so- cial and historical forces behind the origination of a new concept, and creating new concepts. Reasoning, looking for and analyzing facts, synthesizing, and of- fering critiques are important skills for the intercultural communication process.

4. *Develop fluency in speech.* Surprisingly, many people find that their communica- tion skills need improving going from what they think to articulating their thoughts ("I know what I think—I just can't say it."). The ability to develop com- munication of concept and to express that diversity is important. We must explain our meanings in more than one way, especially during intercultural communica- tion. Forcing ourselves into multiple ways of describing our feelings, thoughts, and behaviors is a step in initiating improved intercultural communication skills.

5. *See success with people as success in task.* Effective intercultural communi- cation involves more than getting a job accomplished. Communication rela- tionships must be initiated and cultivated along with our task orientation.

This Chapter in Perspective

Successful intercultural communication converts the drives of perceived dissimilarity (between culture A and B) into applying intercultural competency as part of an adaptive third culture (culture C) leading to communication accommodation strategies ultimately leading to intercultural effectiveness outcomes.

Intercultural communication involves understanding the influence of culture, personal communicator style, and interpersonal relationship attributes as these affect intercultural communication and perception of difference. These factors influence two people in building a third culture or communication climate from which they find commonality, reduce uncertainty and anxiety, and provide a context basis for continued communication. This third culture C is an adaptive area, leading to accommodation strategies for intercultural effectiveness. It is important to discover the imprint of culture on communication.

You may not live in Pongo-Pongo, but you may live in Chicago, in a rural area of the United States, or in a region of the United States culturally different from the place where you grew up. Intercultural communication should, therefore, encompass a number of dimensions where culture and communication come together.

Exercises

1. How have recent trends in terrorism affected foreign travel? Perceptions toward other nations? How are people who are from different countries affected?

2. Interview an international student on changing patterns of communication style within his or her country. What are the differences in communication style between that person's home culture and the current culture in which he or she lives?

3. On your own, read another intercultural communication book. Scan and list all of the assumptions about communication that you can find in the book. What do you see?

4. Conduct an internet search or scan news sources for bias toward ethnic or social identification groups. How can you spot these reflections? How can you define them? What words or symbols would you use to alter perceptions of these groups if you were writing the newspaper story?

Endnotes

1. See Richard Brislin, *Understanding Culture's Influence on Behavior,* 2d ed. (Orlando: Harcourt Brace Jovanovich, 1993).

2. William B. Gudykunst and Young Yun Kim, *Communicating with Strangers* (New York: Random House, 1984); William B. Gudykunst and Tsukasa Nishida, "Theoretical Perspectives for Studying

Intercultural Communication," in *Handbook of International and Intercultural Communication,* ed. Molefi Kete Asante and William B. Gudykunst (Newbury Park, Calif.: Sage, 1989).

3. This approach is rooted in several rich communication research traditions. Uncertainty reduction theory, discussed by communication scholars, Charles R. Berger and R. J. Calabrese, "Some Explorations in Initial Interactions and Beyond," *Human Communication Research* 1 (1975): 99–112, has been applied to intercultural conditions; William B. Gudykunst and Mitchell Hammer, "Strangers and Hosts: An Uncertainty Reduction Theory of Intercultural Adaptation," in *Cross-Cultural Adaptation: Current Approaches,* ed. Young Y. Kim and William B. Gudykunst (Newbury Park, Calif.: Sage, 1988); William B. Gudykunst and Tsukasa Nishida, "Theoretical Perspectives for Studying Intercultural Communication," in *Handbook of International and Intercultural Communication,* ed. Molefi Kete Asante and William B. Gudykunst (Newbury Park, Calif.: Sage, 1989); Gudykunst and Kim, see note 2. Third culture building has been a topic in the field explored by Fred L. Casmir, *Intercultural and International Communication* (Washington, D.C.: University Press of America, 1978); Fred L.Casmir, "Introduction: Culture, Communication, and Education," *Communication Education* 40 (1991): 229–34; William B. Gudykunst, Richard I. Wiseman, and Mitch R. Hammer, "Determinants of a Sojourner's Attitudinal Satisfaction," in *Communication Yearbook* 1, ed. Brent Ruben (New Brunswick, N.J.: Transaction, 1977); W. G. Ouchi and A. M. Jaeger, "Made in America Under Japanese Management," *Harvard Business Review* 52 (1974): 61–69; and Philip R. Harris and Robert T. Moran, *Managing Cultural Differences,* 3d ed. (Houston: Gulf, 1991). The concept has elements from what is called coordinated management of meaning (called CMM), where people are said to develop rules and accommodations to the unique social encounters they experience; W. Barnett Pearce and Richard Wiseman, "Rules Theories: Varieties, Limitations, and Potentials," in *Intercultural Communication Theory: Current Perspectives,* ed. William B. Gudykunst (Beverly Hills, Calif.: Sage, 1983); Vernon E. Cronen and Robert Shuter, "Forming Intercultural Bonds," in *Intercultural Communication Theory: Current Perspectives,* ed. William B. Gudykunst (Beverly Hills, Calif.: Sage, 1983); Vernon E. Cronen, V. Chen, and W. Barnett Pearce, "Coordinated Management of Meaning," in *Theories in Intercultural Communication,* ed. Young Y. Kim and William B. Gudykunst (Newbury Park, Calif.: Sage, 1988). Research in intercultural accommodation and adjustment has been useful; Young Y. Kim, *Communication and Cross-Cultural Adaptation: An Integrative Theory* (Avon, England: Multilingual Matters, 1988); Young Y. Kim, "Intercultural Adaptation," in *Handbook of International and Intercultural Communication,* ed. Molefi Kete Asante and William B. Gudykunst (Newbury Park, Calif: Sage, 1989), *Theories in Intercultural Communication,* ed. Young Y. Kim and William B. Gudykunst, (Newbury Park, Calif.: Sage, 1988); Paul Lakey, "Communication/Social Difficulty of Thai Students in the Process of Cultural Adaptation" (Ph.D. dissertation, University of Oklahoma, 1988); as well as research in newly emerging fields of adolescent and family accommodation and development; David Lewis, Carley Dodd, and Darryl Tippens, *Shattering the Silence* (Nashville: Christian Communications, 1989); David Lewis, Carley Dodd, and Darryl Tippens, *Dying to Tell: The Hidden Meaning of Adolescent Substance Abuse* (Abilene, Tex.: Abilene Christian University Press, 1992). Intercultural competency and effectiveness has been an illuminating area for intercultural communication; Mitchell R. Hammer, "Intercultural Communication Competence," in *Handbook of International and Intercultural Communication,* ed. Molefi Kete Asante and William B. Gudykunst (Newbury Park, Calif.: Sage, 1989); Richard Wiseman and H. Abe, "Finding and Exploring Differences: A Reply to Gudykunst and Hammer," *International Journal of Intercultural Relations* 8 (1984): 185–99; Huber Ellingsworth, "Adaptive Intercultural Communication," in *Intercultural Communication Theory: Current Perspectives,* ed. William B. Gudykunst (Beverly Hills, Calif.: Sage, 1983); Myron Lustig and Jolene Koester, *Intercultural Competence,* 2d ed. (New York: Harper Collins, 1996); Daniel Kealey, "A Study of Cross Cultural Effectiveness: Theoretical Issues, Practical Applications," *International Journal of Intercultural Relations* 13 (1989): 387–428. Other communication theory perspectives have been significant as well including homophily theory, Everett M. Rogers, *Diffusion of Innovations,* 4th ed. (New York: Free Press, 1995); rhetorical theory, Michael H.

Prosser, ed. *Intercommunication among Nations and Peoples* (New York: Harper and Row, 1973); Michael H. Prosser, *The Cultural Dialogue* (Boston: Houghton Mifflin, 1978); Jolene Koester and Carl Holmberg, "Returning to Rhetoric," in *Intercultural Communication Theory: Current Perspectives,* ed. William B. Gudykunst (Beverly Hills, Calif.: Sage, 1983); Barbara Monfils, "The Critical Perspective in Intercultural Communication," (paper presented to the Speech Communication Association, New York, November, 1980); Bernard Blackman, "Toward a Grounded Theory," in *Intercultural Communication Theory: Current Perspectives,* ed. William B. Gudykunst (Beverly Hills, Calif.: Sage, 1983); constructivism as it relates to perception and social categorization, James Applegate and Howard Sypher, "A Constructivist Outline," in *Intercultural Communication Theory: Current Perspectives,* ed. William B. Gudykunst (Beverly Hills, Calif.: Sage, 1983); James Applegate and Howard Sypher, "A Constructivist Theory of Communication and Culture," in *Theories in Intercultural Communication,* ed. Young Y. Kim and William B. Gudykunst (Newbury Park, Calif.: Sage, 1988); Fred L. Casmir, "Stereotypes and Schemata," in *Communication, Culture, and Organizational Processes,* ed. William B. Gudykunst, Lea P. Stewart, and Stella Ting-Tommey (Newbury Park, Calif.: Sage, 1985); William B. Gudykunst and Lauren I. Gumbs, "Social Cognition and Intergroup Communication," in *Handbook of International and Intercultural Communication,* ed. Molefi Kete Asante and William B. Gudykunst (Newbury Park, Calif.: Sage, 1989); C. Gallois, A. Franklyn-Stokes, H. Giles, and N. Coupland, "Communication Accommodation in Intercultural Encounters," in *Theories in Intercultural Communication,* ed. Young Y. Kim and William B. Gudykunst (Newbury Park, Calif.: Sage, 1988); Peter Ehrenhaus, "Culture and the Attribution Process: Barriers to Effective Communication," in *Intercultural Communication Theory: Current Perspectives,* ed. William B. Gudykunst (Beverly Hills, Calif.: Sage, 1983); and face-saving and conflict management, Stella Ting-Toomey, "Toward a Theory of Conflict and Culture," in *Communication, Culture, and Organizational Processes,* ed. William B. Gudykunst, Lea P. Stewart, and Stella Ting-Toomey (Newbury Park, Calif.: Sage, 1985); Stella Ting-Toomey, "Identity and Interpersonal Bonding," in *Handbook of International and Intercultural Communication,* ed. Molefi Kete Asante and William B. Gudykunst (Newbury Park, Calif.: Sage, 1989).

4. Rules and roles theory is reflected in the work of several authors, including Young Y. Kim, *Communication and Cross-Cultural Adaptation: An Integrative Theory* (Avon, England: Multilingual Matters, 1988).

5. Fred L. Casmir, *Intercultural and International Communication* (Washington, D.C.: University Press of America, 1978); Fred L. Casmir, "Introduction: Culture, Communication, and Education," in *Communication Education* 40 (1991): 229–34; William B. Gudykunst, Richard I. Wiseman, and Mitch R. Hammer, "Determinants of a Sojourner's Attitudinal Satisfaction," in *Communication Yearbook* 1, ed. Brent Ruben (New Brunswick, N.J.: Transaction, 1977); W. G. Ouchi and A. M. Jaegar, "Made in America Under Japanese Management," *Harvard Business Review* 52 (1974) 61–69; Philip R. Harris and Robert T. Moran, *Managing Cultural Differences,* 4th ed. (Houston: Gulf, 1995).

6. Michael H. Prosser, *The Cultural Dialogue* (Boston: Houghton Mifflin, 1978).

7. Kathleen M. Galvin and B. J. Brommel, *Family Communication: Cohesion and Change,* 4th ed. (Glenview, Ill.: Scott Foresman, 1996); Judy Pearson, *Communication in the Family,* 2d ed. (New York: Harper and Row, 1993); David Lewis, Carley Dodd, and Darryl Tippens, *Dying to Tell: The Hidden Meaning of Adolescent Substance Abuse* (Abilene, Tex.: Abilene Christian University Press, 1992).

Chapter 2

Exploring Fundamental Axioms of Intercultural Communication

OBJECTIVES   *After completing this chapter, you should be able to*

1. Identify the axioms and presuppositions associated with intercultural messages

2. Distinguish between content and relationship dimensions of an intercultural communication situation

3. Describe the interpersonal attribution process and specific negative outcomes associated with PCDs in intercultural communication

4. Discuss a brief history accounting for aspects of the development of the field of intercultural communication

This chapter continues part 1 of the book's background to intercultural communication, continuing with assumptions about intercultural communication and concluding with a selected history of the development of intercultural communication. This chapter explores beginning points, called *axioms,* that form the foundational principles concerning intercultural communication. We think part of critical thinking and ultimately creativity build on the understanding of what assumptions lie behind a discipline, what theories explain it, and how such a field originated. We feel sure that the ideas described in this chapter are only beginning points, hopefully anchored to your interests and just as hopefully stimulating enough for you to investigate more of these assumptions from other sources.

Axioms Associated with Intercultural Communication

Intercultural Communication Assumes Perceived Cultural Difference

These axioms remind us how important it is to examine why we think about and act toward individuals and groups as we do.

Communication existing in a climate of cultural differences presupposes a range of intercultural principles. As chapter 1 documents and explains in some detail, PCDs (perceived cultural differences) assume that individuals are likely to encounter dissimilarity in some dimension. Consequently, messages and interaction between individuals or groups from two different cultural situations proceed with a number of antecedents and consequences to that interaction, as explained earlier. It is the bridging of the intercultural gap that gives intercultural communication its fullest meaning.

First, PCD implies a principle that people may not immediately share norms, thought patterns, structures, and systems. Thus, that cultural differences intervene in communication is part of the rationale behind the field of intercultural communication. In retrospect, researchers realized that the assumption of difference influenced research efforts to isolate cultural comparisons. These *cross-cultural communication* studies produced a data base of knowledge and understanding. In more recent years, researchers have concentrated less on the study of cultural differences

---

INTERCULTURAL INSIGHT

The Value of Difference

The difference, once recognized, can motivate positive or negative "drives." Successful intercultural relationships recognize differences as resources. An exact copy of ourselves can prove only to multiply our own flaws—the differences of others can provide a renewed resource of insight.

Seeing "difference" is a central facet to intercultural communication. We perceive difference—some would say a decision of similarity or dissimilarity—in one of three screening filters by which communicators size up each other: differences in culture or group, differences in personality, and differences in their view of a particular interpersonal relationship.

---

and comparisons in favor of the interaction between two individuals or groups. As Kim once indicated, to get to the point of contact and communication defines more exactly intercultural communication.[1]

Second, PCD explains two kinds of communication tendencies, involving drives or motivations as you saw in chapter 1. One one hand, a person's "drive" may lead to avoid intercultural interactions. In this case, a person forecasts discomfort and performs in dysfunctional ways which have been identified earlier. On the other hand, an effective intercultural communicator recognizes difference as a positive opportunity to move functionally in ways previously identified.

This PCD axiom ultimately affects our understanding information and relationships. Evaluating the source of difference explains actions or thoughts of another person who appears different. We can explain the source of miscommunication, attributed to difference because of (1) culture ("This is the way my culture does things."), (2) personality ("You and I are from the same culture but we are individuals who think and act differently."), and (3) relationship history ("I thought I knew you, but I can't trust you anymore.").

By its nature, intercultural communication assumes not only the message, but the social relationship associated with an interaction. We label this axiom as communication having content and relationship dimensions. Watzlawick, Beavin, and Jackson emphasized that communication does not exist in content isolation; ultimately meaning results from *what* is said and *who* says it. The relationship between two communicators affects how the message is interpreted.[2] For example, if your best friend said, "Could we get started on this project?" you probably would interpret the statement as a simple request for starting a task. However, if the boss said, "Could we get started?" the meaning likely would be different.

Intercultural Communication Relates to Content and Relationship

Interaction between culturally different people creates a system that demands an understanding of each participant's need to reduce uncertainty.
© 1992 Hazel Hawkin/Stock Boston

Relationship Interpretation

The influence of credibility as one parameter of relationships is illustrated by Nid (not her real name), an international student from Thailand who expressed her negative evaluation of a certain American young man. However, once she reevaluated her attribution of various qualities about him, she perceived him as much more believable in ways that were credible for her home culture. Once that credibility was established, she began to view this same young man's messages as "very important." In the process, her alteration of the credibility relationship subsequently influenced messages between the two.

While it is true that relationships alter meanings, the converse also works: messages alter relationships. For example, it is easier to feel positively toward a co-worker who compliments rather than criticizes. It is easier to like a boss who affirms constructively. In these cases, messages create a relationship, which in turn becomes the beginning for the axiom; the nature of the relationship then sets the stage for interpreting the next message.

The term "relationship" implies a potentially broad array, ranging across dimensions of credibility, interpersonal attraction, personal networks, love, friendship, and so on. These reasons predict relationships. Although relationship formation is a sensitive and complex topic, clearly the message-relationship bond operates.

Communication Style Affects First Impressions

Intercultural communication can be described in terms of a person's communication style. Communication style means the personality qualities we infer from the messages and the manner of a communicator. For example, some people might be described as exhibiting a dominant communicator style; others a submissive style. Some individuals are thought of as warm and caring; others cold and unfeeling. Some seem authoritarian; others open-minded. Some communicators are preoccupied; others are attentive. Other personal communication styles include being extremely friendly, being a mediator between people, being a counselor, being a critic, being a question asker, being an informed opinion giver, and being a victim.

Sometimes these "styles" or forms of social communication are conscious. In such cases, people communicate intending to make a certain kind of impression. More often, people are not aware of their communication style. In this case, they act from habits formed in culture, family, and individual differences. Very few of us remain unaffected by the various communication styles we encounter.

Encountering diversity is an axiom involved in intercultural communication.

Intercultural Communication Involves Uncertainty Reduction

Intercultural communication depends upon reducing uncertainty levels about other people. In our interpersonal encounters, we encounter ambiguity about relationships: "How does he feel about me?" "What are her attitudes?" "What can I expect to happen next in this relationship?" We experience discomfort with questions about relationships, and so to reduce our discomfort, we engage in behaviors that enhance our chances of maximum understanding.

In the field of communication, predictability is something of the opposite of uncertainty and remains an important aspect of relationships. We seem to need a certain amount of redundancy to lessen the entropy (the "new" messages or the unfamiliar part of a message) in communication. In other words, the less guesswork about a message *and* a relationship, often the better we feel about the situation.

Now, here is the problem. Communication in the presence of diversity poses *proportionately more* ambiguities and uncertainties than in communication with predominant similarity. Some form of predictability is needed to combat the uncertainty. Typically, interactants turn to "standard" customs and rules in order to enhance predictability and reduce the impact of the unusual and the uncertain. Throughout the conversation, various cultural rules guide the communication. If we share the same culture, the communication rules are simpler to understand than cultures where the rules are unknown to the participants.

What are the answers? One answer to facing uncertainty is to offer predictability, using communication rules, customs, rituals, phrases, and nonverbal behaviors that match the other person's culture. A second way to face uncertainty is to understand and manage interaction stages typically acting when people meet. They can be described as a process, developing during conversation: precontact, contact and impression, and closure.

Precontact.   The first phase of reducing uncertainty involves precontact impression formation. In coming in contact with another person, we proceed from an unfocused scanning of the environment to a focused scanning.[3] We become aware that another person is a part of the immediate communication climate. At that point, we engage in *reciprocal scanning.* We gain information by interpreting the appearance and mannerisms of the other person, while the other person does the same with us. The strategies can be quite complicated, but the result is that participants reduce uncertainty in a fairly efficient way during this first phase.[4]

Contact and impression.   The second phase of intercultural uncertainty reduction involves the initial impression within the first few minutes of verbal communication. Some researchers suggest that during the first four minutes of conversation, a decision is made to continue or discontinue the relationship.[5] We form some rather important judgments: "Do I like him?" "Is she understanding me?" "Am I wasting my time?" "He sure doesn't look like much." This *four minute barrier* as it sometimes is labeled, may not take exactly four minutes, but the power of early impressions is certain.

Closure.   The third phase of uncertainty reduction involves closure or a final judgment about the intercultural relationship. This is not just a way of exiting or saying goodbye. Closure is the lasting attitude based on the contact stage. The tendency to form a comfortable summary of another person, a mental picture or verbal phrase, profiles a final evaluation concerning another person.

The perceptual processes involving these stages of contact and closure are complicated. Four reasons explain the perceptual logic during these stages.

1. *Attribution.* This theory refers to our summarizing others' behaviors by inferring their motivations. To a positive action or perceived positive value taken by someone, we often attribute a positive motivation. Negative actions, however, can cause a negative inference regarding motivation—"He's manipulative," or "She really is working for a different position in the company." The key phrase is "inferring motives."

2. *Impression consistency.* A related concept is called *implicit personality theory.* This theory implies that we seek a summary of another person consistent with our first assessment of an individual's qualities. A positive first impression usually leads to a projecting of additional positive qualities to that person, even if we are not sure about the other qualities. For instance, if Jim is energetic and assertive, then he will also be _____. What word would you insert? Courageous? Intelligent? The theory predicts that some positive word will follow. In the same way, if the first known qualities are negative, we forecast the unknown with more negative features. If Jim is described as dumb and clumsy, what additional personality adjectives might be included? Probably something negative, according to the theory. In other words, a positive or negative "halo effect" extends from described qualities to unknown qualities consistent with the known.

3. *Incomplete information.* Inadequate data about a person also accounts for less quality perception. Inadequate or poor sampling from which to draw accurate data about a person or a group is often a reason for such hasty and limited generalization.

The Power of Attitudes

When you read about racism, bigotry, and prejudice such words stir emotions. In the close of the twentieth century, how could anyone hold these attitudes, much less feel hatred or act violently toward "out-groups"? The daily news reports such tensions. What attitudes deny peace between coexisting cultures? What causes these attitudes, and what signifies their presence?

Positive intercultural attitudes lead to adaptive, functional outcomes, such as friendship, peace, increased understanding, and lasting bonds. The attitudes and accompanying communication behaviors emerge as openness, affirmation, questioning, supporting, listening, offering feedback, asserting, and suggesting.

Negative intercultural attitudes lead to nonadaptive, dysfunctional outcomes including prejudice, racism, ethnocentrism, discrimination, and negative stereotyping. These are related to communication behaviors such as withdrawing, blocking, closed-mindedness, authoritarian communication, slandering, condemning, and hating.

4. *Following cultural norms.* Some culture's norms reinforce negative social attitudes toward out-groups. Simply following unchallenged caricatures, stereotypes, and attitudes becomes an all-too-easy perception summary about another person. Sadly, one's culture has done the thinking for such a person. One university student once explained, "My hometown and school never had any Hispanics, so I never realized my prejudice and bias toward people 'not like me.' When Armando and I first met, my exclusive attitudes erupted into an ethnic dislike and blocked seeing what a caring, sensitive man he really is." Cultures, schools, and families teach us subtly how to feel about others "not like me." It is all too easy to lift the stereotypes others have invented and unconsciously apply this "in-group" judgment without question.

Culture and Communication Are Inseparable

Cultures inherently contain communication systems. Many years ago, Smith[6] observed that "communication and culture are inseparable," a point echoed in more recent research.[7] One implication of this insight is that cultures generate symbols, rituals, customs, and formats. To use a simple example, every culture has rules for achievement and attainment. In western culture, the symbols of these "rites of passage" include degrees, promotions, certificates, material objects, technology, and other symbols of material wealth. Nationals in rural Botswana use physical symbols also, but the symbols represent recognition in tribal terms and are symbolic of pride in the primary group and not just individual attainment. Cultural misunderstanding occurs when we fail to match the appropriate symbols and general communication system to the culture. Just witness the awkwardness of an expatriate who attends a gathering in a host culture, but fails to wear the appropriate clothes. One cannot escape this inseparability of culture and communication.

A second implication of this axiom implies not only using correct symbols, but also applying the appropriate communication style for the occasion. Communication styles include mannerisms, phrases, rituals, and communication customs appropriate for various situations in a culture. For instance, in Saudia Arabia the correct interpersonal communication style upon meeting one's host is often honorific language loaded with compliments and thanks. Public criticism of fellow workers in this culture is rare, for such a message would appear disloyal and disrespectful.[8] Some West Africans exhibit a friendly and warm interpersonal communication style. Some Asians are described as conscious of propriety, ceremony, and rules of respect and honor. Some U.S. culture members appear informal, uninhibited, and prefer to come to the point quickly in a linear manner. Some Britons display a reserved manner, preferring understatement and control in interpersonal interaction. These examples remind us of the importance of understanding intercultural style.

Intercultural Effectiveness Is the Goal of Intercultural Communication

A final axiom of intercultural communication involves communication effectiveness. The text is dedicated to enhancing knowledge and skills to bring about intercultural competency. But competency in and of itself is actually only what you know and can do. Ultimately, the aim of all this exercise is to achieve positive intercultural outcomes. Success can take many forms: improved relationships, effective management, friendship, training,[9] technology dissemination, and conflict reduction. The model of chapter 1 and later in chapter 9 name three overall intercultural communication outcomes: task, relationship, and cultural adjustment. The *task* outcome results from intercultural job performance. *Relationship* outcome concerns the number and quality of relationships. Understanding others, decreasing tensions, conflict management, and friendship are examples of important relationship aspects.[10] *Cultural adjustment* means going through transitions and adapting to the stresses of a new culture.

The Origins of Contemporary Intercultural Communication

The origins of this area of study are many and complex, so we present here only a brief history selected from a trend analysis of intercultural communication and its genesis in the United States.

Interaction with International Diversity

Some observers claim that, prior to the Second World War, many people in the United States lacked a world perspective. (Today, the low geography scores and language propensity in U.S. culture would suggest a consistent trend.) The experiences of travelers and missionaries were seminal, but the events surrounding the Second World War galvanized a national consciousness of a global, geopolitical and cultural world. Isolationist views continued to erode under a move toward international awareness and interaction manifested in a variety of programs and institutions.

First, during the Second World War, leaders were faced with a strategic problem. How could allied nations cooperate with residents of other cultures when their leaders knew little about other languages or cultures? Anthropologists were then invited to study and discover the culture of many of these new places.

Through these investigations, the focus of cultural anthropology became more popular and took on new meaning. The study of culture became more widely known, setting the stage for the importance of culture and communication.[11]

Second, following the Second World War, programs focusing on world situations and international policy influenced the development of intercultural communication studies. With the advent of the United Nations, governments initiated new programs like the World Health Organization, the United Nation's assistance programs, the World Bank, and other agencies. These generated a need to understand the cultures of developing nations. The U.S. Congress passed a 1953 act instituting the United States Information Agency (USIA). The name was changed in 1977 to the International Communication Agency. This agency was charged with providing information about the United States through various communication media to nations of the world. The familiar broadcast "Voice of America" exemplified those efforts.

Unfortunately, many of their attempts at communication across these cultural boundaries were superficial and sometimes dominated by economic theories of development that cast some doubt upon cross-cultural theories of social change. Otherwise sincere attempts of these super-power organizations were overshadowed by the lack of cultural understanding of the peoples they were trying to serve.

Third, during the 1950s, early pioneers in this effort, such as Edward T. Hall, found that the USIA lacked cultural information, a point echoed in work by Leeds-Hurwitz.[12] The image of the "ugly American" seemed linked to poorly trained foreign service officers and travelers who lacked cultural awareness and intercultural communication insight. During this decade, Edward T. Hall drew upon his vast experience with the Hopi and Navaho Indians during the 1930s and 1940s and with foreign service officers in his capacity with the USIA and wrote the classic *The Silent Language,* originally published in 1959.[13] Many believe this publication marked the birth of intercultural communication, since it synthesized fundamental issues regarding culture and communication.

Fourth, foreign language classes following the Second World War took on new enthusiasm, partly because language had become more "functional." The soldiers' return prompted a social, governmental, and educational awareness of a global society, and this enthusiasm quickly worked its way into school curriculum, mostly as foreign language studies.

In the larger development of cultural studies, the geopolitical aspects and needs presented awakened a segment of the academic culture to the ongoing work of the British and European social anthropologists, such as Malinowsky. Soon, the work of American cultural anthropologists such as Margaret Mead and Ruth Benedict become known, as well as the linguistic work of Edward Sapir and Dell Hymes.

As national attitudes embraced a more robust global view, understanding about multicultural diversity also underwent gradual change. Using the United States as a case, programs designed to meet the needs of multicultural diversity often experienced low quality outcomes. As far back as 1909, for instance, the Bureau of Indian Affairs had arranged "The Last Great Indian Council," a meeting that was supposed to be a type of farewell to the "vanishing race" of Indians, despite

Interaction with Multicultural Diversity

the fact they had been increasing in numbers, not decreasing.[14] This lack of cultural awareness and denial was augmented by various national programs intended to assimilate the Native American into the dominant Anglo society. The handling of educational, welfare, and medical programs on reservations revealed little awareness of most Native American cultures. We don't want to make an unfair analogy, but examples like this one are said to typify the traditional way in which a number of cultural and minority programs were handled in the United States.

The 1960s also marked a cultural awakening. With the Civil Rights Act in 1964, the nation discovered the roots of multiculturalism. The same decade gave birth to many human rights issues in the United States. The questions, and sometimes the conflicts, made us painfully aware that communication between groups and cultures was no longer a matter of international expediency, but a problem of domestic urgency.

Another salient event with severe repercussions for intercultural communication was the Vietnam War. The interactions with Southeast Asians under the conditions imposed by the war overwhelmingly influenced the participants. The consequent overflow of refugees thrust a new generation of Americans into cultural contact never before known to them—overnight, elementary, high school, and college students were in classrooms with counterparts from Cambodia, Laos, and Vietnam. Educators faced a challenge with a cultural group with whom they had no experience, and communication challenges soared.

Events in the 1990s will cause us to determine our future in part by our abilities to understand and to interact interculturally, a point well illustrated by riots in the Los Angeles area following the outcome of the first Rodney King trial and by exclusivist movements motivated by intolerance in several areas of the country.

Of ongoing importance, too, are the continuing intercultural demands of growing multicultural societies throughout the world. In the United States regional demographic changes mean that groups once considered minorities will be the majority, a fact already having occurred in some areas and soon to occur in others. Diversity in the workplace and schools is a current reality. Economic and political oppression from regions of the globe, along with the growing human rights movement and continuing human rights unrest and political unrest in parts of the world, have heightened the concerns for intercultural awareness.

As treaties of economic significance in Europe, Asia, and North America continue to flourish, the intercultural needs accompanying these transactions correspondingly will rise. Furthermore, global ecology agreements require international and macrocultural analysis and finesse to communicate across these cultural boundaries.

Increasing an Academic Culture of Intercultural Communication

From these historical transitions, briefly reviewed, scholars continue to address investigations concerning the reciprocal impact of culture and communication. In the earliest days of intercultural communication, even the name for this area of communication investigation was inconsistent. Scholarly work was limited to pulling from a number of fields including rhetorical and communication theory, mathematics, social psychology, psychiatry, linguistics, anthropology, political science, philosophy, folklore and oral history, literature, rural sociology, and sociology.

Today, numerous works are available from many researchers across the globe, each exploring new dimensions ranging in such areas as international concerns, interethnic and minority questions, dominance-nondominance issues, adaptation and competence, intracultural communication, diversity in the workplace, and intercultural communication training. It is necessary to argue for a culture of learning that insists on the role of intercultural perspectives in educational curricula, where a global and shrinking world needs knowledge and skills to meet the ever growing demands for competency and effectiveness in this field.

In his overview, Hammer concluded that intercultural communication shared a vision that has been cultivated and is still growing.[15] He argues first that we need to employ interdisciplinary and multicultural "maps." Second, the field is eminently heuristic, helping practitioners manage a number of interethnic as well as international needs. Third, intercultural communication addresses the concerns of people wherever groups are found.

Developing Skills in Understanding Intercultural Communication Axioms

1. *Look beyond the surface.* Dress, custom, and presenting conditions (including climate) become superficial ways to judge culture. Go beyond the tourist level.

2. *Develop a curiosity about the internals of culture, such as cultural structure, cultural thought patterns and logic, and cultural relationships.* A sense of internal culture can heighten intercultural experiences and foster better relationships.

3. *Look for ways in which various communication sources mold perceptions of groups.* Family, friends, media, and educational sources all leave us with information about cultural groups. Question your communication sources to develop a sharp focus on the accuracy of their stereotypes.

4. *Discover ways that relationships affect content and content affects relationships.* How we feel about someone colors the message, and conversely, messages can heighten or flatten how we feel about a person. Unfortunately, not everyone means what he or she says, so working through the person-versus-the-message issue can be an important aspect of communicating.

5. *Broaden your views of culture to a notion of collectives.* Where people relate and have tasks, communication bonds emerge. With these bonds develop a set of norms, structure, thought, procedure of relationship, and communication style. One measure of a person's intercultural growth is his or her ability to visualize those kinds of factors in a number of groups and to look for the ways in which a culture exists for that group.

6. *Question negative attributes you might hold toward a group.* Unfortunately, many people selectively perceive negative features about others or what they define as negative features. The idea here is to develop the discipline to select and search for positive attributes to balance your view.

This Chapter in Perspective

This chapter documents a number of intercultural axioms concerning intercultural communication. These include the principle of difference, the content and relationship dimensions of intercultural communication, the role of personal communicator style in intercultural communication, reducing uncertainty about relationships and messages, the nature of perception in sensing differences, the centrality of communication to culture, and the importance of intercultural effectiveness as a goal.

Exercises

1. List as many microcultures as you can. Pick two or three of these cultures and identify the structure and symbols of these groups. How do their structure and symbols foster or inhibit communication with other cultural groups?

2. Rent the movie *Witness,* a story involving the Amish culture. After viewing the movie, discuss the perceptual limitations people have of the Amish culture. What perceptual limitations do the Amish have of the larger macroculture? If you were in a position to resolve problem areas in intercultural communication between the Amish and others, what would you do?

3. Write at least three headlines from a newspaper that indicate culture or "groupness." How do they define culture?

Endnotes

1. Young Y. Kim, "Searching for Creative Integration," in *Methods for Intercultural Communication Research,* ed. William B. Gudykunst and Young Y. Kim (Beverly Hills, Calif.: Sage, 1984).

2. Paul Watzlawick, Janet H. Beavin, and Don D. Jackson, *Pragmatics of Human Communication* (New York: Norton, 1967). This assumption is widely discussed in communication theory and recognizes that what is said does not remain in isolation with who is saying it. The influence of relationship is a powerful mechanism in interpreting information.

3. Dean Barnlund, ed., *Interpersonal Communication: Surveys and Studies* (New York: Houghton Mifflin, 1968).

4. Charles Berger, R. R. Gardner, Malcolm R. Parks, L. Shulman, and Gerald R. Miller, "Interpersonal Epistemology and Interpersonal Communication," in *Explorations in Interpersonal Communication,* ed. Gerald R. Miller (Beverly Hills, Calif.: Sage, 1976).

5. William D. Brooks and Philip Emmert, *Interpersonal Communication* (Dubuque, Iowa: William C. Brown Company, 1976).

6. Alfred Smith, *Communication and Culture* (New York: Holt, Rinehart and Winston, 1966).

7. Michael L. Hecht, Peter A. Andersen, and Sidney A. Ribeau, "The Cultural Dimensions of Nonverbal Communication," in *Handbook of International and Intercultural Communication,* ed. Molefi Kete Asante and William B. Gudykunst (Newbury Park, Calif.: Sage, 1989).

8. Philip R. Harris and Robert T. Moran, *Managing Cultural Differences,* 4th ed. (Houston: Gulf, 1995).

9. Richard Brislin, *Understanding Culture's Influence on Behavior,* 2d ed. (Orlando: Harcourt Brace Jovanovich, 1993).

10. Sharon Ruhly, *Orientations to Intercultural Communication* (Chicago: SRA, 1976).

11. Speech by E. T. Hall, 1980 and personal interview following the speech. Hall explodes with passion about the role of anthropology and its popularizing influence. His descriptions are personal but offer a highly informative perspective on intercultural communication origins. Hall himself is probably credited as the single most important influence in the development of the field.

12. Wendy Leeds-Hurwitz, "Notes in the History of Intercultural Communication: The Foreign Service Institute and the Mandate for Intercultural Training," *The Quarterly Journal of Speech* 76 (1990): 262–81.

13. Edward T. Hall, *The Silent Language* (New York: Anchor, 1973).

14. Robert Faherty, "The American Indian: An Overview," in *Intercultural Communication: A Reader,* 2d ed., ed. Larry Samovar and Richard Porter (Belmont, Calif.: Wadsworth, 1976).

15. Mitchell R. Hammer, "Intercultural Communication Competence," in *Handbook of International and Intercultural Communication,* ed. Molefi Kete Asante and William B. Gudykunst (Newbury Park, Calif.: Sage, 1989).

Part Two

Perceiving the Nature
of Cultural and
Social Diversity

Chapter 3

Elements of Cultural Systems

OBJECTIVES   *After completing this chapter, you should be able to*

1. Define culture

2. Identify elements of culture as a system

3. Describe institutional subsystems within a culture

4. Describe the means by which cultures develop and change

Facing World Events

Cultural differences are certainly broader than the following incidents, but even such unusual examples remind us of a diverse world. For example, Hindu ritual practices of cleansing differ from Islamic rituals. When we consider food and drink differences travelers encounter among different regions of the world, one can identify the meaning of at least a modest level of cultural difference. In 1979 and the early 1980s, during Iran's political transition, dissenters to the resurgence of a Moslem nation sometimes fell victim on a trail of executions and severe punishments. The Kurdish group in Iraq is victimized by an ethnocentric Iraqi power elite. Vandalism at a certain level in Singapore is punishable by "caning." Perhaps such an application of law and social control should be no more surprising than practices in portions of the United States not so many years ago when thieves were hanged for stealing a horse, but released or mildly punished for taking a life. The violation of minority rights and human ethics of fairness in the United States all too often sound like silent cries for the perpetrators but are actually loud cries of minority injustice. The mass suicide of nine hundred persons in Jonestown, Guyana, starvation in Ethiopia, crisis in the former Yugoslavia, war lords in Somalia, and a massacre in Beijing all remind us that ours is a world of different cultures.

Source: Potpourri of news reports.

To discuss "perceived cultural differences" we recognize two presuppositions. One is an affirmation of our common humanity, that is, we live in a global community across nations and cultures and often share common needs, hopes, and technology. A second presupposition recognizes that groups of people, nations, continents represent a world divided—not merely by political boundaries but by cultural barriers. Some vivid reminders of differences occur nightly on each evening's news where examples of diversity in language, ritual, social rules, custom and law, world view, values, and ethnocentrism are but a few categories of dissimilarity.

A recognition of cultural differences is not meant to create despair. Rather, as the central model from chapter one indicates, effective intercultural communicators try to understand diversity in its many forms and to develop competency skills and strategies in order to achieve effective outcomes when encountering contrasting cultures. This chapter should help readers understand how cultures are systems of interrelated elements, beginning on the inside with each culture's identity, beliefs, values, and world view among people who view each other as a group. The elements described in this chapter are found almost universally. They become a common framework to guide our observations of cultural diversity.

Defining Culture and Its Influence on Communication

Almost 200 definitions of culture define it in numerous ways such as community, social class differences, minorities, social groups, nationalities, geopolitical units, societies, and so on. All these emphasize culture's multifaceted nature. However, in our examination of culture, we choose to underscore those features of culture that contribute most to culture's influence on communication. We define culture here as follows:

Culture is the holistic interrelationship of a group's identity, beliefs, values, activities, rules, customs, communication patterns, and institutions.

This chapter explores the implications of these definitional concepts as factors that make up a system or culture. As you will read, people have learned intriguing ways of *doing* and *thinking* that significantly organize their world. You will see how culture is a powerful vehicle for *socialization*. Culture influences how we adapt and learn, language, habits, customs, expectations, and roles—it shapes thinking, acting, and communicating according to group expectations. Many cultural imprints are subtle and elusive, if not beyond conscious recognition at times. Culture is so basic to human behavior that we cannot ignore its pervasive influence which in recent years has been taken into account in communication research.

Before we turn to elements of culture, it is important to understand the overall reasons why culture influences communication. First, culture *teaches significant rules, rituals, and procedures*. Attitudes toward time, how to dress, when and what to eat, when to come and go, and how to work, illustrate this first function of culture. The overall process of learning these things is called *socialization* which refers to developing a sense of proper and improper behavior and communicating within those cultural rules.[1] As an example, think over any one of thousands of rules your culture or your family (an obvious significant cultural unit) may have taught you. What is polite, crude, or expected all fall under this rubric of rules, rituals, and procedures. These are very important, for they become the stuff of inclusion, boundary-setting, and self-worth. They define human development within the context of any one specific culture.

Second, culture *reinforces values*. What is good or evil, what is truth, and core understanding of the world are taught in a cultural context. Consequently, we develop approaches to thoughts and beliefs about the world. Among the Kissi tribe of Kenya, for example, the grandmother assumes special responsibility for telling her grandchildren stories about the importance of family honesty, loyalty, and the nature of good and evil. Culture teaches us what is beautiful or ugly, sexy or unappealing. As one overseas document for living abroad reminds us, culture teaches the value of hard work, thrift, privacy, competition, fair play, and directness.[2]

Third, culture *teaches relationship* with others. These relationships formed in culture generate a dynamic of roles and expectations. For example, where to stand, how to smile, when to visit, and the level of formality in language are highly influenced by the nature of the relationship with the interactant. Culture teaches these and hundreds of other aspects of forming and maintaining relationships. How does this happen?

First, each culture encourages a particular communication style expected within each culture. In the science fiction "Star Trek" series the classic Klingons exhibit a demanding and harsh communication style. In many of the stories most of the Klingons interact ineffectively with other cultures, preferring confrontational

Culture is more than a place. Culture encompasses the identity, values, activities, rules, customs, communication patterns, and institutions. © Jim Harrison/Stock Boston.

if not a warlike style of communication, a style that rarely produces positive outcomes (unless you are a Klingon who likes to blast people out of the universe). Areas like loudness, pitch, rate, and certain stances and gestures characterize communication behaviors. A specific culture expects an "ideal" communication style. The contrasts are striking, such as when an American speaking in a "normal" conversational voice seems loud to a "quiet" Thai national who interprets the American to be angry. This case illustrates the ideal cultural communication styles in conflict, a conflict rooted in each culture's communication expectations.

Second, culture has the power to shape perception. However you describe it, culture shapes perception by exercising the human tendency to categorize others. These stereotypes engendered are not always accurate but they persist as powerful images, feelings, and beliefs our culture impresses.[3]

In sum, culture is something like a glue that bonds people together. There are some tendencies that typify some group members and areas where individual differences persist.[4] In any event, we can describe a culture in terms of its elements or features which we discuss next.

Elements of Culture

Culture is like luggage we carry. From it we unconsciously lift daily needs: survival, information, interpersonal relationships, goals, rules, rituals, communication style, expectations, and institutional expectations. Sometimes that means applying rules, while other times it involves operationalizing values. Or, we engage in a ritual all too familiar "back home" but misunderstood in a new culture. We begin in this chapter to open a cultural suitcase and unfold its contents. As we open each pocket, we explore an interrelated set of group identity, beliefs, values, activities, rules and customs, institutions, and communication patterns arising from these.

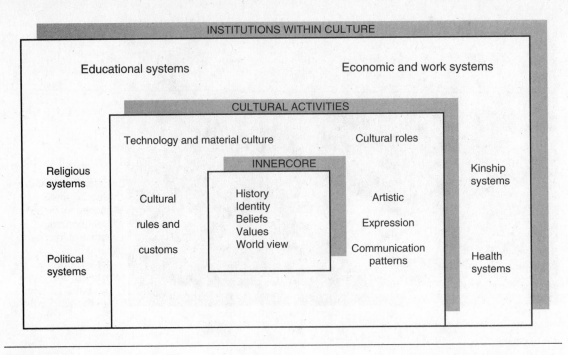

Figure 3.1

This model demonstrates elements of culture composing a system. The inner core lies at the most significant level. The second and third set of elements are tied to the core, but remain an area for some degree of flexibility, fad, and change.

The model presented in figure 3.1 visually expresses these cultural elements. We can describe culture as a system since these elements as major components interact on members of a culture.[5] The inner elements of a cultural system are the mainspring that deal with the identity, beliefs, values, and world view of a culture. The next level out from the inner section can be described as the areas of activity, rules and customs, and communication patterns of a group. Finally, the outer boundary of a cultural system involves the institutions of a culture. The next sections of the chapter explore these elements.

The Inner Core of Culture

History. A culture's identity, often associated with its historical development and tradition, is a cornerstone to understanding culture. In the United States, for example, a family tree and family lineage afford identity and purpose, perhaps more in some regions than in others. Cultural history generates insight into norms of groups and individual behavior and explains many attitudes that seem to be shared by cultural members.

Among the Ga and Ewe tribes of Ghana, a high respect if not fear exists toward the neighboring Ashanti tribe who are described with unusual "strength and power." Their attitude has historical origins. In the slave trading days, the Ashanti outnumbered

Traditions and historical roots, illustrated by these Mayan ruins in Guatemala, are a part of culture that contribute to the current life of a group of people. © Peter Menzel/Stock Boston.

and conquered neighboring tribes and sold them on the coast as slaves to European and American dealers. This historical origin permeates contemporary relationships of the Ashanti and their tribal neighbors. As another example, communication with various tribal Indians from Central and South America would be incomplete without a knowledge of their ancestral heritage, which includes being conquered by Spaniards and a 450-year history of submissiveness to social and economic domination.

Cultures have various ways of expressing their history, heritage, and traditions. Among some cultures, a totem—often displaying elaborate artistry—may show tribal history. The totem's importance lies in its symbol as a record of the past, a reminder that for some cultures is a pervasive part of the present. In other cultures, the past is written or perhaps recalled orally by local historians who specialize in memorization of a culture's history. This was the case for the noted American author Alex Haley whose quest for his African heritage led to interviews with West African tribal members who had memorized generations of orally recorded history.

In any case, the roots of history for most cultures are long extending from the past to influence the present. The power of origins and history provides a social continuity, an identity, as if to say, "This is who I am," a point we turn to next.

Identity. Members of every culture have a sense of social identification: who they are and why. In other words, cultures can be likened to a group personality. The idea is akin to theorists who make an analogy between groups and individuals, declaring both have a "personality."[6] Raymond Rodgers once explained that, through its folklore, a culture identifies itself with archetypal figures, such as heroes, and that these ideals become models to measure personal and group success.[7]

The Past Meets Modernity

No matter how a culture records its history, the point for the intercultural communicator is to appreciate a culture's past. For example, many European visitors to the United States wonder at the North American's fascination for the new and innovative. Enthusiasm for more efficient buildings, to replace old structures that could be remodeled, along with a quest for the latest gadgetry or technology contrast with cultures that believe in preservation and sufficiency of existing material objects. In many cultures, tradition is so important that anything new is viewed suspiciously. The effective intercultural communicator appreciates these emphases and sources of cultural pride and seeks to learn the history and geography of another person in order to understand possible attitudes and values, which are essential elements in intercultural communication.

One's cultural identity affects interpersonal relationships and expectations of individual activity. From a sense of social identity (who *we* are), one receives a sense of personal identity (who *I* am). That principle is seen especially clearly in those cultures described as collective rather than individual, where individualism is often subjugated to group decisions made by the leaders in that culture. Among the Ashanti tribe, individual decisions are made with the approval of the maternal uncle, maternal grandfather, and one's father, and rarely by the individual acting alone.

Cultural beliefs. Each culture has an interpretation of reality, or perceptual "window," through which people see self and others. In this sense, beliefs are a culture's view of what is true or false. They also hold conceptions of how to arrive at the difference between truth and falsehood.

Beyond what is merely truth, cultures have concepts of ultimate significance and of long-term importance, known as values. Finally, what a culture believes about nature and the workings of the cosmos is called world view. World view is a specific belief system about the nature of the universe. More than just an outlook or philosophy of life, world view functions as a central construct related influencing how much control one believes is available (see chapter 5 on values and world view details).

A final area of cultural belief is a culture's pattern of thought and its sense of logic. For instance, many people in the Western Hemisphere accept cause-effect reasoning. Solutions to problems are simply a matter, they reason, of altering or controlling the causes to alter or control the desired effects. In contrast, some eastern cultures reason that no one can know the causes of life events and that the events are part of a natural plan that humans should not try to understand completely but to accept. Thus, the intercultural difference in this example is the divergent approach the interactants experience in the use of evidence. Cultural interactants may differ in a variety of ways including linear-sequential, time-ordered patterns vs. configurational picture patterns, cause-effect vs. no cause, spiritual relations vs. nonspiritual factors, etc. All these remind us of cultural differences in what philosophers call ontology (the study of being and reality) and epistomology (the study of how we learn truth). These are not merely differences perceived in far-away cultures in exotic continents, for failure in working with cultural diversity in many regions of the globe has been traced to failure to examine learning style differences sometimes associated with minority cultures.[8]

From the inner core of cultural history, identity, and beliefs, we move to identifying a culture's activities. These can be expressed in several ways, particularly in technology and material culture, cultural activity roles, and artistic expression.

Cultural Activities

Technology and material culture.   Probably the most salient features to most tourists abroad are the perceived cultural differences in a culture's technology, often viewed as its material culture—food, clothing, travel methods, tools, and other technology. Unfortunately, some travelers offend host cultures by making light of their cultural methods of working out their basic material needs. Since technology is usually a matter of cultural invention and of intercultural contact with other technologies, it might be argued that no opportunities have arisen for acculturation of a technology, or perhaps the culture has rejected the technology.

Too often, we prematurely judge a culture by its material features. A person who values technological features may overlook a rich cultural heritage in such areas as art, language, and interpersonal relationships. Unfortunately, such myopia can damage intercultural communication.

Sometimes a culture's technology and social functions intersect. For instance, an observer once described how women in a rural area of one East African country walked over a half mile to a river that supplied their families with water—two buckets at a time. One of this nation's governmental agencies decided that a water pump and a central water system would enormously benefit the villagers. However, the water-gathering routine was a means of social interaction and a very important method of making new relationships, enjoying friendship, and keeping up with village news. The government field staff also did not recognize the fact that routine excretory functions were performed off the beaten paths to and from the river. When the new water system failed because no one used it, the government was shocked to learn the reasons. The water system was abandoned, and life continued as before. This case illustrates that some methods and procedures are not always amenable to change without entire cultural imbalance and repercussions.

Material culture does not exist merely as a feature with functional value. *Overt* material culture may reflect a more subtle, *covert* peculiarity (much like the tip of an iceberg revealing only a small part of the total iceberg). For example, the Yir Yoront tribe of Australia had a central tool—the stone axe—for securing food, shelter, and warmth. Beyond its function of value as a material object, however, the stone axe symbolized masculinity and respect for elders. In short, the stone axe represented authority, which was a controlling feature for these people, bonding together

Food preparation and eating habits are a significant area of difference for sojourners to new cultures, as for example in rural Jordan. © Owen Franken/Stock Boston.

elements of their culture. Although the men owned the stone axes, women and children borrowed and used the tool according to customary rules of social relationships, and, in the process, reinforced the cultural glue of respect and authority. In fact, this artifact of material culture had such symbolic value that the subsequent introduction of the steel axe totally disrupted the social and economic bases of the cul-

Cultural technology and customs, shown here in Thailand, differ between global regions, as each culture meets its needs in a variety of ways. © Cameramann International, Ltd.

ture.[9] The culture literally disintegrated as thievery, drunkenness, and selling wives and daughters as prostitutes became commonplace once social order was removed.

Of course, the meaning behind material culture is often complex. Effective intercultural communicators typically first try to understand existing customs, and second, seek to avoid a biased reaction from their own cultural standards. For example, the early dinner in some northern European cultures strikingly contrasts with the late evening meals in Spain. You can well imagine the scene as hungry people in a new culture cannot understand why dinner is not served at the right time. Simple observation and adaptation are keys to interacting in any host culture. Like the stone axe, we should remember Everett Rogers's description of technology. Technologies have *form* (what it is or how it looks), *function* (what it does, how it works), and *meaning* (what it represents).[10]

Cultural roles.   Cultural roles revolve around categories of people and their expected pattern of performance or activity. People in various roles often must play prescribed scripts and expected behaviors in these roles. Each culture has its catalog of expectations of various roles.

1.   *Age roles.* One obvious example of how culture determines role relationships centers on views toward the aged. Japanese students show respect for the elderly in various ways, including the use of greeting terms that show respect. The Ashanti of Ghana have a form of greeting any elderly man as, roughly translated, "my grandfather." The numerous examples demonstrating respect for the elderly and ancestral generations are well documented in many cultures. By contrast, global cultures in the Western world are often said to lack respect for the elderly. Sometimes a senior person is perceived as nonproductive, an

intruder in the lives of a busy, younger generation. This attitude is changing, but these role expectations have enormous emotive qualities, and contribute to acting out these societal conceptions. In a type of self-fulfilling prophecy, some elderly people actually perform less efficiently, develop more health problems, and feel alienated because of societal expectations.

2. *Occupational roles.* Occupational role behaviors are also culturally defined. The consequence is that a person in a certain occupation is expected to perform in a role-prescribed manner. Police officers, lawyers, doctors, and salespersons play certain roles congruent with social expectations. For instance, a police officer usually does not crack jokes while handing out a citation, not because of lacking a sense of humor but because of the social role.

3. *Friendship roles.* Even our relationships with friends, professors, family, and strangers are mediated by societal expectations. We usually communicate in full accordance with those unspoken but expected cultural rules for each role. For instance, bowing in certain Asian cultures correlates with the perceived social relationship: the higher the status of the person, the lower one should bow.

4. *Gender roles.* Role differences also involve the differing expectations of males and females. Not only are gender roles organizing factors for a culture, they also widely vary from culture to culture. Almost every culture, for example, has a division of labor decisively determined by the individual's gender. Among the Boran herdsmen of Kenya, women are expected to complete all household duties, gardening, and milking while the men tend to the herds. Traditional Vietnamese women are expected to eat smaller quantities of food than men at each meal, no matter how hungry they are.[11] In a research study investigating Hispanic males and Anglo females in North American dual cultural marriages, Baldwin suggested that the wife's overinvolvement in the community or at work runs contrary to a perceived ideal role type and contributes to communication dissatisfaction.[12] In other words, gender role expectations are culturally variant and when the ideal cultural expectations are not met, conflict arises.

The decision making and authority positions of men and women are constantly changing within cultures. Power, often associated with decision making, comes in variant forms. The Boran women of Kenya, again, decide who in the family gets the greatest allotment of milk. The role and the power attendant to that role hold survival significance in that culture. Power-status relationships, traditionally associated with gender, are decreasing at a rapid rate among world cultures. Nevertheless, norms and cultural roles still are highly defined and stylized in a number of regions. Effective communication adaptation requires understanding and cultural sensitivity to these norms.

Roles serve in three ways to embody a culture's activities. First, roles help guide personal and social behavior. Second, they serve as standards in a stabilizing function, allowing members to predict certainty about what otherwise would amount to ambiguity in role relationships. Third, they give identification, as if to satisfy a need to know self and others. However, roles can be a source of stress, especially if (1) a person does not fit a cultural role, (2) there appears to be no adequate role model or if the guidance is too ambiguous, or (3) if a person is attempting to play multiple roles.

A culture's artistic expressions become one keyhole through which to view and understand a culture. © Robert Frerck/Tony Stone Images-Click/Chicago Ltd.

Artistic expression.   Another element of cultural activity is the relevant artistic expressions of a particular culture. When we consider music, sculpture, painting, and weaving as reflections of underlying themes of a culture at a given time in its history, this element assumes deeper significance. The myriad of aesthetic differences and explanations of why one culture's view of "beautiful" is another culture's view of "ugly" go far beyond the scope of the artistic object or its manifestations. Artistic expression can reflect current, relevant themes of a culture, by which the investigator gathers more and better insight. Or an investigator may discover a bit of artistic work to hold only *vestigial* significance, meaning the art once held unusual significance but no longer holds the original meaning. For instance, a particular design and color of cloth among native Central Americans once identified tribalism but now means little more than pretty colors and design.

The relation between language and culture is significant. Language and its categories filter, shape, and organize reality by the boundaries that linguistic systems draw, a point discussed in chapter 6. Of the thousands of language communities on earth, over one-fourth have yet to be written.

Communication Patterns

Language and culture.   Every culture has a language and a set of interactional rules for conversation. In terms of language, we should understand the importance of categories of experience captured in a language that may not transfer to other cultures. For example, a Chinese man who spoke immaculate English was conversing with a North American who kept referring to words like "unique," "individual," and "self." Although his English was proficient, he had a puzzled look on his face during the conversation. He finally asked, "What is this 'individuality' you keep referring to?" Although the grammar and vocabulary were similar, the concepts inherent in the North American's use of English were quite different from the Chinese concept of humility wherein individuality is rarely brought forward. The example illustrates that intercultural communication is more than knowing the right words. It involves a vast array of cultural knowledge including application of meaningful experiences and categories within a culture.

As a side note to language and culture, we should point out how some cultural members use codes understood by only their fellow members in the culture. The use of jargon, slang, or "in-house" codes allow shorthand-type communication. Using such telegraphic code may convey great meaning for people who have experienced the in-house communication, but it obscures meaningful communication from individuals outside the culture.

Conversational rules. In addition to language and code, there are many conversational and interaction rules associated with communication patterns in a culture. This notion of interaction implies a set of communication rules expected in every interactional context. For example, there are certain words and phrases expected in greetings and leavings. In many African cultures you are expected to give signals of respect to other people who are older. For example, the word in one West African language that refers to older people is roughly translated "My grandfather" or "My grandmother," conveying the idea that a person who is not really your grandfather or grandmother deserves the same respect as your own family.

Leave-taking rules also illustrate this principle of conversational and interaction rules. You can abruptly stop a conversation, or you can proceed with culturally appropriate rituals. For instance, Americans end briskly with a minor apology, such as, "Well, I have an engagement, and it's time for me to go," or "I've got to leave right now." We typically thank people for the time together and offer summary statements, concluding the interaction with friendliness and smiles. However, for many cultures, leave-taking is a matter of the higher-status person breaking the conversation. Often there are more elaborate forms, and all of them take a great deal of time. Every culture has rules about forming relationships and using linguistic codes. The right form shows up not only in word choice, but in the tone of voice, pitch, volume, and number of expected words. For example, Middle Easterners are highly verbose, while Germans are more to the point. Furthermore, many cultures rely more on nonverbal cues than verbal codes. Great skill is necessary to read the situation and understand the use of silence, the flicker of an eyebrow, or the depth of a bow. However, in American culture, such features are not as important as the actual words spoken.

Adaptability and change. Another aspect of communication patterns in culture asks the likelihood of adaptation to changing circumstances. When circumstances dictate is there a tendency for members of a culture to adapt effectively? Cultures that adapt to change are often not afraid of *innovation*. Others are *resistant*. As a whole, adaptable cultures can be explained by apparent historical and traditional reasons. For example, Japan has demonstrated extraordinary adaptation into the world economy since World War II. Japanese values traditionally stress flexibility. By contrast, the ethnic wars of the mid-1990s in Europe and in Africa exposed traditional cultures that place little value on communicating about change and adaptation. Conversely, adaptive communication stresses cultural competencies and intercultural motivation of effort and interpersonal communication opportunities.

Ethnocentrism.   Ethnocentrism is considered a negative element of communication patterns in a culture. More than simply an attitude, ethnocentrism refers to culturally shared notions of superiority in comparison with other cultures. Sadly, almost every culture exhibits some tendencies to judge others. The us-versus-them attitude is easily observed in interracial interactions when cultural categories remain stagnate or inflexible. In many nations, urbans look down upon rurals, elites scorn peasants, and white-collar employees devalue blue-collar employees. Sometimes national policies and activities favor practicing ethnocentrism. As an example, consider typical headline news stories: Iraqis Feel Superior to Iranians, Indians Belittle Pakistanis, Thais Devaluate Malaysians, Germans Isolate Turks, and Serbs Violate Croatians. Ethnocentrism causes war, takeover, and stands as the primary reason for incompetent and ineffective intercultural communication.

Nonverbal communication.   Every culture has some system of nonverbal behaviors—gesture, touch, facial expression, and eye movement. The collective pattern of such behaviors, while usually in concert with spoken communication, is itself a symbol system. Nonverbal behavior, in this sense, becomes nonverbal communication and is loaded with cultural expectations. Researchers agree that a culture's nonverbal communication system is the most powerful communication system available, although not without its liabilities. The differences in nonverbal behavior among cultures can cause breakdowns in intercultural communication.

1. *Spatial relations.* One facet of nonverbal behaviors involves use of space. As a part of the dynamic interrelationship with other cultural elements, space is correlated with information and meaning inferences. Space is related to relationship development, perceptions of feelings and moods, inferences about intentions, and generalizations about personality. Inferences about spatial usage also leave wide ambiguities. For example, when a male from Saudi Arabia stands close to a U.S. male from the Midwest, the U.S. male may be conditioned to back away. The Saudi is confused by this cool and abrupt reception. How quickly intercultural communication fails!

2. *Time.* Time is also considered a facet of nonverbal behavior. Time's implications for intercultural communication begins with understanding how time is culturally rooted, and our use of time is wedded to our culture's cognitive perceptions surrounding time. Some cultures view time with great precision and expect you to be precise also. For example, Americans, Britons, Canadians, and Germans expect punctuality. A large share of these peoples' relationships are governed by the clock—and with some rigor: "Sorry I arrived a few minutes late," "Wow, look at the time! I've got to go." Furthermore, impressions in a time-conscious culture are based on one's ability to adhere to cultural rules about the time system.

By contrast, some cultures, such as African, Latin American, and Malaysian, are less time conscious. In these cultures, time does not dominate, except for situations where punctuality is the rule. Norms in the less time-conscious cultures seem to address the issue of people first, schedules second. Cultural rules in these cases are centered around internal relationships rather than external schedules.

Intercultural communication problems between time-conscious cultures and less time-conscious cultures involve task-conscious people, externally shaping their relationships with time and schedules, and interpersonal-relationship-conscious people, motivated by saving face and social lubrication. The task-conscious individual communicating with the people-conscious individual may experience unexplainable rebuffs. Such cool relationships are expected when our cultural time rules do not match those of the cultural system in which we are communicating. The powerful outcomes of nonverbal intercultural communication remain an area related to one part of adaptive communication competencies and skills.

Communication of rewards, recognition, and gifts.   Every culture has communication norms for offering gifts and rewards. Rewards, for instance, are obviously culturally conditioned with the norms of each culture in how it expresses recognition and reward. Initiation rites, when successfully completed, represent a cultural method for advancement in tribes and clans. Proper behavior is usually recognized in some way. In the case of an American manager working in Japan who insists on individually recognizing an outstanding employee may inadvertently create embarrassment. Traditional Japanese norms emphasize rewarding the group, not individuals who are singled out. Offering money, gifts, personal praise, written statements, future contracts, new titles, promotions in rank, acceptance into a group, initiation completion, and equality are but a few additional ways of showing recognition.

Exercising reward or recognition follows communication norms conditioned by culture much in the same way as gift-giving. The communication norms for giving gifts vary widely between cultures. To not bring flowers or a beverage in some cultures is an insult. In other cultures, bringing gifts could seem to be "over-achieving" or trying to compensate in some way to your host. From experience, I have learned to ask lots of questions about gift norms and to be a good receiver as well as a good giver.

The most usual problem in intercultural communication concerning reward, recognition, and gift behavior is that an intercultural participant simply does not know the communication rules and expectations. Consequently, a manager representing a multinational corporation hires, makes assignments, and offers promotions according to his or her corporate culture's methods: management by objectives, participatory decision making, and the like. However well-intentioned such methods often fail because they simply lack cultural fit.

Cultural Rules and Customs

Every culture has rules of behavior ranging from everyday activity to the law of the land. Rules in this discussion generally refer to the regulations and expectations guiding the conduct about how things are to be accomplished. Many rules are expressed in everyday operations and interactions as customs. Customs in this sense are the procedures and operational habits assumed within a culture. For example, consider cultural rules and customs regarding opening a bank account. Perhaps for you the custom involves a few minutes of basic identification, signing a file copy, issuing checks, and depositing money. However, in many cultures the procedures of establishing a checking account can be rigorous and exasperating, involving extensive documentation, perhaps a character reference is summoned, and waiting for long periods before writing checks or withdrawing money are standard. For months the account might be scrutinized. Banking exemplifies numerous differences in cultural rules and custom.

Most people are aware of the way we are expected to perform in a culture. Unfortunately, the rules of a culture are rarely stated; nevertheless, we are expected to develop communication competence with those rules. In the American culture, for example, there are simple, but important expectations in the ritual of greeting. You are supposed to look someone in the eyes, touch them a certain way, and offer verbal recognition such as "Hello." However, such a simple procedure is totally different in another culture. No wonder visitors experience uncertainty and anxiety for those accustomed to the American style of greeting. In other cultures, such a procedure may be marked by lack of eye contact and lack of touch with few spoken words. In some parts of Japanese culture one bows, presents a business card, and waits for the person of higher status to initiate the conversation.

Another aspect of cultural rules is called rituals. *Rituals* refer to activities customarily followed in a culture conditioned by the standards and rules of that culture. Some rituals are formal, as in ceremonies, rites, formal occasions, initiations, solemn observances, or liturgies. Examples include weddings, births, funerals, baptisms, graduations, and a host of others. Other rituals are informal customary observances and lack the stiffness and solemnity of formal rituals. Examples include meeting friends after work, going to lunch at a certain place every week, crossing your fingers for good luck, or throwing bird seed at a wedding. In general, these are more casual. Rituals can be mixtures of formal and informal or be marked by a series of punctuations of formal/informal rituals (even routines) within a larger ritual.

Institutions Within Cultures

Most of us recognize that every culture has formalized systems to handle numerous aspects of a culture's ultimate survival in ways that are accepted and often sanctioned by law. These formalized, sanctioned systems within a culture are called institutions. The ones we discuss here can be argued to be basic to life and survival. That is why cultures often present these as fundamental to the economic, legal, social, and spiritual nature of a culture.

Economic Institutions

Every culture has various mechanisms of dealing with economics and work, known as economic systems. Examples in most parts of the globe are well known, so let us mention a few of the more unusual illustrations of economic systems. A practice among farmers in certain parts of the United States is to "swap out" work, whereby one farmer helps another harvest crops and the second reciprocates. Money is seldom exchanged in this process, although a system of informal record keeping keeps both parties aware of who owes whom. While monetary economic systems play a dominant role in most cultures today, this example reminds us that other methods of exchange exist according to unique cultural situations. Highlanders in Papua

New Guinea traditionally used the sweet potato as one unit of exchange. A missionary once described the mild surprise of foreign visitors to a church meeting where the indigenous church members contributed a large pile of sweet potatoes instead of money for a Sunday collection.

Family as Institution

Like many other cultural elements, kinship is a highly integrated part of cultural experiences. The forms and institutions regarding family vary culturally, but family needs are universal. That is why institutions and laws regarding family exist. Although models of family organization and system change constantly, theorists believe that the family functionally serves to meet the demands of a particular cultural group. Anthropologist Robin Fox summarized this position:

> I have tried to show how kinship systems are responses to various recognizable pressures within a framework of biological, psychological, ecological, and social limitations. Many anthropologists write as though kinship systems have dropped from the sky onto societies—they're there because they're there because. . . . In truth, they are there because they answer certain needs—do certain jobs. When these change, the systems change—but only within certain limits.[13] Clearly, societies organize the family as they would any other aspect of a social group—to meet needs practically.

Because they face common problems and needs, family units adapt to meet those needs. For example, in cultures where economic needs exist for labor, a marriage model of polygamy has developed. (As an aside polygamy is the generic word for the more specific *polygyny* or two or more wives and *polyandry* for two or more husbands). Functional need-meeting may account for some of these models, but other cultural factors also account for marital norms: superstitions, magic, status, etc. Other basic models of marital units, such *monogamy* (one husband and one wife), and *serial monogamy* (a series of monogamous marriages with different partners) become institutionalized at various levels of acceptance within a culture.

Researchers describe family units under two major classes. The first unit is the *nuclear family,* a unit referring to father, mother, and siblings. The second unit is the *extended family,* which includes the nuclear family and extends to incorporate the grandparents, uncles, aunts, cousins, and so on. *Descent groups* refer to a common ancestry for group members. A collection of lineages where common descent is often demonstrated is a *clan.* Collections of clans may become a *tribe* in some cases. Marriage only within the clan (or any significant unit) is called *endogamy.* Marriage from outside the clan (or other significant unit) is called *exogamy.* Both endogamy and exogamy formats can result in social and economic relationships between the units involved.

Kinship systems also involve the role of authority. Male-dominated authority patterns in the family are called *patriarchal,* while female-dominated authority patterns are called *matriarchal.* Finally, qualities of inheritance or naming, or both, that come through the mother's side are found in *matrilineal* cultures. *Patrilineal* groups foster inheritance or naming, or both, emphasizing the father's side.

Universally, societies have some form of governing organization functioning on both a formal and an informal level. On the *formal* level, such governing organizations originate because of self-appointment, inherited rights, vote, consensus, or political takeover. A less obvious *informal* method of accruing perceived power, status, and leadership also exists. In various cultural groups, some leaders are assumed to have a certain degree of supernatural power. Many years ago, a group of South Sea islanders considered the power of *mana* (special power or magic) to dwell in certain individuals. This impersonal power was believed to cause its recipients to possess the equivalent of what we might term "power," since persons who were perceived to have high degrees of mana usually had greater financial prowess, inherent status, and attributed power. Individuals believed this power also resided because of some special charm or incantation formula. The term for this perceived power stuck—the word can still refer to a special leadership.

Aside from the concept of impersonal supernatural power residing in or near a person, traditional leadership in political organizations among traditional cultures seems closely linked with age and economic qualities. In Ghana, for example, village chieftainship and eldership appear to be related closely to man's age (usually over 50 years old), economic ability (usually higher economic status), and family.

Related to formal and informal political systems in a culture is the concept of social control. All cultures have methods of dealing with violations of norms (accepted modes of behavior) and laws. Societal punishment appears to be universal, although consequences vary from fines to banishment or death. For example, two visitors in an African country unknowingly walked through sacred African *ju-ju* ground, a religiously special place, and were fined the national equivalent of one month's wages. Physical punishment also exemplifies differing cultural solutions to the universal need for order as "caning" in Singapore illustrates.

Like every other element of culture, social control develops from specific cultural contexts. This chapter opened with several examples related to social control. A difficulty arises when we compare social control in one culture with its counterpart in another culture. Many international persons, for example, believe that the United States is far too lenient in its punishment for certain crimes; conversely, many U.S. citizens believe that some countries have enacted overly strict laws. Evaluation of cultural methods of social control depends on examining each culture from its own perspective.

Health Institutions

How a culture addresses the health of cultural members also poses a significant cultural system. As Harris and Moran observe, the very concept of meaningful health can differ among cultures.[14] The methodologies by which people are medically treated can range from chemical medication by highly educated medical specialists to herbal application by village practioners.

Hospitals and medical clinics are relatively new innovations in some cultures, and sometimes an interesting mixture of the traditional medicines with the modern medicines appears in hospital rooms. In Papua New Guinea, family medical tradition has sometimes combined with modern hospitalization as family members take turns in groups staying with a patient, cooking food, and practically camping out in the patient's room. Health information is a topic currently significant for those working in developing countries. Not only is it important to understand the health system of a culture in order to manage it effectively from within, but the nature of health delivery is equally important in order to disseminate health information.

Cultural differences related to health care delivery unfortunately correspond to differential quality of life questions. Traditionally disadvantaged ethnic populations in the United States have higher than average infant mortality rates and overall fewer life span years on the average. While socioeconomic factors play some role in these differences, other cultural factors intervene. We have adapted several of Richard Brislin's observations concerning reasons for poor physical and mental health associated with culture:[15]

1. lack of financial resources causes people to wait too long before calling a health professional;

2. traditional remedies may be used either because modern medicine is too expensive or because it is seen as ineffective;

3. little trust in health subsystems or in health professionals;

4. inadequate or inaccurate information provided for families;

5. cultural values toward the age at which mothers pay more attention to their infant's health needs;

6. accurate indicators of physical or psychological distress are not viewed as significant indicators of illness to report. In other words, symptoms a certain culture looks to as a sign of illness may be inaccurately linked to the real illness, and conversely, symptoms that modern health professionals look for in examinations may seem irrelevant to an acculturated individual;

7. nonverbal signs typically associated with certain psychological disorders (like depression) are culture-bound, especially clinical diagnoses that involve interaction and rapport qualities and facial expressions. Mental health experts must conduct clinical evaluations using cultural base lines of normality.

8. world view intervenes in preventing modern medicine; for example, a person who believes in animism (witches and spirits) needs to be evaluated in light of the entire culture's beliefs. By western psychological standards, a person having a vision may seem mentally unstable, but by certain traditional African standards the person would be normal. We also can add fatalism, ancestor worship, the importance of silence, stoicism, language norms, and a host of other variables related to world view and values that intervene in accurate physical and mental health assessments.

Educational Institutions

Cultural educational systems widely differ. In the British educational system, for instance, students are either university or vocational bound, influenced by testing by about age twelve or fourteen. Also, many nations emphasize more than one language in education from early childhood through high school. Many foreign universities are structured differently from those in the United States. At some universities, subjects are studied a year at a time, not by semester or quarter unit credits. The critical point for intercultural communication is recognizing diversity in educational subsystems and how those differences alter our perceptions and messages.

Religious systems involve beliefs, ceremonies, places of worship, norms of respect, and linguistic concepts surrounding worship and spiritual issues. Many visitors to mosques and temples, for instance, neglect basic etiquette by failing to remove their shoes or observe other norms of respect. Recognizing the external elements of religiosity in a particular culture not only prevents cultural mistakes but also can affect insights into macrocultural patterns, cultural beliefs, and cultural values. For example, during the holy month for Moslems, fasting occurs from dawn to dusk. As told by a Thai participant, several Thai workers (mostly Buddhist) who worked side by side with Islamic workers failed to appreciate the significance of the period of time and the rituals associated with the fasting. Consequently, the organizational climate during that month was tense and negatively altered communication patterns, work productivity, and morale. Understanding basic religious beliefs, significant holidays, and religious practices can facilitate effective intercultural communication. Elements and institutions around which cultures are organized have been identified. What phenomena account for a culture's changes? The topic of explaining culture shift is complex. Our discussion of cultural elements would be incomplete without briefly exploring social forces and theories leading to change.

How cultures have developed, and more specifically, how they have dealt with innovation and adaptation during that development over time is a topic that can assist our understanding of culture as a variable in the communication process. In this closing section, we highlight several main directions to explain cultural development and change.

The first explanation involves what occurs when cultures borrow or in some other way come into contact with innovation in its many forms. External contact of one culture meeting another can produce change in one or the other or both. When the Pilgrims ventured to the United States, some of their habits changed; partially because of culture contact, they borrowed survival skills from Native Americans, such as planting and eating corn and other foods. Sometimes, cultural borrowing occurs deliberately as part of someone's agenda or strategy. In the case of the Australian stone axe culture mentioned earlier in this chapter, acceptance of a culturally foreign object proved disastrous.

Many years ago, blackbirds were brought into the United States from England to control insects. However, today in some mid-southern states, these birds are creating an enormous health problem and millions of dollars of grain loss each year. Another example also illustrates this point. A hearty ground cover useful in Japan was imported to the United States for planting along roadsides. For some reason, the plant life grew so well that it became uncontrollable, covering fence lines, large trees, and waterways.

There is little question that cultural borrowing can significantly alter culture. We only have to think of a few cases of imported products to illustrate this consequence: international foods, technology, and clothing all represent significant

Religious Institutions

Theories of Cultural Development and Change

Cultural Borrowing and Innovation Acceptance

ways cultural borrowing affects our lives. Culture contact that leads to change can be planned or unplanned. When planned, the culture contact typically is part of a strategic plan or special effort.

Cultural Crisis

Sometimes, cultural changes are the result of uncontrollable forces, such as floods, hurricanes, volcanic eruptions, and other spontaneous events that cause physical relocation or psychological alteration. Just as disasters create a need for cultural realignment, these cataclysmic changes and crises in the life and history of a group of people can also forge a new culture from the old. For example, the severe Guatemalan earthquakes of a few years ago, toppled entire barrios built on hillsides and engulfed mountain villages, and led to cultural change in the massive relocation that followed. The settled villagers of the mountains became the new settlers in plains regions. This shift has caused alteration of endogamy, authority structure, and language.

Contrived, human-made forces can be just as cataclysmic, and at least as forceful, as natural disasters in shaping cultural destinies. Wars, political coups, and installation of high dams along rivers seriously alter culture. For example, war-torn Vietnam, among other things, left a trail of refugees, many of whom settled in the United States. In some cases, highly skilled physicians, lawyers, or engineers worked at menial jobs as a result of their immigration. Family structures were also altered. Many of the younger Vietnamese showed greater acculturation capabilities than their elders. Despite family pressure to let the elders make decisions, pressure from the new culture sometimes pushed the younger generation toward family leadership and individualism.

As World War II encroached upon the South Pacific, New Guinea islanders were dramatically confronted with strange new ways. The war brought guns, machines of all sorts, vehicles, and hundreds of other things needed for life support and battle. The alien aircraft dropping their packaged cargoes from the sky surprised the islanders and yet enticed them toward these "miracles." When the hardware was removed at the war's end, an unusual cult developed. This new culture was termed the "cargo cult," and one of its tenets rested on the expectation of a return of the cargo. To this day, the quasi-religious culture still anticipates the return of the cargo.

Some economic changes induce social change. The Aswân High Dam on the Nile River has affected Egyptian rural life. Some observers believe that the many economic benefits of the dam may be partially balanced by its social effects. Many villagers have shifted occupations and live in newly formed towns, a move that has eroded traditional lines of authority. The farmer, now a factory worker at a fertilizer plant, sometimes loses his personal pride as his superiors devaluate his former life. Once prosperous river villages now lie under water, swept by the currents of a lake newly formed for a developing nation.

Ecological Change

While cultural cataclysms have an immediate crisis-centered impact on a culture's development, cultural experts recognize that a culture's ecology also has a long-term, gradual impact. Certain environmental features may influence a culture's diet, dress, religion, and marriage partnerships.

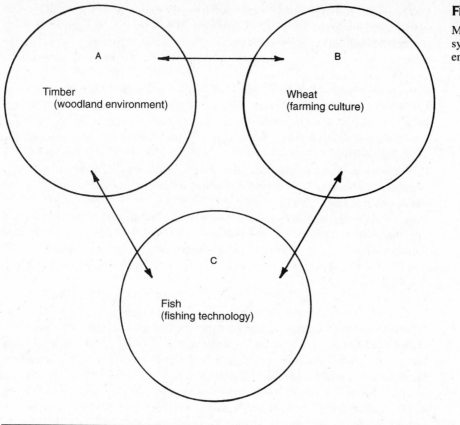

Figure 3.2

Model of cultural
symbiosis based on
environmental factors.

Ecological environment is important to culture for at least two reasons. One is that, as population increases, available land decreases. This population pressure pushes natural boundaries to their limit, and new frontiers are colonized. We see that today in news stories about the rain forests. As a result of the new frontier environment, changes in agricultural practices, dress, diet, and word usages emerge. Also, hierarchy and structure, power, economic, and political changes occur.

A second reason that environment influences culture involves the distribution of products, services, and materials in the importing and exporting with other cultures. For example, if the environment of culture C contains necessary items for cultures A and B, a symbiotic relationship develops. *Symbiosis* refers to fulfilling mutual needs between two or more cultures. Suppose that groups A, B, and C contain environmental productions of timber (A), wheat (B), and fish (C) (figure 3.2). Inasmuch as all three cultures desire these things, economic exchanges develop and symbiotic relationships crystallize.

As economic interplay heightens, significant social changes may occur, different from cultural traditions. Members of a submissive culture may now become fierce bargainers or symbiosis may escalate; or, endogamous cultures (marrying inside their own group) may find attractive marriage partners outside their traditional social units.

| Dominant Theme Analysis | Another theory for explaining culture examines the major themes of a culture. The renown anthropologist Ruth Benedict explained how dominant ideas and themes of a culture not only signify values but serve to guide activities, rules, and customs. In other words, these fundamental cultural themes act as a dominant force on action and thought. |

Among the Zuni Indians, for instance, two cultural themes stand out. According to Zuni tradition, men submerge their activities into those of the entire group and claim no personal authority. A second theme is nonviolence. Even under attacks of insult and abuse, accepted behavioral systems provide nonviolent outlets.

National and regional cultures illustrate key themes that drive the nature of a culture. In Asian cultures, group harmony and subjecting self to the group is a predominant theme, a value strongly influencing culture. Some employees in Japan so identify with the company, for instance, that they introduce themselves with the company name first and then their own name. In one case, a Japanese engineer with an electronics firm so identified with the company that he called himself NJT Kanakamani, where NJT refers to the corporation and Kanakamani to his name.

| Functionalism | Another theory of culture is called functionalism, developed by Bronislaw Malinowski around 1944. From his work with the Trobriand islanders, he reasoned that cultural systems are an outgrowth of three underlying human needs: basic, derived, and integrative. Culture develops and organizes its values and practices around what the culture considers ways to deal with those needs. *Basic* needs refer to survival needs, such as food, water, and shelter. *Derived* needs refer to "social coordination," including division of labor, distribution of food, and social control. The third need is *integrative,* or, as Nanda continues, the need for security and social harmony met by magic, knowledge, myth, and art.[16] Malinowski's fundamental notion was that every aspect of culture can be summarized by one of these three needs and that cultures develop to satisfy these needs in ways functional for their situation and with their particular resources.[17] |

Developing Intercultural Skills in Knowledge of Culture's Workings

1. *Respect the dignity and personhood of others.* Even if you disagree with a culture's values or any other aspect of a culture, you may wish to avoid arguing. Respect the rights of others in their cultural situation, and seek to understand the culture rather than to criticize it. Try to focus more on the people rather than their system.

2. *Do not let others' criticism get you down.* In your attempts to learn a new culture, you will always find people who criticize your efforts to adapt and practice skills in intercultural communication. Be a bit thick-skinned. Even a friend's criticism can be misguided if that person is unwilling to try to understand a new culture. Of course, if they are trying to tell you that you are reacting inappropriately, then be aware of their honest feedback. Keep in mind

there are times you could be experiencing culture shock, and friends can help a person keep balance and perspective.

3. *Do not feel as if you have to be liked everywhere by everyone.* The outgoing American may feel alienated in some cultures where members do not act as gregarious as the visitor may prefer. Everyone cannot be liked everywhere. Even if you feel that people do not like you, keep trying to communicate.

4. *Work on adaptability.* Studies show that being able to adapt quickly to new and different situations is essential to becoming a good intercultural communicator. In many circumstances, you may prefer to suspend judgment and listen to other people—and avoid merely reacting. Emotions quickly blind us, especially when frustration and emotional tensions are high anyway because of our arrival in a new culture.

5. *Work on initiative.* Be willing to take social risks. Try to open yourself to new cultural experiences. The principles in this chapter, including this suggestion, do not apply only to cultures outside the United States. Showing initiative and creativity can help you in everyday interpersonal communication and relationships. The words of Shakespeare seem particularly important as you ingratiate yourself with others: "Our doubts are traitors and cause us to lose the good we oft might win by fearing to attempt."

6. *Be observant.* Part of becoming proficient in intercultural communication involves watching and listening. You may find it helpful to write in a diary or notebook the things you observed each day. Write down things people say, stories you hear, or anything you think is important. Later reflection can be an amazing tool for learning.

7. *Be ready for lack of privacy.* One of the things many people value without realizing it, is personal privacy. In many cultures, privacy is viewed differently than you might expect. Rude as it may seem to you, personal privacy simply may not be significant in another culture or may be expressed in very different ways than you have thought before.

8. *Do not superimpose your political values.* All too often a person in an intercultural contact converses about political systems to the exclusion of other topics of conversation. In fact, some people get into violent arguments about politics and misjudge a culture because of its political norms. Remember, a culture can be appreciated for topics and areas other than politics.

9. *Recognize perceived roles of women.* A number of cultures hold attitudes toward the role of women that may vary greatly from your attitudes. Though you may disagree with these attitudes, try to demonstrate respect for cultural traditions, whether you think they are right or wrong. Many intercultural relationships are lost trying to win ideological battles. You may win the argument but lose the relationship.

10. *Respect tradition.* Most of us who grew up in the United States have not learned the same respect for tradition that many members from other cultures hold. Many cultural members believe that traditional ways are tried and proven and that to disregard these matters is highly disrespectful.

This Chapter in Perspective

This chapter defines culture and explores the key points of that definition through a systems model and a discussion of the many elements implied in the model. Beyond an appreciation for cultural elements, the chapter's goal is to introduce the inner culture including a culture's history, identity, beliefs, values, and world view. Culture can also be expressed by elements that surround a culture's activities, rules and customs, and communication patterns. Cultures also develop formalized institutions surrounding the insuring continuation of basic survival needs in areas of economics, family, politics and governance, health, education, and religion. The chapter concludes with five major theories explaining how cultures develop and change.

We do not become experts in intercultural communication because we now know that culture is a system composed of interrelated elements and institutions. This discussion, however, may help set the stage for understanding. Sensitization to another person's culture is a prerequisite for effective intercultural communication.

Exercises

1. Interview an international student on your campus. Then explain, to your class or a small group, a cultural element, a cultural theory, or a system of culture from the international student's home culture.

2. In almost every issue of *National Geographic* there are articles on other cultures. Pick an article that describes a culture of some interest to you, and give a brief synopsis. What theoretical point of view did the author of the article take concerning his or her description of the culture? Can you identify the major cultural variables uncovered in the article?

Endnotes

1. Richard Brislin, *Understanding Culture's Influence on Behavior,* 2d ed. (Orlando: Harcourt Brace Jovanovich, 1993). Brislin explains how culture is learned through contact in numerous ways ranging across personal contacts, family, and numerous institutions in culture. Socialization thus occurs in context, not in isolation.

2. *Overseas Diplomacy,* U.S. Navy, Bureau of Navy Personnel, 1973.

3. Michael L. Hecht, Peter A. Andersen, and Sidney A. Ribeau, "The Cultural Dimensions of Nonverbal Communication," in *Handbook of International and Intercultural Communication,* ed. Molefi Kete Asante and William B. Gudykunst (Newbury Park, Calif.: Sage, 1989).

4. David Matsumoto, Harald G. Wallbott, and Klaus R. Scherer, "Emotions in Intercultural Communication," in *Handbook of International and Intercultural Communication,* ed. Molefi Kete Asante and William B. Gudykunst (Newbury Park, Calif.: Sage, 1989).

5. R. Becvar and D. Becvar, *Systems Theory and Family Therapy* (New York: University Press of America, 1982).

6. R. Cattell, "New Concepts for Measuring Leadership, in Terms of Group Syntality," *Human Relations* 2 (1951): 161–84. In his approach to groups, Cattell likened groups to individual personality. Knowing the group personality can be useful in understanding how a group might act or how its members might think in certain situations.

7. Raymond Rodgers, "Folklore Analysis and Subcultural Communication Research: Another View of World View" (paper presented to the Society for Intercultural Education, Training, and Research, Phoenix, Arizona, February 1978).

8. Anita K. Foeman, "Managing Multiracial Institutions: Goals and Approaches for Race-Relations Training," *Communication Training* 40 (1991): 255–65.

9. Lauriston Sharp, "Steel Axes for Stone Age Australians," in *Human Problems in Technological Change,* ed. Edward H. Spicer (New York: Russell Sage Foundation, 1952).

10. Everett M. Rogers, *Diffusion of Innovations,* 4th ed. (New York: Free Press, 1995).

11. Nguyen Kim Hong, "Vietnamese Themes," (paper presented to the Regional Indochinese Task Force Workshop for the New York City Board of Education, New York, January, 1976).

12. John Baldwin, "Self-Monitoring, Cognitive Complexity, Stereotypes and Role Perception as Correlations of Communication Satisfaction in Intercultural Marriages" (master's thesis, Abilene Christian University, 1991).

13. Robin Fox, *Kinship and Marriage* (Baltimore: Penquin, 1971), 25.

14. Philip R. Harris and Robert T. Moran, *Managing Cultural Differences,* 4th ed. (Houston: Gulf, 1995).

15. Richard Brislin, *Understanding Culture's Influence on Behavior,* 2d ed. (Orlando: Harcourt Brace Jovanovich, 1993).

16. Serena Nanda, *Cultural Anthropology* (New York: Van Nostrand, 1980).

17. Marvin Harris, *Cultural Anthropology* (New York: Harper and Row, 1983).

Chapter 4

Cultural Diversity

Within Culture

Microcultures and Intercultural Communication

OBJECTIVES   *After completing this chapter, you should be able to*

1. Identify the models associated with perception of cultural diversity and microcultures

2. List the rhetorical strategies used between in-groups and out-groups in their communication

3. Identify communication strategies for effective relationships with microcultures of cultural diversity

4. Identify types of racism

5. Apply communication solutions to prejudice and racism

6. List factors that block effective intercultural communication concerning cultural diversity

Dealing with multicultural pluralism is a major goal for every culture.

The model for this text begins with PCDs, perceived cultural differences, and the consequent direction individuals take when encountering these differences. To highlight cultural variability is to underscore the reason why intercultural communication occurs. The last chapter defined culture and described elements and institutions within larger macrocultures. In this chapter, we move to a discussion concerning cultures within a culture.

The term we use throughout this book is *microculture* which refers to one or a combination of (1) groups we choose to associate with, (2) collective identities we prefer to maintain, (3) demographics we may represent, and/or (4) ethnic and family origins we may experience based on birth. Together or singly, microcultures form a matrix of cultural diversity within a culture. In other words, we focus in this chapter on social groupings within a culture, their role in perceived differences affecting relationships, how they serve as a "group identity," and how they influence communication. It is easy to recognize how group identities form a part of culture and how they influence communication. Consider the many ethnic tensions in schools and in the workplace. Or, think about the many group categories whose labels become a basis for inclusion and exclusion in many relationships. These dynamics are associated with group membership. By exploring those factors, we think the study of microcultures and their influence on perception and communication is fascinating and illuminates our developing effective intercultural communication.

We are making two observations the reader will be reminded of at this point in the text. One is that cultural membership can influence communication. The second is that the PCDs between people can influence the drive to communication constructively or destructively in a perceived intercultural encounter. This chapter begins by helping us see first the social categorization process often leading to the PCDs, and second, the various social groupings that typically constitute microcultures.

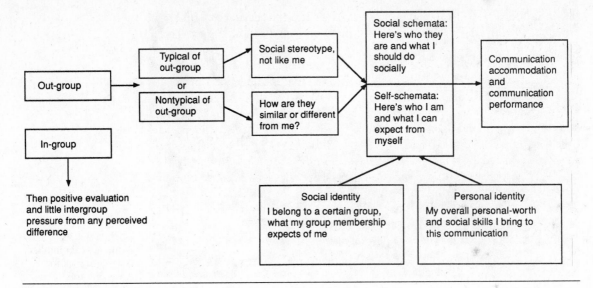

Figure 4.1

A model of social categorization.

Understanding Social Perception and Its Influence on Intercultural Communication

Explaining Social Perception Through Social Categorization and the In-group/Out-group Model

We begin this discussion by describing the perceptual theory leading to perceived cultural differences as they pertain to experiencing cultural diversity and the microcultures that constitute that diversity.

The process of perceiving cultural differences, especially related to experiencing cultural diversity, involves a series of stages as the model in figure 4.1 reveals. The first part of the process involves *social categorization* where we decide if the other person can be defined as within my social grouping or outside such a social unit.[1] This process of classifying into in-group or out-group initiates a set of consequences for the communication to follow. In a way, this part of the model is similar to stereotyping. We put people in different boxes, and, unfortunately, build fences around the boundaries related to in-groups and out-groups. For example, a person is either a Hispanic or an Anglo, an Asian or a black. Over time, we tend to build a set of expectations of how Hispanics, Anglos, Asians, and blacks are supposed to act. Some folks have more permeable boxes than others, but the point is the tendency to build these perimeters.

The second step of the model shows how we further refine the categorization by asking if the "out-group" person is typical or nontypical of the out-group stereotype. Here, individuals project various traits, emotions, roles, abilities, and interests of out-group members. Mental tapes are played and images resurrected that can stimulate our beliefs about the group. As a person said recently, "She must like a certain kind of music, because she is from _____ group (a particular ethnic group)" or "He is probably a good athlete because he is of a particular racial heritage."

In the third step, the model indicates that we test further on how similar or dissimilar *from me* in addition to how typical or nontypical of the out-group they seem.

The fourth step in the model points out that we mentally evaluate what is *expected of me* in two ways. One way is what social role am I expected to play in this relationship. Researchers call this the *social role schemata*. The belief factors in expectations of how I should perform socially given this situation. The second expectation is what personal worth or competency I bring to the encounter and what consequent actions and communication I should take based on my personal beliefs and competencies. Underlying what is called this *self-schemata* are two identity issues.[2] My *social identity* asks my belief of my group membership's expectations of me in this situation. And, my *personal identity* asks, "What can I expect of myself in this communication situation?" given my feelings and personal worth and competency for this situation.

Based on a cumulative processing of all this, a final stage results in *communication accommodation*. This means that we typically engage communication strategies to deal with the encounter. As we have repeated since chapter 1, sometimes the strategies we engage are functional and lead to positive and effective outcomes. However, sometimes the strategies and our communication performance are dysfunctional and lead to negative, ineffective outcomes.[3] The effectiveness dimension is measured as we indicated in chapter 1.

The effectiveness outcome of this process is altered by several factors:

1. When arrogance is perceived or present on the part of one or both interactants.
2. When anxiety or uncertainty remains high following the stereotyping process.
3. When personality factors mediate the process rigidity (high dogmatism, low category width), low self-monitoring (a person who adjusts with less awareness to communication needs in various communication settings), low in cognitive complexity (or a person who lacks ability in discerning aspects of people and their interpersonal relationships).
4. When the interactants lack motivation to pursue the communication or to foster a relationship.
5. When stereotypes are premature and draw upon negative attributions.
6. When our identities are insecure, lacking robust social or personal identification.[4]

As stated earlier, social categorization leads to inclusion of in-groups and exclusion of out-groups. In many parts of the world, cultural diversity and microcultures frequently define in-group and out-group relations. The strife in the former Yugoslavia exemplifies, almost to the extreme, the in-group/out-group distinctions based on what has been called ethnic cleansing.

Responses to social categorization reflect a rhetorical pattern often experienced under conditions of in-group/out-group relations. We will summarize these patterns by calling them the *social response* model which is best explained by four metaphors: the "S" of suspicion, stereotypes, solidarity, and separation.

Explaining the Consequences of Social Perception with the Social Response Model

In-group and out-group communication is often characterized by alienation. Photo by Tu Deng/Eastfoto.

Suspicion.   Some situations are marked by mutual suspicions of group *A* toward group *B*. The erupting racial tension in schools, cities, and the workplace in the United States illustrates the intense feelings resulting in not only poor communication, but avoidance and hostility. The level of suspicion aroused is clearly irrational in most cases and is fueled by specific features, such as the "we-they" syndrome and mistrust.

1.   We-They distinction. When suspicion hovers over the communication context, a rhetorical distinction emerges in the communication about the out-group. Win-win language gives way to win-lose language. Distinctions between the "we" and "they" grow large. Minnick made this point and illustrated the principle with the words of Malcolm X:
    No, I'm not an American. I'm one of the 22 million black people who are victims of Americanism. One of the 22 million black people who are victims of democracy. . . .[5]

2.   Mistrust. Suspicion also correlates with attitudes of mistrust. Unfortunately, since contacts are often limited, people selectively perceive out-groups and affirm their misconceptions often by continuing to avoid contact. In circular fashion, mistrust is strengthened.

Research such as Broome's case analysis of Greek in-group/out-group communication documents many of the outcomes we have described. His study, for instance, described protection, trust, support, cooperation, sympathy, and admiration among in-group members. His analysis contrasts these positive factors with attitudes toward out-groups reflected by suspicion, mistrust, rejection of out-group influence, avoidance, hostility, concealment, deception, and general lack of helpfulness.[6]

Stereotypes.   Stereotypes develop as a way of organizing our world. Categorizing is a necessary part of daily functioning. However, stereotyping of people can be misleading, since all people within a category are not alike and since we may not always fully understand what we perceive.

Experimental studies confirm anecdotal notions of stereotypes and specify the ways in which those stereotypes operate. In a classic study of stereotypic attitudes toward Mexican Americans, one group was shown slides of a Mexican American male in various scenes—in a yard behind a frame house, carrying trash cans, raking leaves around a tree, and putting the leaves into a wagon. He was dressed in a work shirt, work pants, and an outdoor work hat. A second matched group was shown exactly the same scenes, except that the man in the slides was an Anglo male dressed exactly as the Mexican American stimulus figure. The respondents perceived the Mexican American stereotypically: having less education, working for others not self, and having a large family. Sadly, evidence continues to support a general insensitivity.[7] (See Jack Condon's *Good Neighbors,* or Deneve and Condon *Hispanic Cultures: A Kaleidoscope in Intercultural Communication.*) The problem is complex, but we can improve this problem starting with some simple skills.

1. *Seek a common task.* By seeking a common task we can maximize our chances for a heightened overlap of experiences. In those experiences we see the other person more fully, we experience the emotions of knowing another.

2. *Practice empathy.* Empathy comes from trying to put yourself in the other person's shoes. Asking for information, following-through, keeping promises, and showing trust are but a few of many ways to better understand another person.

3. *Suspend judgments.* If interaction with a person from an out-group raises negative attitudes toward that group, then make a conscious effort to suspend those attitudes. Consider the uniqueness of each individual by carefully listening, expressing your view honestly, and then continuing to listen.

Solidarity.   A third social response involves a group's expression of solidarity. They view themselves in the same social condition, a condition often described in crisis. Minnick again illustrates this rhetorical response, this time in the timeless and honored words of Martin Luther King, Jr. when he declared:

> But one hundred years later, the Negro still is not free. One hundred years later, the life of the Negro is still sadly crippled by the manacles of segregation and the chains of discrimination.
>
> One hundred years later, the Negro lives on a lonely island of poverty in the midst of a vast ocean of material prosperity. One hundred years later, the Negro is still languished in the corners of American society and finds himself an exile in his own land. So we have come here today to dramatize a shameful condition.
>
> In a sense, we have come to our nation's capital to cash a check. When the architects of our republic wrote the magnificent words of the Constitution and the Declaration of Independence, they were signing a promissory note to which every American was to fall heir.[8]

The point of solidarity so eloquently stressed in this excerpt, was the mutual suffering and the future promise of mutual reward by remaining loyal to the culture. The speech and the movement itself highlights some important communication factors associated with solidarity.

1. *In-group code.* By using a code system that only in-group members understand, a sense of belonging and uniqueness can result, facilitating solidarity.

2. *In-group symbols.* To the extent that the group encourages high levels of solidarity, use of symbols such as colors, musical lyrics, slogans, and significant objects, also foster solidarity.

3. *In-group expectations.* Solidarity also results from clear expectations. Whether one is a member of the group or not, norms and performance standards often are known.

4. *In-group enemies.* The racial tensions of our age starkly remind us of instances where in-groups portray out-groups in negative, hostile, enemy-like terms. Broome and others again remind us that such tensions are global, illustrated by his study of Greek negative attitudes toward out-groups mentioned earlier.

Separation.   A final theme of in-group/out-group communication is best expressed in the metaphor separation. Evidence points to isolation, exclusion, and feelings of loss among heritage cultural members. This exclusion theme is elevated when out-groups find themselves uninvited or disengaged from in-groups. In the case of minorities as out-groups, Gonzales addresses this point from a Mexican American analysis. According to his research, the separation theme is painfully experienced in light of a Mexican cultural quality which values "otherness," a value that typically embraces friendship and openness. But the culture has experienced hatred and fears rebuff, exclusion, and even demolishment. The social response to this Mexican experience, notes Gonzalez, is ambivalence, self-conscious resignation, withdrawal, and feelings of betrayal. These themes are rooted in the Spanish Conquest, but no doubt have streams of present reality as Mexican Americans interact throughout North America.[9]

Explaining Social Perception with the Social Attitudes Model

We have examined earlier how dysfunctional attitudes arrest the development of effective intercultural communication. This section identifies attitudes that consistently limit intercultural relationships.

Ethnocentrism.   The first of those social attitudes is one you may recall from chapter 3. Ethnocentrism is an evaluation of one's culture as better than or superior to another culture. This attitude represents much more than technical or quantitative assessment, such as recognizing that a culture has more technology or more resources than another culture. It is cultural arrogance, loaded with emotions, and broadly applied to out-groups. The resulting "my culture is better than your culture" belief weaves its way into thoughts and actions, such as arrogance, avoidance, withdrawal, faulty attribution, and faulty categorizing. Although the term normally appears in discussions comparing global macrocultures, it is easy to recognize how ethnocentrism surrounds numerous diversity cultures.

In chapter 2, one of the axioms concerning attributions or summary motives and impressions about groups and individuals was noted. Sometimes the information about a culture is accurate. For example, to state that in general Japanese politely respect elders or that traditional Thais bow as a form of greeting to elderly persons is essentially correct about many members of those cultures. You can always find an impolite Japanese or an inhospitable Thai person, but the trend toward frequent actions is accurate. In this sense, stereotypes can refer to data and trends that are correct.

Stereotypes also can be inaccurate. How then does this inaccuracy occur? First, the facts may be based on incorrect observations of a culture, perhaps overly subjective. Second, extrapolation of qualities and intentions from trends may be unwarranted leaps of interpretation. For example, to say "Rural people are friendly," may be accurate regarding many rural settings and values. However, to go beyond cultural observations and add "Furthermore, they must not be too smart," is an outrageous extension of the first value (friendliness) into a different domain (intelligence). Third, stereotypes which assume that what is true of the group is true of every member, violates a significant rule of logic: each individual is not like the entire group, even if you accept the first premise about the group.

I am sure we also recognize the many *affective* or feeling components regarding stereotypes. Even to discuss this subject in the book may seem offensive because of the cultural tension some of our readers undoubtedly have experienced. Look at racial and ethnic tensions in the United States expressed between some urban blacks and Koreans, Hispanics and Anglos, Skinheads and Jews, Italians and Puerto Ricans. The in-group/out-group hostilities are explosive and leave little doubt of the deep-seated feelings lying underneath the diversity cultures' clash.

Racism and prejudice.   A third social attitude explores attitudes of dislike and hatred toward out-groups. Richard Brislin writes on the origins of prejudice, as a *socialization* process where pervasive negative stereotypes are passed on to children. If Brislin is right, the consequent intergenerational outlook is bleak. In this sense, emotion, not reason, captures our feelings of who is good and bad and how to feel about out-groups. Brislin's analysis forms a significant framework to understand the obvious and subtle ways of prejudice's forms, particularly as these evolve into hatred toward ethnic or racial groups, or racism.[10]

1. *Intense racism.* People believe or act in a way indicating their belief that certain groups were born as outcasts. Consequently, they are viewed as being of low worth. Clusters of negative beliefs surround intense racism, beliefs that discriminate, devalue, ignore, withdraw from, and perpetuate negative or injurious myths toward the target of racism.

2. *Symbolic racism.* Brislin uses this term referring to out-groups as devalued not because of inherent inferiority, but because the group is seen as blocking basic cultural goals. In many cases, individuals are not disliked, but again, the out-group is perceived as causing trouble, disrupting habits and values, or moving too fast.

3. *Tokenism.* This subtle form of prejudice involves a person's small participation in activities appearing nonprejudicial as self-convincing proof of not being prejudiced. As an example, Brislin indicates giving small amounts of money or limited time and effort toward minority group activities in order to make participants

The Contact Hypothesis

Research shows that developing the right kind of contact between people who perceive cultural diversity can facilitate improved communication.

1. *Make the contact personal.* Group meetings with little opportunity for sharing views and conversation beyond mere introductions does little more than allow for arms-length prejudice to continue. Contact alone does not work, but contact with intimacy has significant potential.

2. *Make the contact positive.* Sometimes structuring events that ensure positive contact and pleasant contact work best. A number of strategies exist to make the contact seem rewarding.

3. *Put people together with similar status.* In this case, role positions of similar rank or value are important. Pairing a lower positioned employee with an executive, for instance, works against the desired outcomes for the intergroup contact.

4. *Put people together with similar values.* As indicated in the last chapter, similarity of values fosters more rapid acceptance and assists credibility. For contact, the principle works to heighten positive evaluations toward an outgroup member.

5. *Reduce personal goals and agendas.* If the conversation pursues goals or agenda items that are relevant more to one than the other person in an intergroup contact session, this lack of empathy, perspective, and faulty listening make it less likely to experience positive communication adaptation outcomes.

6. *Show openness and respect.* These dual qualities work about as effectively in numerous intercultural contacts as almost any observation suggested. Openness implies response to differences that lead to inquisitiveness, willingness to learn, and tolerance of ambiguity. Respect carries an air of appreciation for differences and allows mistakes without judgment, expecting and creating mutual growth emerging from honest communication.

Source: Adapted from different studies by various authors.[11]

---

feel good. Actually, the feeling is superficial, and hiding beneath the surface because of lack of involvement is a potential or latent prejudice or racism.

4. *Arms-length prejudice.* A final category chosen from Brislin's work is the behavior where nonprejudicial actions are clearly demonstrated in public, social settings, but warmth, friendliness, and intimacy are withheld in private settings. For instance, going to a party and being nice to out-group members, but later acting uncomfortably in a one-to-one visit over coffee or ignoring roommates, neighbors, in potential interracial/interethnic friendships in any private settings.

For many years, researchers and practitioners have explored the boundaries of how intergroup contact can work best.[12]

Now that we have examined the dynamics of perception applied to cultural diversity and microcultural encounters, let us turn to the microcultures themselves. Again, the term microculture implies perceived cultural difference concerning the mileau of cultural diversity within a larger culture. These many group memberships are the source of many PCDs, or because of perceived differences, trigger intercultural communication responses when encountering cultural diversity.

Ethnic groups are identifiable bodies of people noted for their common heritage and cultural tradition, usually national and/or religious. Examples include Polish American, Italian American, and Mexican American. These examples can be misused or occasionally misleading because the naming process to identify ethnic groups changes frequently, and some members of ethnic groups may not like the names offered by the media and others. Nevertheless, the idea is to indicate a person's origin, without any preconceived value to the naming intended.

Racial groups are defined by genetically transmitted and inherited traits of physical appearance. Examples include African American (or "blacks"), Native Americans (or American Indians), Asian Americans, and so on. Since these examples focus from a U.S. cultural perspective, and differ within countries outside the United States, we give only a few suggested examples to illustrate the concepts.

There are two myths at work when these topics are brought up. One is the dynial myth, as if to say that ethnic and racial matters are not even problems. We recognize for some people these issues do not pose a problem. But, research and experience indicate that ethnic and racial labels persist, leaving unresolved problems in society. A second myth is to oversubscribe to ethnic and racial injustice. Such arguments in the extreme command power and social class interpretations in their communication theories. It is true that glass ceilings exist and invisible walls block progress. In many situations equality and fairness must be further implemented. But logic also dictates that not every problem can be laid at the feet of hierarchy, power, and inequality variables.

In any case, evidence continues to mount that ethnic or racial perceptual differences are one source initiating the intercultural communication process positively using functional approaches or negatively using dysfunctional approaches. In writing on race relations, Foeman commenting on an article from the *Harvard Business Review* about black managers states that, "After years of cross-cultural training activity many organizational members of color still report disappointment, dismay, frustration, and anger because they have not gained acceptance on par with white peers." She continues, noting that African American movement into upper ranks is unimpressive and that "while legal and political milestones may have been met, interpersonal acceptance has tended to lag behind."[13] Casmir reminds us that despite efforts to conceive of intercultural communication as individuals in interpersonal communication contexts, "it is the differences that create major challenges." While we think of ourselves as independent, Casmir argues that "human beings have always been *inter*dependent. . . . Along with the awareness of required interaction comes the recognition that we also have to deal with ethnic and racial diversity or even confrontations, because interdependence means that we 'cannot leave each other alone.' "[14] Other studies also indicate the importance of facing cultural pluralism in multicultural contexts in education and for the multiple communication encounters in the workplace involving cultural diversity.[15]

Intercultural Marriage as Microculture

In a chapter on cultural diversity, we choose to include a topic of growing interest, intercultural marriage. Intercultural marriages, sometimes called dual cultural marriages come in various forms, including rural, urban, interethnic, interracial, national and global macrocultures, mixed social classes, mixed religions, and mixed regions of the United States.[16] Where there are significant group differences that mark the marriage, we choose to call it *intercultural marriage,* and refer to the partners as *intercultural couples.*

Studies examining intercultural couples reveal a similar theme: intercultural marriage partners experience normally expected marital adjustment problems and unique cultural adjustment problems. The cultural adjustment problems in intercultural marriage manifest themselves in a variety of ways as follow.

The Romeo and Juliet effect.   This concept refers to intense feelings of attraction because family prejudices essentially deny the couple's blessing for marriage. Like the familiar Shakespeare story, the forbidden relationship seems to intensify attraction,[17] and in the early stages can be stronger than that of intracultural couples. Unfortunately, over time the intercultural couple, once so intensely in love, now face increased and unexpected criticism, unwelcome and unusual interference by parents, low acceptance among the community, and ultimately decreased trust between the couple. One study compared 170 intercultural and intracultural couples, including Caucasian, Samoan, Hawaiian, Tongan, New Zealander, Filipino, Chinese, and Japanese couples. The results indicated a general satisfaction with the marriage, for both the intracultural couples and the intercultural couples. However, the intercultural couples reported 63 percent negative responses toward the marriage compared to 36 percent negative responses among the intracultural couples.[18]

Role expectations.   In this same study wives felt pressured into accepting their husbands' culture. That is, the pressure to assimilate into their husbands' culture and to make greater adjustments was greater for wives. John Baldwin at Illinois State who began several years ago to forge several studies in this area found a similar result with Anglo-Hispanic couples; when the wife became "over-involved" or when other activities detracted from her husband's expectations about home, ratings on communication satisfaction dropped.[19]

Extended family intrusion.   Problems surrounding intrusion or evaluation by the extended family are often more frequent for intercultural couples. North American and Western cultures may not fully recognize the extended family influence in marriage.

Collective-individualistic cultures.   Some cultures engage in a sharing/caring approach because of group commitments and group obligations, while others are more concerned with themselves and are more individualistic. For instance, the intercultural couples in the study by Graham, Moeai, and Shizuru revealed a strong extended-family pattern for all the South Pacific (Polynesian) groups, which was described as a sharing culture. The interpersonal commitments of those from the sharing culture toward their extended family became an economic drain upon the family finances. Such a value system was a direct clash with their marriage partners who were from the "keeping" values of U.S. dominant nuclear families.[20]

Language and misunderstanding.   When two languages were spoken in an intercultural marriage, conflicts obviously resulted, particularly in instances of literal misunderstanding in language or wording, a psychological power struggle over who is going to control the household, and a question of which language will be used at home. According to Graham, Moeai, and Shizuru, when two languages are spoken in an intercultural marriage, the children tend to learn the mother's tongue more fluently when the wife retains the dominant influence over the child or when she does not adjust as quickly to the husband's language or both. However, if the wife is bilingual, speaking her husband's language as well as her own, and the child is exposed to both languages, then the child is slower in language acquisition and comprehension. Furthermore, the authors reported that if the child is forced to decide his cultural identity, he will most likely follow the mother. In one case in which a Samoan mother was married to a Tongan father, the child was asked, "What are you?" The reply was, "I am a Samoan."

Conflict styles.   Differences in styles of conflict resolution also mark a significant point of departure for intercultural couples. We can anticipate, as chapter 5 describes, how directness-indirectness, high context-low context cultures, monochronic-polychronic styles, and power distance are factors related to conflict in intercultural marriage.

Child rearing attitudes and practices.   Attitudes toward children and child-rearing methodologies represent another difference between the intercultural couples. Some cultures are much stricter with rules than other cultures, creating a value difference and a difference in the way values should be communicated and reinforced with children.

Negative expectations from the community.   Bizman asked 549 subjects to evaluate a carefully devised description of three conditions of Jewish intercultural and intracultural marriages: a western Jew married to a western Jew, an eastern Jew married to an eastern Jew, and a western Jew married to an eastern Jew. In other words, the study afforded a case of outsiders looking in on an intracultural and an intercultural couple. The conclusions indicated that intercultural marriages (East-West) were expected to be 25 percent less successful in the marriage.[21]

Overall, while intercultural marriages pose unique problems, a proactive intercultural communication approach can help prevent many of these problems from becoming serious. In fact, Beulah Rohrlich's review of intercultural marriage concludes that communication is the single-most prevalent issue. Her solution? Rohrlich describes a continuum from one extreme, in which a partner gives up his or her culture to adopt the ways of the other, to the other extreme, where both partners give up something of their old culture, producing still a new culture between the two of them. Consider the options she presents for adjustment:

1. One-way adjustment: one partner adopts the cultural pattern of the other;
2. Alternative adjustment: at times one cultural pattern is consciously chosen and at other times the other is chosen;
3. Midpoint compromise: partners agree on a solution between their respective positions;
4. Mixing adjustment: a combination of both cultures is consciously adopted;
5. Creative adjustment: partners decide to give up their respective cultures in favor of a new behavior pattern.[22]

Rohrlich is calling for solutions usually at level 3, 4, or 5, in the ideal. To marry an individual from another culture is to marry that culture. Lack of interest on the part of the spouse in the other's culture is damaging. To assume that the spouse is attached to the new culture is a serious mistake. The fundamental theme of the culture must be raised, discussed, and valued, if not shared, by both parties. As Gudykust and Kim remind us, intercultural marriage involves adapting to a "stranger."[23]

Microcultures of Chosen Identity and Group Membership

Microcultures of social identity are defined as group loyalties and memberships usually based in choice of association and membership. They are sometimes called primary reference groups or association groups. Examples include friendships, family groups, religious groups, unions, educational associations, professional groups, club memberships, and so on. In essence, they act as reference anchor points for information and decisions, depending on the intensity of the decision and loyalty to the group. For instance, research indicates that voting in the United States is often influenced by reference groups. They also can precipitate PCDs in stimulating the intercultural process.

When these group memberships are significant, what is the influence of reference groups on their participants? How does this influence affect intercultural interaction? Researchers believe these kinds of groups intervene as microcultures within a larger macrocultural environment in several important ways.[24]

1. They create interpersonal bonds and loyalties that command obligation.
2. They mediate information.
3. They interpret and reframe messages on various issues.
4. They offer self-worth and identification.
5. They set rules and customs.

When do reference groups influence group members? This communication web of influence is most meaningful and works to *create conformity* under certain conditions:[25]

■ When groups are small
■ When there is frequency of contact
■ When members are cohesive

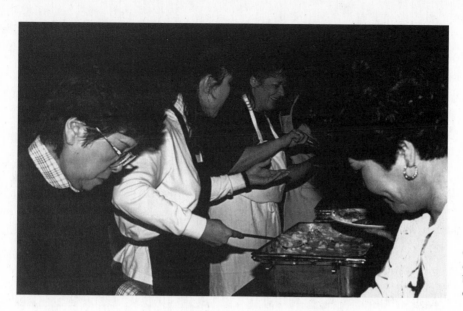

Group membership offers an anchor for beliefs and evaluation of information.

- When the group is important to an individual member
- When group expectations are clear and unambiguous
- When a high degree of similarity exists
- When issues confronting the group are complex and/or important
- When a member has a high need for inclusion, that person is more influenced by the group
- When the group is instrumental, or a stepping-stone, for a person's ultimate goals

Regional and Residential Microcultures

Regional differences are not merely geographical but often imply social attitudes and communication differences. Regional diversity in attitude, speech patterns, and lifestyles illustrate a few of the perceived differences raising uncertainty between potential intercultural communicators. To illustrate the diversity involved, consider attitudes and speech patterns.

Regional accents and speech.   Attitudes and values differ regionally within a national culture. Northern Germans differ in several social values from southern Bavarian Germans who in turn differ from East Germans. The regions within the national boundaries of Japan vary in several cultural and social values.

Evidence indicates that regional cultures within national cultures not only differ in attitude and values but in speech patterns and accents. Hundreds of examples exist. Spanish differs significantly from Castillan to Andalusian. Japanese language in Okinawa differs from Japanese spoken in Tokyo; Spanish in Mexico City varies slightly from Torreon; Chileans in the mountains differ from the coastal areas. Bostonian English is different from midwestern and from Appalachian English accents in the United States.

Friendships create a major part of our social identification in culture.

Not only do attitudes and accents differ regionally, but regional cultures apply varying approaches to information management and communicator style. Observation concerning diversity of communicator style in the United States illustrates the point:

1. Perceived abruptness; speed of getting to the point versus delaying the main point.

2. Rate of speech delivery.

3. Amount of verbal buffering; that is, how many introductory phrases before getting to the point.

4. Amount of interpersonal buffering, level of informal rapport.

5. Amount of eye contact, touch, space, and verbal pausing.

6. Amount of verbal and nonverbal behavior surrounding phrases and messages before leaving a conversation.

7. Amount of perceived warmth and openness.

8. Amount of animation.

9. Amount of dominance.

10. Amount of contentiousness.

While these categories do not represent all possible regional differences, they highlight a number of common communication questions.[26] Regional differences can silently keep people apart. Some of the most sophisticated people seemingly let the subtle prejudices of regional differences affect their attitudes and relationships. This unfortunate waste of human resources is preventable.

Communication Apprehension in the Rural Setting

A study by Charla Tichenor showed a higher degree of communication apprehension among persons from rural settings. She also found higher cognitive complexity for rural individuals, which indicates a higher ability to form accurate interpersonal impressions. This also means that rural individuals possess a more diverse set of categories by which to finely judge interpersonal relations. In fact, as Perrin writes, rural people can judge rather quickly according to some intuitive interpersonal rules.

Source: Charla Tichenor's thesis on rural-urban differences and communication[27]

Rural culture.   In addition to regional differences, it is possible to identify characteristic norms of rurality. First, rural cultures emphasize personal know-how, practicality, and simplicity over complexity in approaching decisions. Skills at doing rather than being or knowing are often valued; perhaps such skills relate more to survival. Like all groups we attempt to describe, rural cultures are not all alike. Some favor innovation and change, while others embrace traditionalism. In some of my international field work and research, I spent time in a number of villages in West Africa and in southern, central India. Villages separated by only a few miles differed vastly on norms of innovation and change.

Second, norms toward interpersonal relationships persist within rural cultures. Indications are that bonds of friendship differ from urban cultures. It may not be surprising that norms of rurality in the United States hold traditional American values and themes of people-helping activity and friendliness.

Third, rurality is a mindset. One can stay rural in the middle of urban life, or for that matter stay urban living in a rural region. For example, there are pockets of originally rural southerners in the greater Detroit area. According to personal interviews reported by Bill Goodpasture, many have retained some of the unique characteristics of their roots, despite a long passage of time.

Fourth, communication style differences of rural individuals can clash interculturally with stylistic features others are not accustomed to. For instance, a General Motors plant in the United States relocated into a traditional southern rural area from an urban, midwestern region. The most evident problems were related to the communication style differences. Beyond accent and dialectical differences, some diverse approaches to managerial style of communication illustrate intercultural communication issues:

1. Requests occur in a less demanding style.

2. Messages tend to be phrased in personal terms, rather than objective terms.

3. Respect is shown for the free will of the other person.

4. Story, image, and background scenarios play an important role in the communication style. Communication is filled with anecdotes and stories, often about family or friends.

5. Messages are usually related to a unified theme deemed typical of the person or event. There is a kind of implicit theory about how this person or that event fits into the whole picture from a cultural point of view. For instance, "He acted kind of crazy. Probably because he's been working long hours."

6. Personal history behind events, people, and conditions serve organizing functions for messages, for instance, "He almost fell off the hay wagon. That's no surprise, considering his grandpa did the same thing twice when he was a boy."

Urban culture.   Obviously, urban life is complex, if nothing else given the massive numbers of people involved. From historical analysis we find a need to separate suburban culture from inner-city culture. Among *suburban* residents, those living on outlying areas of urban regions, a number of communication needs seem prevalent: (1) identification and joining behavior, (2) community integration, (3) high idealism. Witness the soccer moms and little league dads, the multiple group memberships, church attendance and so on that abound in studies about this group. Affluence may explain this partly, but evidence also indicates a high social motivation that is qualitatively different from inner-urban or rural residents.[28]

Inner-city cultures tend to be composed of isolated members with pockets or enclaves of group cohesion. Social participation outlets are limited, and isolation remains a significant theme. Housing problems, less affluence, and high crime rates affect social participation in urban areas and foster less dependence on interpersonal communication networks.

Anomia, a generalized isolation and loneliness, may result partly from crowded physical surroundings. Such conditions can easily lead to urban fears and suspicions predicated upon an urban dweller's experience with such things as increased crime and decreased personal territoriality.

Social Class Cultures

Social systems usually stratify according to what are called socioeconomic status variables, typically composed of occupation, income, and education. That is, members of a society rank people into higher or lower social positions, producing a hierarchy of respect and prestige. Respect is conferred to individuals according to their conformity to a society's ideals. The result is a role-related position determined by the prestige, esteem, and value that other members of the social system place on the individual's social class and, therefore, on the individual. It is easy to see how intercultural communication perceptual differences result.

Overall, classes are inclined to depreciate the social differences between themselves and higher classes and to magnify differences with lower classes. Sometimes, this perceptual set is heightened so that a certain unity of outlook exists by allusions to "people like us" and to persons that are "not our kind." A feeling of "we-ness" especially occurs when expressing dissatisfaction with the upward mobility of the lower classes or resentment toward the higher classes. Unity is further intensified through common beliefs and patterns of overt behavior. The Indian caste system is an example of a highly ordered and rigidly determined class ranking, which in turn predicts attitudes and communication between different castes within the larger context of India's culture. Labor and management differences also reflect the attitudes that some classes hold toward other classes and of the importance of communication in resolving those differences.

Research also reveals unique tendencies concerning socioeconomic differences, friendship, prestige, and trust. First, compared with stationary members, those members climbing upward in the class system are not as likely to maintain close personal friendships. This phenomenon can partly be traced to their more frequent geographical movement, as Alvin Toffler's classic book *Future Shock* and recent data on high mobility in the United States remind us. Second, prestige and achievement become more valuable to middle-class members than to lower-class members and, especially, to upwardly mobile middle-class persons. Third, lower classes seem to be more distrustful of authority used by more powerful classes.[29]

A type of economic and social microculture is what we will term here poverty culture. This group refers to individuals who suffer from a lack of financial and material resources. Associated with this economic condition is a broad array of beliefs and values. We do not know if these social attitudes caused poverty, the poverty caused the attitudes, or there are unknown causes. In any case, these themes appear in many poverty conditions across many national cultures. These are not necessarily racial, ethnic, or minority issues, but poverty issues with central tendencies characterized from available research. Everett Rogers originally proposed some of the following categories, offering factors from a five nation study profiling attitudes among the poor.[30] Researchers have added helpful insights to the list.[31]

Poverty Culture

Limits of potential economic upward mobility. Some individuals view economic potential to be something like a pie with a limited number of slices. If someone prospers, it is perceived to occur only at others' expense, since it is assumed that prosperity means one has taken an inordinate amount of the pie. Keeping people the same and holding things down, so to speak, avoids an uncomfortable suspicion toward a community member who financially succeeds and thus violates the unspoken norms of this culture.

Familism outweighs individualism. Some members of poverty cultures subordinate personal goals to the wishes and perceived good of the family. Called familism, family needs outweigh personal and individual needs or wishes.

Fatalism. Fatalism is a believed degree to which we cannot control the future. In many cultures, the future is often viewed as unknown and certainly uncontrollable. Success and failure are seen as matters of luck. Unseen forces control destiny and people may see themselves as victims of these forces. As one interviewee once told me, "Once you've been beaten down, you don't believe anything will ever work again."

Poverty cultures worldwide can experience a similar outlook.

Unwillingness to try new things. Newness can be risky and members of poverty cultures typically cannot afford innovations. Over time, resistance to innovation may happen to turn to change in general and values develop toward traditionalism using tried and proven ways.

Goals are limited.   Some individuals caught up in the poverty cycle have a low achievement motivation. Perhaps they have been burned or have developed a belief that they do not deserve raising their economic status. Some may have given up trying to find a job or improve their current job. Many poverty-level individuals find that lack of education thwarts economic opportunity. The result in these cases is to experience limits concerning the future.

Buying now with little regard for the future.   More than poverty cultures, there are a lot of people who do not consider future consequences of present actions. In the case of a person who struggles within the poverty limits, spending today may be the only survival strategy. That's all you have as a choice. However, there is also a here-and-now syndrome of reward without future consequence where immediate satisfaction overrides waiting for future rewards. As Daniel indicated, the future is difficult to envision, so live for here and now.

Low empathy.   Members of poverty cultures have a difficult time projecting themselves into any situation or role other than their present one. This lack of empathy explains why traditional poverty cultures around the world seem otherwise resistant to well-intentioned attempts at health treatments, nutritional practices, and agricultural innovations.

Victimization.   Some poverty cultures envision institutions or out-groups as out to get them. The lines encircling legitimate cases where individuals have been victimized by prejudice or policy are real and frequent. Denial of fair treatment occurs often around the globe: South African blacks being denied fundamental human rights; prejudice in policy toward Hispanics in the United States; civil rights denied African Americans; abuse toward immigrant Irish Catholics; put-down of American Jews; and hostility toward immigrant Swedes in the United States. It is easy to see how such cases can create a victimization outlook. However, we should also point out examples where reframing and reorientation leads to positive and fulfilling expectations, despite difficult circumstances.

A counterculture is a group that stands in opposition or performs resistantly toward the larger culture. Features that serve to bind countercultural members include common code, common enemy, and common symbols.

**Countercultural
Microcultures**

Common code.   Counterculture group members often develop common linguistic usages, such as jargon and slang, that are meaningfully interpreted usually only in light of the group members' assigned meanings to the code system. Street language, while constantly changing, is an example of specialized code usage in antisocial groups such as gangs.

Common enemy.   In a number of countercultures, there is a perceived common enemy, usually the dominant culture itself. When attention is focused on the common enemy, who allegedly is responsible for some ill affecting the countercultural group, the group then has a rallying point. In this way, group members are reinforced in their beliefs, and the reinforcement tends to bond the group into an even more cohesive unit. The numerous terrorist groups found throughout the world clearly employ such images of enemy hatred.

Common symbols.   Many countercultural members use symbolic objects, such as colors, highly prized objects, and so on. These symbols emphasize commonality and unification.

Microcultures of social identification also include work cultures. In recent years, organizational culture has proven a rich metaphor to describe organizations. The potential for organizational culture to influence individuals or the larger macroculture is growing. These examples illustrate the confluence of organizational culture with other microcultural conditions:

**Organizational
Cultures as
Microcultures**

> A top manager from ARAMCO in Houston goes to work in Saudi Arabia for a branch office.

> A high school principal is promoted to an assistant superintendent position and must adjust to central office norms.

> David received his master's degree in his native Michigan and has been hired by Delco to work in their regional office in Oklahoma.

Deborah, a Canadian, works for the Canadian Development Office but has just been hired by Algoma Steel in Ontario, Canada to work in their computer division.

Samuel is joining a Japanese car sales force in his native Nigeria.

These examples call up differences these people may encounter while attempting to reconcile the demands of one's organizational culture.

In this discussion, *organizational culture* refers to the system rooted in a common set of norms and interpretive frameworks about the things people encounter in their work environments. Like any other culture, we are dealing with organizational beliefs, activities, rules and customs, communication patterns, and institutions within the organization.[32]

Organizational culture holds a powerful influence in communication. When you consider the many hours people spend at work, it is no wonder organizational cultures influence communication between people. Just how does that influence work? Several reasons explain how.

The influence of message through metaphors and slogans. Peters and Waterman's now classic work *In Search of Excellence,* portrays culture as the dominant idea behind the organization. They cite Delta's "family feeling," Maytag's Iowa work ethic, Levi Strauss's predominantly people-oriented philosophy, and Texas Instrument's innovative culture. These themes are so strong that productive, successful companies rely on fundamental image and metaphor to guide and influence employees' productivity and morale.

The influence of message through story. Organizational cultures have significant communication systems involving stories.[33] The retelling of stories in a variety of settings reinforces values, heroes, and norms. The storytelling itself helps shape organizational culture.

These stories are incredibly powerful and coupled with clear expectations, shape us more than we may realize. Some of the top performing companies, as Peters and Waterman explained, have "a rich network of legends and parables of all sort." A number of these stories surround the originators of the companies, such as J. C. Penney and his values toward business, honesty, and quality.

The influence of explicit and implicit information. A low-context culture makes meanings and information available and explains expectations. Information in these low-context cultures is explicit. Meanings are not in the context but in the verbal explanations provided. High-context cultures are the opposite. Expectations are inferred from the context. One is expected to know appropriate behaviors. Meanings are not explained but are implicit (details are in chapter 5).

In this way organizational cultures are no exception. Consider the case of the college graduate who was told by a major corporation, "You should know what to do within a couple of days. You have your accounting degree, and it should be no problem for you." While the manager in this case was intending to allow the new employee to be independent, the college graduate felt adrift. There was no orientation defining expectations or how the company typically engaged in certain procedures. Passing on corporate insights and defining the norms are functions of a low-context organizational culture. However, this culture was high-context—the accountant was expected to automatically know what to do and how to accomplish the task.

The influence of filtering. Organizational cultures impose definitions of identity that oddly enough creates a perceptual filter regarding outside information coming into the organization.[34] While there are many advantages in a culture having a clear view of itself, organizational identity can become a powerful screening device to interpret messages, acting in this case like any primary reference group.

The influence of organizational socialization. Successful organizational cultures encourage employees to adapt to the organizational culture. The kind of organizational adaptation envisioned here involves orienting typical management functions to cultural formats and methods of operation. A form of socialization into the life of the group includes cultural elements accepted across a variety of topics of organizational concern as for example: how to dress, communication slogans and codes, leadership style, identity formation, planning, goal setting, motivating, controlling, negotiating, training, evaluating, and selection.

Developing Skills in Interacting with Microcultures

1. *Treat cultural differences as a resource.* All too often, we treat cultural differences as something highly negative and thus approach intercultural communication with something of a jaundiced eye. We should look upon differences as an opportunity, a resource from which to learn exciting things about a new culture, a new person, and ourselves.

2. *Do not rely on past experiences to deal with every new situation.* The past comes from your own cultural background. The new culture represents a situation where your familiar cues are not present, and thus, to respond to features in the new culture as if you were in the old culture would be misleading.

3. *Competition may not work.* If you like competitiveness, do not be surprised if cultural differences preclude this value from being mutually appreciated.

4. *Progressivism may not work.* You may also hold strong attitudes toward goal orientation and progressivism. That is, you may expect a culture to be moving in a linear manner toward some goals that you have predetermined are good. Do not be surprised should such a direction not work for you.

5. *Do not assume that your needs are like everyone else's needs.* Because you feel a certain way, do not assume that your feelings reflect anyone else's opinion. By listening and asking questions, you can quickly discover how your personal frame of reference does not match another person's viewpoint. That discovery is the beginning of effective intercultural communication between cultures.

This Chapter in Perspective

This chapter begins with the assumption that microcultures are often encountered as a cultural diversity. Microcultures provide a source of identity, a sense of rules and customs, and can impose intense influence. Perception of cultural diversity is explained with models of in-group/out-group perception, themes presented in the social response model, and expressions indicated in the social attitudes model. These explain the adjustments people make regarding others and the perceptions they have about others and self.

This chapter highlights awareness of group membership and identification as essential components of a larger culture. To understand group differences is to increase insight into intercultural communication. Many intercultural communication problems emerge from reference group barriers. Understanding the dynamics of reference groups is partially a matter of realizing their importance. Under a number of conditions, reference groups have an enormous influence on individuals. Also, individuals can affect reference groups.

Exercises

1. Interview intercultural marriages, or dual-culture couples as they are sometimes called, and ask for their evaluation of the ways they have worked out their differences and how their relationship has been affected.

2. Draw your own family tree showing as much extended family as you can. What influences came down through whom? What roles do you see yourself encompassing perhaps because of one or two major influences of family members?

3. Trace the influences of prejudice in your neighborhoods, schools, and workplace. Perhaps do library research about your community or conduct interviews to find out when attitudes have changed and why. People who have been around a company for many years are great sources for highlights and events over the years that resulted in heightening or reducing racial tensions. This assignment can be developed in a lot of ways, not limited to this brief description of target or resources.

4. Look at a cross sample of television programs, including reruns of older programs along with contemporary programs. What are the influences of group memberships in these instances? What are the group stereotypes? How are reference groups depicted, if at all?

5. In a public place, like your campus student center, observe people interacting with various groups. What patterns of behavior and interaction do you observe?

6. Interview someone from a poverty culture. Ask that person questions about his or her life conditions. What conceptions do people have about the group? What conceptions does the poverty culture member have concerning people with financial resources? Are there different kinds of poverty cultures?

7. When you read newspapers, what kinds of articles about organizational cultures do you find? What model of organizational life is portrayed frequently in the popular media? Do you think these are accurate or inaccurate?

Endnotes

1. William B. Gudykunst and Lauren I. Gumbs, "Social Cognition and Intergroup Communication," in *Handbook of International and Intercultural Communication,* ed. Molefi Kete Asante and William B. Gudykunst (Newbury Park, Calif.: Sage, 1989) identify important perception factors in intergroup relations; one of those factors is social categorization.

2. Gudykunst and Gumbs 1989 (see note 1) along with C. Gallois, A. Franklyn-Stokes, H. Giles, and N. Coupland, "Communication Accommodation in Intercultural Encounters," in *Theories in Intercultural Communication,* ed. Young Y. Kim and Wiliam B. Gudykunst (Newbury Park, Calif.: Sage, 1988), and Stella Ting-Toomey, "Identity and Interpersonal Bonding," in *Handbook of International and Intercultural Communication,* ed. Molefi Kete Asante and William B. Gudykunst (Newbury Park, Calif.: Sage, 1989) have produced various perspectives which are adapted here from their perspectives.

3. Gallois and others, 1988 (see note 2).

4. Ting-Toomey, 1989 (see note 2).

5. Wayne Minnick, *Public Speaking* (Boston:Houghton Mifflin, 1979), 143.

6. Benjamin J. Broome, "Pavelome: Foundations of Struggle and Conflict in Greek Interpersonal Communication," *The Southern Communication Journal* 55 (1990): 260–75.

7. William England, "The Stereotype of a Mexican American: Analysis by Semantic Differential Technique" (unpublished paper, Department of Anthropology, University of Texas, 1977).

8. Minnick, 1979, 140–41 (see note 5).

9. Alberto Gonzalez, "Mexican Otherness in the Rhetoric of Mexican Americans," *The Southern Communication Journal* 55 (1990): 276–91.

10. Richard Brislin, *Understanding Culture's Influence on Behavior,* 2d ed.(Orlando: Harcourt Brace Jovanovich, 1993), 85–91.

11. William B. Gudykunst, "Intercultural Contact and Attitude Change: A Review of Literature and Suggestions for Future Research," *International and Intercultural Communication Annual* 4 (1977): 1–16; Richard Brislin, 1993 (see note 10); Benjamin J. Broome, "Building Shared Meaning: Implications of a Relational Approach to Empathy for Teaching Intercultural Communication," *Communication Education* 40 (1991): 235–49.

12. Intercultural authors such as William B. Gudykunst, "Intercultural Contact and Attitude Change: A Review of Literature and Suggestions for Future Research," *International and Intercultural Communication Annual* 4 (1977): 1–16; and Brislin, 1993 (see note 10); Benjamine Broome, "Building Shared Meaning: Implications of a Relational Approach to Empathy for Teaching Intercultural Communication," *Communication Education* 40 (1991): 235–49; along with numerous authors from social psychology and sociology, have recommended strategies for enhancing intergroup contact, applied here to interracial and interethnic relationships. Others have contributed in excellent ways to this discussion including Arthur L. Smith, *Transracial Communication* (Englewood Cliffs, N.J.: Prentice-Hall, 1973); Andrea Rich, *Interracial Communication* (New York: Harper and Row, 1974); Jon Blubaugh and Dorothy Pennington, *Crossing Difference: Interracial Communication* (Columbus, Ohio: Charles Merrill, 1976); Oscar H. Gandy, Jr. and Paula W. Matabane, "Television and Social Perceptions Among African Americans and Hispanics," in *Handbook of International and Intercultural Communication,* ed. Molefi Kete Asante and William B. Gudykunst (Newbury Park, Calif.: Sage, 1989); Dorthy L. Pennington, "Interpersonal Power and Influence in Intercultural Communication," in *Handbook of International and Intercultural Communication,* ed.

Molefi Kete Asante and William B. Gudykunst (Newbury Park, Calif.: Sage, 1989); Molefi Kete Asante and Alice Davis, "Encounters in the Interracial Workplace," in *Handbook of International and Intercultural Communication,* ed. Molefi Kete Asante and William B. Gudykunst (Newbury Park, Calif.: Sage, 1989).

13. Anita K. Foeman, "Managing Multiracial Institutions: Goals and Approaches for Race-Relations Training," *Communication Education* 40 (1991): 255.

14. Fred L. Casmir, "Introduction: Culture, Communication, and Education," *Communication Education* 40 (1991): 231.

15. Jolene Koester and Myron W. Lustig, "Communication Curricula in the Multicultural University," *Communication Education* 40 (1991): 250–54; Asante and Davis, 1989 (see note 11).

16. Robert Shuter, "The Centrality of Culture." *The Southern Communication Journal* 55 (1990): 237–49.

17. R. Markoff, "Intercultural Marriage: Problem Areas," in *Adjustment in Intercultural Marriage,* ed. W. S. Tseng, J. K. McDermott, and T. Maretski (Honolulu: University of Hawaii Press, 1977).

18. Morris Graham, Judith Moeai, and Lanette Shizuru, "Intercultural Marriages: An Intrareligious Perspective," *International Journal of Intercultural Relations* 9 (1985): 427–34.

19. John R. Baldwin, "Self-Monitoring, Cognitive Complexity, Stereotypes and Role Perception as Correlations of Communication Satisfaction in Intercultural Marriages" (master's thesis, Abilene Christian University, 1991). Baldwin has developed extensive research in the area of dual culture marriages and interethnic communication in general. I am indebted to Dr. Baldwin for many of these sources and for his work.

20. Graham, Moeai, and Shizuru, 1985 (see note 18).

21. Aharon Bizman, "Perceived Causes and Compatability of Interethnic Marriage: An Attributional Analysis," *International Journal of Intercultural Relations* 9 (1987): 387–99.

22. Beulah Rohrlich, "Dual-Culture Marriage and Communication," *International Journal of Intercultural Relations* 12 (1988): 35–44.

23. William B. Gudykunst and Young Y. Kim, *Communicating with Strangers* (New York: Random House, 1984).

24. Raymond Rodgers, "Folklore Analysis and Subcultural Communication Research: Another View of World View" (paper presented to the Society for Intercultural Education, Training, and Research, Phoenix, Arizona, February 1978); Kenneth Boulding, *The Image* (Ann Arbor, Mich.: University of Michigan Press, 1972); Brewster M. Smith, Jerome S. Bruner, and Robert White, *Opinions and Personality* (New York: John Wiley & Sons, 1956); *Attitude, Ego-Involvement, and Change* ed. Carolyn W. Sherif and Muzafer Sherif (New York: John Wiley & Sons, 1967); Bernard Berelson and Gary A. Steiner, *Human Behavior: An Inventory of Scientific Findings* (New York: Harcourt, Brace & World, 1964); Herbert I. Abelson, *Persuasion* (New York: Springer, 1959); M. Sherif, C. Sherif, and R. Nebergall, *Attitude and Attitude Change: The Social Judgment-Involvement Approach* (Philadelphia: Saunders, 1965).

25. Erwin P. Bettinghaus, *Persuasive Communication,* 4th ed. (New York: Holt, Rinehart and Winston, 1987).

26. R. W. Norton, "Foundation of a Communication Style Construct," *Human Communication Research* 4 (1978):99–111. Norton brought to the forefront communication style issues that are also indicated here in this list and in the application of this microcultural feature.

27. Charla Tichenor, "Rural and Urban Factors in Communication" (master's thesis, Western Kentucky University, 1980).

28. Gordon McDonald, *Ordering Your Private World* (Nashville: Thomas Nelson, 1985).

29. Bernard Berelson and Gary A. Steiner, *Human Behavior: An Inventory of Scientific Findings* (New York: Harcourt, Brace & World, 1964); Jack Daniel, "The Poor: Aliens in an Affluent Society," in *Intercultural Communication: A Reader,* 2d ed., ed. Larry Samovar and Richard Porter (Belmont, Calif.: Wadsworth, 1976).

30. Everett M. Rogers, "Elements in the Subculture of Traditionalism" (paper presented to the Society for Applied Anthropology, Mexico City, April 1969); Rogers has been a classic paradigm by which to investigate the global factors concerning poverty culture.

31. Daniel, 1976 (see note 29) along with Camille Parrish's helpful qualitative analyses involving reviews of hundreds of welfare cases by this single-parent, African American manager working in a social services agency. Camille Parrish, "Observations from Department Human Services Client Load," interview by author, Abilene, Texas, June 18, 1993. We gratefully acknowledge her confirmation and insights.

32. Donald Carbaugh, "Cultural Communication and Organizing," in *Communication, Culture, and Organizational Processes,* ed. William B. Gudykunst, Lea P. Stewart, and Stella Ting-Tommey (Beverly Hills, Calif.: Sage, 1985); Beverly D. Sypher, James L. Applegate, and Howard E. Sypher, "Culture and Communication in Organizational Contexts," in *Communication, Culture, and Organizational Processes,* ed. William B. Gudykunst, Lea P. Stewart, and Stella Ting-Toomey (Beverly Hills, Calif.: Sage, 1985).

33. William B. Gudykunst, Lea P. Stewart, and Stella Ting-Toomey, eds., *Communication, Culture, and Organizational Processes* (Beverly Hills, Calif.: Sage, 1985); Peter J. Frost, Larry F. Moore, Meryl R. Louis, Craig C. Lundberg, and Joanne Martin, eds., *Organizational Culture* (Beverly Hills, Calif.: Sage, 1985); Robert D. McPhee and Phillip K. Tompkins, eds., *Organizational Communication* (Beverly Hills, Calif.: Sage, 1985); Linda L. Putnam and Michael E. Pacanowsky, eds., *Communication and Organizations: An Interpretive Approach* (Beverly Hills, Calif.: Sage, 1983); M. Lee Williams, "Cases in Organizational Culture," (paper presented to the Southern Communication Association, San Antonio, Texas, April 1992); Sypher, Applegate, and Sypher, 1985 (see note 32) call this feature of an organizational culture its "implicit organizational communication."

34. Philip R. Harris and Robert T. Moran, *Managing Cultural Differences,* 4th ed. (Houston: Gulf, 1995).

Chapter 5

Underlying Dimensions

of Culture

OBJECTIVES   *After completing this chapter, you should be able to*

1. Discuss the importance of underlying themes and values of culture as they influence communication

2. Understand monochronic and polychronic cultural orientations and their effects on communication

3. Differentiate between high-context cultures and low-context cultures and how they affect communication

4. Identify Hofstede's four factors of culture

5. Discuss concrete examples of how a culture's world view affects intercultural communication

6. Identify cultural values that influence perception and communication

Culture is more than just cultural elements and issues of perception of cultural diversity. Culture includes how people think—their beliefs, values, world view, and information processing. These are underlying dimensions of culture which are part of a less obvious yet highly significant area sometimes called cognitive culture. There is a less tangible but undeniably powerful system of belief behind a cultural system that involves vision, beliefs, truths, and outlooks. Your beliefs and assumptions about the nature of the universe and themes and values all may sound a bit grandiose, but they illustrate the considerable forces which guide cultural activities. Asians who value hard work and group responsibility take actions and process information in ways congruent with those values. Hispanic views of hospitality translate into marvelous care for family and others. A U.S. dominant cultural value toward time, reflected in phrases such as "Time is money" and "A stitch in time saves nine," influences communication patterns creating a shared perception about what is right and wrong, what it means to be late, and what happens if you fail to be careful.

These illustrations of cognitive culture remind us that some fundamental ways of processing information are involved as we encounter cultural differences. So, the first part of this discussion begins with Hall's influential theories about the nature of time.

Monochronic and Polychronic Cultures

Monochronic Culture

Edward T. Hall's classic book *Beyond Culture* expresses an important theory about the way cultures process time— and consequently information and communication— including everything from irritation at being kept waiting to the very thought framework of time as a cultural perception. According to Hall, the element of time structures our interaction. Indeed, there appears to be a continuum of time orientation, with monochronic time on one end and polychronic time on the other. Monochronic time urges people to do one thing at a time. Time, for them, is like a long ribbon of highway that can be sliced into segments. Monochronics believe that accomplishments and tasks can and should be performed during each segment. Monochronics have a high need for closure—completing a task or coming to a conclusion in a relationship.

For example, one U.S. dating couple had diverse cultural outlooks in informational processing. The man was operating from a polychronic orientation, trying to process many of the couple's future relationship decisions all at once. The woman, on the other hand, was monochronic. She tended to focus on a single issue at a time and wanted closure, or completion, on each issue that the couple confronted in their dating relationship. Her need for closure was so high, in fact, that her demands for answers pressured the man into breaking up the relationship.

Monochronics are not all demanding, but they prefer seeing things finished. They are dissatisfied with dangling loose ends. Also, as a result, their tolerance for ambiguity is not high. As uncertainty rises, monochronics tend to articulate solutions and to work toward resolution, whether in conflicts or ordinary, everyday decisions. Monochronics usually think in a linear fashion. That is, they internally process information in a sequential, segmented, orderly fashion. For instance, monochronics schedule appointments linearly—arrival, meeting, conclusion, action—and they cycle through this same pattern all day long.

Being a monochronic is great if you are in a monochronic culture. However, when a monochronic is placed in a polychronic situation, or overall, in a polychronic culture, stress and poor communication usually result. For instance, a colleague and I once traveled in India and on one occasion waited for a transportation ticket. We got there early (like good Americans) and secured our place in front of the ticket window. Nobody else was around, so we felt confident that our waiting would be minimal once the window opened. However, when the ticket window opened, about one hundred people came out of nowhere and crowded around us, squeezing us out of what we thought was our place in line. After a half hour of standing in the same place while everyone else crowded in front, we finally realized that in this culture there was no such thing as a line—it was everyone for himself or herself. Once we understood that, we soon had our tickets. We had structured our space just like our monochronic time orientation. The Telegu people of India, however, had a more polychronic view and apparently ordered their spatial relations accordingly.

If we examine situations in our lives that seem frustrating or nonproductive, we may find that part of the problem involves monochronic/polychronic conflicts. For example, many monochronic managers are faced with polychronic demands and must work with people who think polychronically.

Polychronic Culture

Although monochronic individuals think in terms of linear-sequential, time-ordered patterns (1, 2, 3, or *A, B, C*), there are cognitive cultures whose members think in terms of pictures or configurations. The holistic pattern of thought that follows a nonlinear order of attention to stimulus is called polychronic time orientation. Here, the stimulus items may follow an attention pattern unique to that culture, as for instance, 1, 16, 37, 2, or *A, M, Z, B*. The issue involves how we collect and process information and is being addressed in the learning style literature.[1] The process of information processing, however, appears to be culturally dependent as well as individually derived. Thus, a significant part of understanding cultural differences involves examining methods of thought.

Polychronic individuals tend to think about and attempt to do a number of things simultaneously. In Latin America, for example, a businessperson may conduct business interviews by inviting a number of unrelated clients into his or her office at once, entertaining them for hours, and jumping from one to another and back again. Sound unusual? Well, the one-at-a-time method seems unusual to polychronic cultures.

Actually, it appears more correct to talk about *individuals* who are monochronic or polychronic. While American, British, Canadian, and German cultures are largely monochronic (as evidenced by the school systems and the organizational patterns of most businesses and the military), Latin American, African, Middle Eastern, and southern European cultures tend toward polychronism. Clearly individuals tend one way or another.

Research indicates some fascinating results involving university students and microcultures. For many years I have conducted critical incident surveys at my university and with a sample currently numbering over 900 upper division college students, one half of the Anglo respondents report extreme or moderate levels of polychronic style. Latin American and Asian students typically report over 60 percent of polychronic style. In a field study of 212 Mexicans and Anglos, Charles Phipps

Differences in Personal Style

In what way do you and your friends use M-P styles differently? Do you think you are a high- or low-context individual? What about your family? Discuss with friends or family these differences. Ask your professor in a class discussion or in private consultation how these cognitive factors influence your communication, relationships, and approach toward tasks.

found that about half of the U.S. Anglo adults were slightly monochronic and statistically were not significantly different from both a Mexico sample and a Mexican American sample. However, 62 percent of the Anglo students in this study were polychronic. Within the Mexican sample, the Eastern Mexican sample from Merida were slightly polychronic (53 percent) while the Monterrey sample was monochronic (76 percent). Furthermore, comparing monolingual Anglos with bilingual Anglos indicated a fascinating trend: monolingual Anglos were about half monochronic and polychronic (51 percent M-culture, 49 percent P-culture) while two-thirds of bilingual Anglos were polychronic (34 percent M, 66 percent P).[2]

Most people describe a basic style or an overriding tendency to prefer either a monochronic or polychronic cognitive style. While that may be true, M or P cultural style also depends on the situation. For instance, as Phipps adds, a person may function polychronically because of roles to play or other demands.

We should point out that monochronic tendencies can become dysfunctional in situations that demand polychronic performance. Some organizational cultures, groups, systems, and families think, schedule, and operate in a monochronic fashion. Thus, a polychronic person can feel rather stressed, even depressed, in such a group.

Polychronics may experience high degrees of information overload. That is, they are trying to process so many things at once that they feel frustrated. They may also experience procrastination. They seem to struggle harder to articulate abstractions without visualization. In fact, they seem to be very visually oriented people. These observations may in further research be found to correlate with the theories of left- and right-brain orientations, where it is asserted that right-brain-dominant people think creatively, visually, and artistically, while left-brain-dominant people think mathematically and linearly.

In any case, how we process time seems both cultural and personal, and this monochronic-polychronic continuum has an important influence on communication behavior. You might choose to measure your information processing style at this point with the M-P scale in the appendix of the book.

Another way that cultures process information revolves around how much its members are expected to know about procedures and rules without being told. Some cultures expect you to know what to do in certain situations. Other cultures do not make these assumptions. To put the idea another way, some cultures

High- and Low-Context Cultures

High-context cultures use implicit meanings without necessarily overt communication of rules and explanations. Each person in an HCC knows what to expect from another. © Sujoy Das/Stock Boston.

more commonly provide a lot more information about their rules, practices, and expectations than other cultures.

Edward Hall describes a culture in which information about procedure is not overly communicated as a high-context culture or HCC.[3] Members are expected to know how to perform, so information and cultural rules remain *implicit*. The context is supposed to be the cue for behavior. For example, a supervisor says, "Here's the task—you have a college degree, so get started on this project." In situations like this, procedures are incompletely stated.

In a low-context culture, or LCC, information is *explicit*; procedures are explained, and expectations are discussed. For instance, a supervisor says, "Here is the task, and here is our procedure for accomplishing this task." Information levels are adequate for performance.

The most frequent intercultural communication difficulty, considering high-context and low-context systems, occurs when one person assumes a high-context mind-set, while the other person expects an explanation, looking for a low-context condition. These assumptions are rarely understood, much less discussed between intercultural participants.

This high/low context phenomenon is evident in macroculture encounters around the globe. For instance, while the Japanese may be considered to express HCC tendencies, American culture is considered to be on the low-context side. By comparison with other cultures, a relatively large amount of information provides cues for how to respond. For instance, some Americans use signs, instruction lists, and standard operating procedures. In contrast, some Japanese expect one to sense the context and act in an expected manner, whether the situation calls for proper bowing, silence, nonverbal expression, or observance of conversational rules. Although there are numerous exceptions, in general, northern Europeans, western Europeans, and North Americans tend toward the low-context condition; Middle Easterners,

Africans, and Latin Americans tend toward the high-context culture dimension, but somewhat less than Asians; Asians tend toward a high-context condition.

In her excellent work on conflict styles and culture, Stella Ting-Toomey's research sharpens our understanding of additional communication principles concerning low- and high-context cultures.[4] First, low-context cultures encourage communicators to separate the issue from the person, sometimes however, at the expense of personal relationships. Often, the rhetorical ideal of avoiding attacking the person is clearly the ideal: "Just get the facts." By contrast, high-context cultures tend not to separate the person from the issue. If you attack the issue, you are assumed to be attacking the person and would create embarrassment or ill will. Such perceived attacks, from a high-context culture viewpoint, need smoothing. Thus, the motive to *save face*, that is to decrease the chance of embarrassing someone else, is usually very strong in high-context cultures.

Second, members of low-context cultures typically do not like things they do not understand. That is, they typically avoid uncertainty, which explains the small talk in conversations. Comfort results from answers to cultural questions: Who is this person? What makes that person the way he is? How can I be accepted and succeed with this person? What is the product and its workings? In contrast, high-context cultures live with more ambiguity. They want information, of course, but they can process information amid uncertainty. Often silence is used as a major part of the strategy in high-context cultures.

Third, low-context culture members use a very direct style of communication. They seek and absorb quantities of information and direct the communication process. A good example is a conflict style that centers around an informational and somewhat confrontational approach. In contrast, high-context cultural members use more indirect styles of communication. For instance, among Japanese cultures, extreme politeness and extreme tact are standard. They are concerned about group harmony, and a nondirective social style may be the best way to engage in communication accommodation. Given that cultural motivation, one can understand strategies of cooperation and participation.

Fourth, negotiation approaches differ based on these styles. People in low-context cultures tend toward linear logic. Analysis is essential for such cultures—in short, a cognitive, using-the-head approach marks the bargaining style. In contrast, high-context cultures use a soft bargaining approach, preferring communication involving feelings and intuition; it is a communication style of the heart (intuitive) rather than the head. On one occasion in Hong Kong I was interested in buying an opal necklace for my wife. I went from one store to the next, scanning necklaces and gleaning all the facts I could, only to be frustrated when it seemed my opponents in bargaining—namely the store owners—did not negotiate in an American style. Looking back, I can see that they were engaging in an intuitive style of bargaining, while I was much more interested in a logical, analytical style. I finally managed to strike a good bargain and came home with a beautiful opal necklace. (See, my dominant U.S. culture side indicates I need to assert how competitively successful it turned out.)

Fifth, low-context cultures seek interpersonal data emphasizing personal, individual aspects, not social or group aspects.[5] In contrast, high-context cultures emphasize social factors in their interaction. In other words, each culture searches for different categories. Because they are scanning for totally different categories, what is heard may not be what was said. An LCC person wants prediction about this individual (who he is, what he does, his worth, his competency). An HCC person is listening for group loyalties (organization, family, national loyalty, value) in order to answer questions of trust and respect. No wonder communication opportunities fail. One person's communication expression surrounds the presentation of self and others, while the other person is clearly looking for harmony, social participation, and issues surrounding trust. These low-context culture members tend to be verbose and open and to center on data, while high-context culture members seem more cautious. After all, mistakes could be made that cause shame or loss of face. In low-context cultures errors are part of the risk one takes in getting good, solid information. After all, an LCC might think such errors can be corrected by adequate explanation.

Hofstede's Cultural Dimensions

During the 1980s, a great deal of research uncovered factors related to cultural themes. One of the major works during this decade was by Hofstede in which he analyzed questionnaire data from multinational corporate employees in over forty countries. He asked extensive survey questions and applied these to a statistical process resulting in four central factors. The relevance for our text and this chapter of underlying cultural dimensions involves the communication qualities associated with these culture types. These four factors were called individualism-collectivism, masculine-feminine, power-distance, and uncertainty avoidance.

Individualism-Collectivism

The concepts of individualism and collectivism have encouraged a significant amount of research. For example, Harry Triandis surveyed anthropologists and psychologists from many parts of the world and concluded individualism-collectivism is one of the most powerful relationship indictors.

Individualism concerns personal achievement. In contrast, collectivist cultures are those that emphasize community, groupness, harmony, and maintaining face. We would expect the accompanying communicator style to be correlated with each of these cultural dimensions. For instance, one could expect a great deal more assertive behavior, self-disclosure, and other personal-advancement issues to arise in an individualistic culture. On the other hand, we could expect far more strategies of people pleasing, solidarity, relational issues, and face saving to occur in a collective culture.

Empirical research by Kim, Sharkey, and Singelis confirms the interactive or communication qualities associated with each facet of this cultural dimension in their study of Koreans (collectivists) and Americans (individualists). They indicate significant communication expectations across a number of studies, which have been adapted and summarized here.[6]

Individualists emphasize:

—concern for clarity, directness

—truth telling, straight talk

—meeting personal needs and goals rather than group needs and goals

—self-referent messages, more "I" than "we"

—more independent

—linear pattern of conversation

Collectivists emphasize:

—indirect communication

—concern for others' feelings, avoiding hurting others, saving face (not causing embarrassing situations)

—avoiding negative evaluation from a listener

—less goal direction

—more interdependent, group concerned

—fewer linear patterns of conversation

Hofstede statistically identified the cultures that fit into these categories. Among the top individualistic cultures are the United States, Australia, Great Britain, Canada, the Netherlands, New Zealand, Italy, Belgium, and Denmark. The top collectivist cultures are Columbia, Korea, Pakistan, Peru, Taiwan, Thailand, Singapore, Chile, and Hong Kong. Notice that the collectivist cultures tend to be Asian and Latin-American, while the individualistic cultures tend to be North American and European.

Although Hofstede is frequently credited for this factor, individualism-collectivism, Harry Triandis also has numerous pioneering works applied to this area. He observed that people can act collective-like (he calls them *allocentric*) or individual-like (he calls them *idiocentric*) across any culture.[7] Also, Sudweeks underscored the importance of the individualism-collectivism dimension in developing more effective intercultural communication and sensitivity. For instance, she reminds us to be familiar with in-group norms, be aware of the collectivist's discomfort with competitive situations, and generally avoid saying "no" or criticizing in environments such as in U.S. classrooms.[8]

Masculine-Feminine Cultures

Hofstede's work borrowed a gender metaphor to describe differentiation in cultures. By suggesting characteristics traditionally associated with masculinity or femininity, Hofstede's masculine cultures are those that exhibit work as more central to their lives, strength, material success, assertiveness, and competitiveness. Masculine cultures also differentiate gender roles more than feminine cultures. Feminine cultures are those that tend to accept fluid gender roles, embrace traits of affection, compassion, nurturing, and interpersonal relationships.[9]

There are also communication style differences that seem to emanate from these cultures. The masculine cultures tend to use more aggressive styles of communication. Their problem-solving methods and conflict-management techniques would center around bottom-line issues, strict coping and debriefing information techniques. In contrast, the feminine cultures are probably much more capable of reading nonverbal messages and are better prepared to deal with ambiguity. Perhaps not so surprising is that masculine cultures display higher levels of stress and also have lower percentages of women in technical and professional jobs when compared to feminine cultures.

The highest masculinity index scores come from Japan, Australia, Venezuela, Switzerland, Mexico, Ireland, Great Britain, and Germany. The countries with the highest feminine scores are Sweden, Norway, the Netherlands, Denmark, Finland, Chile, Portugal, and Thailand. Hofstede observed that machismo is present in the Caribbean, but not particularly evident in the remainder of South America. This point could be debated at some length, based on evidence from other sources. Also as stated by Lustig and Koester, we would agree with their alternative label "achievement-nurturance" as preferred terminology for this factor.

Power-Distance

Still another dimension of Hofstede's research involved what he called the power-distance index. Cultures with a high power index are said to accept inequality as the cultural norm. In other words, these cultures are vertical—that is, they are hierarchical cultures. People expect hierarchy, and authoritarian style communication is more common in these cases. We could expect much more oppressive behavior in high power-distance cultures, as well as more formalized rituals signaling respect, attentiveness, and agreement. Countries highest in the power-distance dimension are the Philippines, Mexico, Venezuela, India, Singapore, Brazil, Hong Kong, France, and Columbia. In general, many of the African and Latin American countries exhibit a high power-distance index as well.

Those cultures that are low in power-distance are more horizontal. That is, they are not fundamentally organized around hierarchical relationships. The countries with the lowest power-distance scores are Australia, Israel, Denmark, New Zealand, Ireland, Sweden, Norway, Finland, and Switzerland—mostly European-style countries.

Several theorists are grappling with the reasons to explain the power-distance phenomenon, including ecological, technological, and climate issues.[10] Such arguments have merit along with other potential causes such as migration patterns, tribal and ethnic origins, and religion. Data are incomplete at this time but the cultural roots of power would be fascinating in any discussion in future research.

Uncertainty Avoidance

Our central model in chapter 1 and an axiom in chapter 2 referred to uncertainty and ambiguity. Hofstede questioned the extent to which a culture would avoid or tolerate uncertainty. Obviously, some cultures have a high need for information and certainty. For them, avoiding uncertainty would be very difficult without increasing the number of rules of behavior to compensate for the uncertainty. These cultures include Greece, Portugal, Belgium, Japan, Peru, France, Chile, Spain, and Argentina.

Other cultures, however, seem more comfortable dealing with diversity and ambiguity. These include Singapore, Denmark, Sweden, Hong Kong, Ireland, Great Britain, India, the Philippines, and the United States.

Hofstede's work concerning this factor reminds us that cultures which value avoiding uncertainty will probably exhibit more direct styles of communication. Such a person may seem insistent or even overly aggressive in pursuit of certainty. Identifying with a cultural communicator in a way that allows him or her to feel the most comfort and commonality with the communication interactant is a positive strategy. Anxiety is reduced to the extent that a match is created between communicators and another person.

World View and Intercultural Communication

A Nigerian student attending a major university spoke to his faculty advisor about a scene he had witnessed in his home country. Many onlookers, including the Nigerian student, observed a demonstration where one person allegedly brought a razor-sharp sword down upon the arm of another person wearing a special charm, but the person wearing the charm suffered no harm. The student then described the amulet and the secrets connected with this cultural phenomenon.

This student was reflecting on one of the most fundamental dimensions underlying a culture, called cultural world view. World view is a belief system about the nature of the universe, its perceived effect on human behavior, and one's place in the universe. World view is a fundamental core set of assumptions explaining cultural forces, the nature of humankind, the nature of good and evil, luck, fate, spirits, the power of significant others, the role of time, and the nature of our physical and natural resources. Because it is so fundamental, world view affects communication encounters and perceptions of difference.

A holistic interpretation of this definition implies a culture's belief regarding various forces associated with daily events and rituals. For instance, many tribal Kenyans believe that disease is the result of evil spirits. Some Latin Americans believe wealth comes from a pact with the devil or possibly luck in finding buried treasure. The Nigerian discussed previously believed in what is called "ju-ju" in West Africa. Voodoo and the evil eye are well-known belief systems in Caribbean cultures. In another example, a middle-school teacher working among a group of economically disadvantaged students faces examples of fatalism in communication with such language as "Why try?" and "No one else will let me." Our interactions may be less than perfect for a number of reasons, but differences in world view intervene as one cause of misunderstanding in intercultural communication.

Elements of Cultural World View

By examining some of the typical concepts by which cultures order their worlds, we have assembled a category system with which to assess some fundamental belief structures of a group of people. A knowledge of those belief structures can improve intercultural communication, a point reviewed extensively by Cecile Garmon for whom we are indebted in this portion of the text for significant contribution adapted here for this discussion.[11]

Shame and guilt cultures.   Some cultures can be characterized by their perceived sense of personal guilt (usually found in individualistic cultures) and shame (usually found in collectivist cultures). This organizing feature of shame suggests that cultures feel a sense of obligation when things go wrong. In Asian cultures, for instance, shame is not good, almost as bad as losing one's group identity. In traditional Japanese culture, disgrace potential is an important element in decision making. If a policy or a person has the potential for bringing about shame or loss of face, then such risks are not likely to be sought. In one study, Japanese American cultures revealed a greater sensitivity to shame than Caucasian Americans.[12] In fact, Japanese chief executive officers have been known to commit suicide if the organization experiences financial failure.

Shame cultures have a way of looking inwardly for obligation and responsibility. If duty is overlooked, it could cause shame to someone else, which in turn would cause you to be shamed. In Thai culture, for instance, it is especially important not to engage in any behavior that would show disrespect for parents or elders. To do so would bring shame.

In contrast, guilt cultures (often individualistic) experience remorse for personal actions but not for group mistakes. These cultures feel a need to reduce guilt and lean more toward personal blame than for group blame.

Both guilt and shame cultures develop systems for atonement and purification and often rituals to expiate those needs. Jimenez noticed this sense of guilt in his therapy practice with upwardly mobile Mexican Americans. His analysis revealed that economic mobility set in motion a number of guilt-provoking messages for certain individuals: "I don't deserve this; why am I so lucky and others so poor?" He based his analysis, in part, on his recognition that the culture in which his clients lived emphasized qualities that provoked guilt, but the culture simultaneously inculcated a sense of group loyalty. Thus, clients experienced a combination of guilt and shame.[13]

The general theme of saving face, identified earlier in this chapter, is also related to the guilt-shame continuum. Several Middle Eastern, African, and particularly Asian cultures engage in communication styles that enhance relationships and avoid embarrassing another person. To publicly communicate personal attacks, to apply negative statements, or to display inadequate listening would likely not only be personally ineffective, but such behavior could trigger shame emotions among nonwestern friends.

Task and people cultures.   Some cultures emphasize task accomplishment over relationships, while other cultures emphasize relationships over task. Task cultures often express an underlying world view defining matters related to "doing" and "action." In some cases, working hard and successful task completion express self worth. In general, task cultures typically approve action and results as a higher priority than people, although the opposite is true in people cultures. There are very many expressions representing surface structures of a deeper, underlying cognitive dimension of how people are viewed in comparison with tasks. We are not suggesting that task cultures experience no relationships or that cultures emphasizing people over tasks do not experience task productivity. We simply recognize that some cultures are driven by priorities that vary on a task-people continuum.

Values ranging from individuality to social responsibility are culturally rooted. Zigy Kaluzny © Tony Stone Images.

Spirit and secular cultures.   Another important cultural world-view continuum involves the role of spiritual factors. This element implies that some cultures accept the presence of culturally defined spirits and beings, while other cultures reject or devalue a spiritual dimension in their world view. Marshall Singer describes a Guatemalan village whose water source ran dry. The government arranged to pipe water from a nearby village who had ample water. The government levied a water tax on the village, but the villagers refused to pay. A friend of the villagers, Mr. Green, visited the village and discovered the reason for the refusal: Everyone knows God gave water for free. When Mr. Green explained that while God gave free water, humans made metal pipes, and would the villagers mind paying back the government for the pipes and installation. The villagers then had no problem and gladly paid the tax. The story illustrates how cognitive beliefs impact relationships and how a secular view (the government framed the problem as purely economic) can counter a spiritual view (the villagers framed the issue initially from a sacred perspective).[14]

This continuum explains a fruitful area of cultural difference rooted in individual as well as cultural world views. Francis Schaeffer, a noted European philosopher, concluded that a secular culture has an implicit faith in the presupposition of the uniformity of natural causes in a closed system. A spirit culture accepts the presupposition of an open system, implying the alternative of categories for God and spiritual dimensions. Essentially, a spirit (or sacred) culture places meaning in the spiritual realm. A secular culture may not accept the category of spirituality as meaningful.[15]

The role of ancestors and the dead.   Some cultures are characterized by their view of the relationship between the living and the dead. The well-known ancestor rituals in certain Asian and African cultures remind us that some people see death as an event that can be bridged with ceremony and ritual. The world view of

Figure 5.1

World-view structure among Ashanti of Ghana, West Africa.

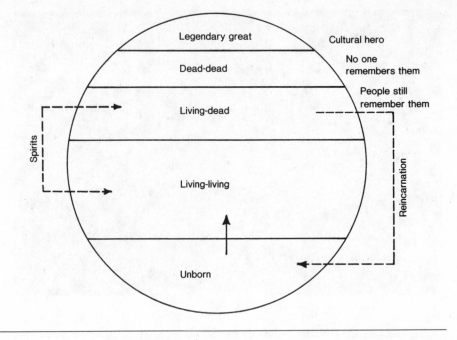

the Ashanti of Ghana, for instance, is diagrammed in figure 5.1 and shows how ancestors are considered as a part of an Ashanti's daily life. Thus, at weddings and funerals, palm wine is poured on the ground to satisfy the thirst of ancestors. This case study indicates a world view layered with ancestral power available to be called upon to perform certain things on behalf of the person asking. At another layer of world view, power also is believed to involve impersonal spirits, magic, formulas, and rituals that serve the living.

Like the Ashanti, the Yaruro of southern Venezuela, view their gods and the dead in a sacred level of existence but who are believed to have a potential role to assist those who are living. Among the Navaho, the ghosts of the dead are greatly feared, and anything connected with death is carefully avoided. Not only do the Navaho have no desire to contact the dead, but they practice rituals to drive away the dead spirits and ghosts; certain illnesses are believed to be caused by contact with death. Navaho patients have even been known to flee a hospital upon learning that a death has occurred there. The Kai of New Guinea customarily swindle their ancestral ghosts, just as they try to swindle each other. In some cultures, the members try to outsmart the ancestral spirits by lying to them. Cajolery, bribery, and false pretense are common means of influencing the supernatural. In other cultures, ancestors are appeased in hopes that offerings and special ritual treatment will please the ancestors, who in turn will offer some benefit to the worshipper.[16] In the funeral rituals of the Mapuche Indian tribe in Chile, the dead person's life history and ancestry are recounted in a loud voice, not for the benefit of the living, but to invoke the ancestors to accept, help, and protect the dead person's spirit from attack by the lurking evil spirits. Spirits are supposed to go to the spirit world and live tranquilly. However, if a spirit were to stay longer on earth, it may be cap-

This photo of Lake Atitlan in Guatemala reminds us of a perceived mystical link of humans to earth, a link traditionally valued by Native Americans. © Ellis Herwig/Stock Boston.

tured and put to a bad use by a sorcerer. Therefore, an unpropitiated spirit returns to earth to haunt relatives, not to do them harm, but to remind them of their obligation to him or her.[17]

Nature of humankind.   According to researchers, culture can influence our perception in the nature of good and evil in humans.[18] One position is to consider the goodness of humans, while the second way is to consider humankind as intrinsically evil, and a third is to perceive humankind as a mixture of good and evil. The point right now is to forecast the implications of these possible world-view elements. If you assume people are basically good or evil, what kind of information could you give to others? Systems of control might vary if you were supervising employees. Can you trust people? What controls are needed based on your assumption about people if you are a supervisor in an organization? Quickly, you can image the many implications of this aspect of world view in our relationships and communication.

Humans and nature.   Another element of world view is the control over nature one believes is appropriate. There are three possible positions. One cultural position is that humans are subject to nature. As Sarbaugh explains this position, a person's culture may emphasize that nature was not meant to be controlled and should not be tampered with. A second position is that humankind should be in harmony with nature, preserving and working in coordination with natural conditions. A third position is that humans should control nature especially in ways that benefit humankind, such as placing dams in rivers or cutting forests.[19]

Doing and being cultures.   The doing-being duality is another world-view difference between cultures. One cultural pattern is to prefer activity and productivity and measurable accomplishment. In fact, a doing culture often develops strategies to invoke guilt on its members for inactivity and loss of productivity. Such cultures emphasize goals, functional information, and less interpersonal dimensions. Many of the world's technology cultures typify this type of culture.

Being cultures emphasize a meditative value, stressing personal thought, discussion, interpersonal relationships, spontaneity, and harmony. Consider, for example, a couple where one person is a very meditative person, preferring quiet time, but the other person enjoys going places and being constantly on the move. Their communication difficulties may relate partially to their cultural differences on the doing-being continuum.

Life cycle. Several examples noted in this text imply that life can be viewed in two ways. One view suggests that life is linear—that birth, life, and death mark each person's existence. According to this view, there is no rebirth, only this life in which to accomplish. Therefore, use of time is considered important. Individuals who maintain this linear view may or may not believe in an eternal existence after death.

A second view suggests that life is cyclical—that birth, life, death, and rebirth mark each person's existence. This view also affects use of time. Since this view posits that another earthly life follows, cyclical cultures may believe that time pressures are not as important. Some analysts have argued, for example, that the United States was at an immediate disadvantage during the Vietnam War because of differences in these two time views. The North Vietnamese were prepared to fight for scores of years; the United States was accustomed to war's quick end and grew weary when such an ending seemed illusive. These expectations justifiably may have resulted from each culture's view of time and life cycle.

Fatalism. Fatalism has been defined as "the degree to which an individual recognizes a lack of ability to control his future," so that a fatalistic outlook on life "results in a failure to see a relationship between work and one's economic condition. Having enough is thought to be almost entirely due to luck and is never believed to be brought about or furthered by personal initiative."[20]

Fatalism is said to produce two totally different results. It can influence qualities such as passivity, pessimism, acceptance, endurance, pliancy, and evasion. However, it can also be credited for success, bringing good luck, wealth, ability to go on, new opportunities, and new relationships.

Fatalism results from a perception that something beyond our control causes our immediate circumstances. That cause may be random luck or manipulation of spiritual forces directed by someone else. The important point is that high fatalism suggests a low degree of control over one's actions and one's environment.

In addition to the elements of cultural world view, we also can identify the mechanisms by which world-view beliefs are said to operate. These mechanisms are said to represent the methods by which members engage their world view.

Animism. Another aspect of world view is called animism, the belief that spirits can dwell in or animate material forms of nature, such as rocks, rivers, plants, weather, and special places. These spirits are believed to be capable of a benevolent or a malevolent influence. Among some Ghanaians, it is believed that proper respect for animism can bring about certain benefits by the power of ju-ju. Voodoo and the evil eye in Caribbean cultures invoke similar forces. Sometimes a special ambassador, called a shaman, is believed necessary to manipulate the spirit world.

Shamanism.   A shaman is an individual who acts as a diviner, curer, spirit medium, or magician. The belief in a shaman's power to manipulate the spirit world is called shamanism. Shamans are recognized by others in a culture as securing an unusual place in the culture and often by expressing leadership in religious ceremonies, magical arts, or curing. It is believed the shaman's power enables contact with spirit beings who in turn may exercise control over supernatural forces. Sometimes, spirit possession and entering a trance are believed to be a part of a shaman's activities. While in this condition, the shaman in some societies acts as a medium, transmitting messages from the living to the dead and vice versa, predicting the future, finding lost objects, identifying the cause of an illness, prescribing cures, or giving advice.

Scholarly interest in recent years has turned toward how individuals internalize their beliefs about world-view-type issues and the influence any personal application of world view has on communication. The term applied to this question is personal communication world view (or acronym PCWV), defined as how much control a person believes characterizes his or her communication encounters. The fundamental theory of PCWV posits that individuals organize a communication construct about themselves and others that reflects fundamental beliefs about perceived control within communication contexts. Consequently, one end of the PCWV continuum relates to helplessness, powerlessness, external locus of control, lack of initiative, and fatalism, while the opposite is true for the other end of the continuum.[21]

Personal World View Influencing Communication

The research connecting personal world view to intercultural communication holds far-reaching implications.[22] First, this construct appears to influence values.[23] Second, PCWV explains specific communication qualities such as openness, relationship initiative and assertiveness, innovativeness, high self-worth, organizational cooperation, cognitive complexity, and opinion leadership. Since these communication qualities also are associated with intercultural communication competencies, the concept appears very useful in understanding intercultural communication encounters.

A growing body of research compares cultures and world-view differences. For example, Long, Javidi, and Pryately found that communication control (defined in their study from a concept called communication motives) differentiated communication styles comparing Japanese, Ukranians, and Americans.[24] Ukranians were the highest on communication control, followed by Americans, and then Japanese. Their results of the survey produced predictable results consistent with the theory regarding world view and with the trends of behavior expected from each culture. Ukranians with high communication control are contentious and place importance on impression leaving. Americans with high communication control are contentious, dramatic, dominant but less friendly in their communication. Japanese with high communication control exhibit dominance and friendliness but less relaxation in their communication. The study leads us to conclude that not only culture but also world view account for communication differences.

World View

Interview several people to assess more about world view. For instance, ask five people about their feelings about luck or owning personal property or about their views of the past. There is certainly much more to world view than these items imply, but the responses you receive may help you to understand more of how people view themselves in relation to forces in the universe as we perceive them.

The Dodd and Garmon research efforts reveal an average 20 percent of U.S. Americans and 30 percent of Latin Americans and Asians experience low communication control according to the instrument's scale. In independent studies, both Garmon and Cardot found significantly higher communication control among faculty than administrators in American colleges and universities.[25] Roper found that entering university students who expressed a degree of high communication control were less likely to drop out of college their first semester.[26] Driskill and Dodd reported that high communication control college students in a dorm environment were more likely to be opinion leaders and express an open communication style.[27]

You can assess your own tendencies in communication control by taking the PCWV scale in table 5.1. According to norms (based on testing over 2,400 people), individuals below 60 may exhibit less communication control, 60–80 moderate control, and 80 or above high communication control. As you might expect, your score depends on your immediate life's circumstances: broken relationships, failures, difficulties. Finally, the instrument predictably differentiates individualistic cultures from collectivist cultures and high power-distance cultures from low power-distance cultures.

Values and Intercultural Communication

Values refer to long-enduring judgments appraising the worth of an idea, object, person, place, or practice. While attitudes may change, values are long lasting. For example, a political candidate supporting humanitarian aid to an impoverished nation may win your vote because that person holds values similar to your values of altruism. This value even might relate to some of your other values. Fundamentally, values relate to questions of whether something ought or ought not to be—when we discover the why of those questions, we discover the values.

Value differences affect intercultural communication. For example, a person may elevate the importance of extra effort and hard work, believing it produces success. Imagine the potential difficulty if this person were teamed with an individual who devalues hard work, believing that just getting by is enough to have time to enjoy life. Their communication may be strained under this system. An understanding of values, therefore, can pinpoint the differences between two individuals from separate cultures—-intercultural communication can be more successful with an understanding of those differences.

Table 5.1   Personal Communication World View

Read each item carefully to be sure you know what that item is stating. Then circle your response to the item. The responses range from strongly disagree (SD), to a less intense disagreement (D), to a position of being right in between agreeing and disagreeing (N), to a position of agreement with the item (A), to strongly agree (SA). You are being asked to indicate your attitude/belief about each item, honestly expressing your personal opinion.

	5	4	3	2	1
1. No matter how much effort I make to communicate clearly, it really seems my level of happiness is not changed by what I say or do.	SD	D	N	A	SA
2. Both the bad things and the good things that happen to me are beyond my control.	SD	D	N	A	SA
3. In my view of the world, the future is already set in motion, so my choices are limited; even if I communicate convincingly, or use helpful decision processes, it will not do much to change the way my future looks now.	SD	D	N	A	SA
4. Frequently, other people have more effect than I do on whether or not I attain my goals.	SD	D	N	A	SA
5. Luck and circumstances play a major role in my life, regardless of my communication efforts for influencing my situation.	SD	D	N	A	SA
6. Many times I could be described as a victim of people or circumstances beyond my control.	SD	D	N	A	SA
7. There is not much use in trying too hard to please people; if they like you, they like you, and if they don't like you, you can't do much to change the situation.	SD	D	N	A	SA
8. My destiny depends mostly on the plans of others, who alter many of my decisions.	SD	D	N	A	SA
9. Getting a job or being promoted in a job depends on my being in the right place at the right time, not on my personal ability or personal communication skills.	SD	D	N	A	SA
10. Many times I could describe myself as having little influence over the things that seem to happen to me or over the people in my life right now.	SD	D	N	A	SA
11. The future lies before most people like a long ribbon that cannot be altered or shaped very easily but mostly just followed.	SD	D	N	A	SA

Table 5.1 Personal Communication World View *(continued)*

	5	4	3	2	1

12. With people who just don't respond well to me, even if I try to pay more attention, listen better, and interact the best I can, my efforts don't work; the relationship seems already set and I can't seem to do much about it.   SD   D   N   A   SA

13. I've found that when I make choices to help or influence people, my decisions really do not change them—usually it's the circumstances and not what I say or do.   SD   D   N   A   SA

14. I wish I could take more control over the direction of my life, but people, groups, and circumstances regulate me too much.   SD   D   N   A   SA

15. It is not always wise to plan too far ahead because many things turn out to be a matter of good or bad fortune anyhow.   SD   D   N   A   SA

16. The way I see it, I can try to communicate and interact, but I'm finding that changing my circumstances is not very likely.   SD   D   N   A   SA

17. In reality, I tend to think and do things the way my family does things.   SD   D   N   A   SA

18. I often think that few of us have a control or predetermined purpose that we understand clearly.   SD   D   N   A   SA

19. My culture, friends, and circumstances usually direct and influence me more than anything else.   SD   D   N   A   SA

20. What is going to happen will happen, regardless of what I say or do.   SD   D   N   A   SA

Scoring:

All SD = 5; D = 4; N = 3; A = 2; SA = 1. Add the rating for each item, and total across all twenty items.

20–59 = low communication control; personal choices and communication management not as strong as relationship, luck, circumstances

60–79 = moderate communication control; personal choices and communication management equally as strong as relationships, luck, circumstances

80–100 = high communication control; personal choices and communication management stronger than relationships, luck, circumstances

(reliability = .86, Cronbach's alpha)

Carley Dodd and Cecile Garmon, introduced in this text, 1991.

A number of values center around evaluations concerning family and kin, especially values toward elders, parents, and ancestors.[28]

Respect for elders.   Almost every culture shows some degree of respect for its elders. In North America, for many years the young used last names in a formal manner when addressing older or respected persons. In some rural areas of the United States, the practice existed not too many years ago of addressing an older person as "Aunt" or "Uncle," even though no actual kinship was evident. Among North American family members, there is a degree of respect for age—up to a point. Some seem to lose respect for their senior family members and senior citizens in general, from retirement age on.

The respect North Americans have for their elderly is indeed pale compared with the high value placed upon the elderly in other cultures.[29] For many Asian and African cultures, age and its accompanying wisdom stand as a salient element—in some cases, a focal point—of culture. Many African men under twenty-five years of age will not make decisions without consulting older family members. Someone recently observed to me that North American parents value their children and their needs more than the parents' parents or grandparents. Just the opposite is true in Asian cultures where the elders are honored ahead of the children. This concept plays out in many circumstances from eating habits to resource management in the family.

Respect for parents.   Value of parental authority also varies culturally. North Americans typically stress individuality and making one's own decisions by the midteens. Accompanying this emphasis seems to be a disregard for parental authority and much less communication with parents—at least in a large number of cases. Such actions would be regarded as dishonoring parents in African and Middle Eastern cultures. In these cultures, to honor one's parents throughout life is considered one of the highest virtues.

Respect for ancestors.   Although most North Americans typically do little more than occasionally remember a deceased relative, many cultures emphasize homage to ancestors. This value partially stems from some world-view beliefs that ancestors can influence one's life and provide special benefits, as indicated earlier in this chapter. In some parts of Africa, family members take out large newspaper ads featuring a picture of a deceased family member and a personal letter addressing the deceased. This form of communication with immediate ancestors or other deceased family members reflects not only an interesting communication form but also the importance of values. Respect for ancestors sometimes coincides with life cycles, illustrated in the ancestor-reincarnation view of the Ashanti (figure 5.1).

Source of identification and self-worth.   Family serves as an organizing social unit from which to develop personal identification. "I am a Martinez," or "a Schleyermacher," or "I am from the family of Chan," or "My family is Abramson," represent examples relating to identity and ultimately a source of self-worth in many cultures. The cultural vitality of the family as a source of personal worth depends on respect and dignity factors offered in two-way processes of affirmation and confirmation between parents, grandparents, and children.

Obligation.   Another family value varying across cultures is obligation to family. In many cultures families must take precedence over self. Obligation in many cultures, however, is broader than just family. A PBS special on African culture entitled "Legacy of Lifestyles" emphasized how successful, urban Africans take their obligations to their rural tribes of origin seriously. An African with good income often makes frequent visits to the village and helps with things like fertilizer, school fees, conflict resolution, and pays respect to older villagers. This example is but one of many cultures where the migration from rural to urban life does not exclude obligation to family and friends. When I was in Papua New Guinea, I observed the won-tok system, whereby material wealth brought with it the culturally accepted obligations to family. In fact, won-tok is so pervasive, that any villager or good friend is allowed to enjoy the material advantages of their friends.

Shame.   The collectivist concept of shame, in contrast to individualistic cultures that experience guilt, recognizes how family members in certain cultures cause group embarrassment, or shame, for all family members. Anytime a child violates norms or law, the shame potential exists. In some Asian and Latin American cultures, a daughter who dates a young man without the parents' approval brings dishonor to the entire family. In certain cases, the dishonor forces the father to disenfranchise the daughter. Shame, embarrassment, and loss of face also can be broader issues than just family, often affecting entire communities.[30]

Values and Interpersonal Relationships

Another set of values focuses on interpersonal relationships. One's personal dealings with others is considered a sacred trust in some cultures but is treated casually in other cultures.

Equality of people.   In the United States, people generally accept the norm of equality among people, at least philosophically. Many other cultures accept inequality and status differences as the norm. As the discussion on power-distance earlier in this chapter indicated, there is a value placed on hierarchy in some cultures. In a number of those cases, the vertical differences between people is explained in terms of harmony and good for all in the culture.

Humanitarianism.   Cultures vary on their obligations to people outside their family, tribes, and friends. In some cases, it is assumed that each significant social unit, like a family or tribe, can help its own members. Thus, obligations are not extended beyond those units to outsiders. Other cultures operate on the assumption that altruism operates broadly and is expected to persist for strangers as well as associates. Most cultures have a sense of altruism, compassion, and sympathy, as these values affect helping others, but the cultural rules for operationalizing these values differ.

Honesty.   Most cultures have some taboo against dishonesty—under certain conditions. A Middle Easterner who values slyness and cleverness, for example, may be fully acceptable as long as he is considered sly in bargaining and not perceived as dishonest. Of course, one person's definition of honesty becomes another person's definition of cleverness—the United States businessperson who can cheat and not get caught is sometimes considered shrewd. That person's foreign counterpart is considered dishonest. In some cultures, a bribe is perceived as dishonest; other cultures view the same activity as a courtesy, as payment for a favor, or as an extended tip.

Harmony.   Earlier discussions already have alluded to the importance of harmony with others. East-west relationship building often stresses this consideration and requires communication activity accompanying this important value. In Asante's research regarding traditional African court and trial procedures, communication and trust are essential to producing harmony (see note 28). Overall, a number of important communication strategies relate to interacting with cultures emphasizing harmony:

> —*face-saving at all costs; regardless of who is right or wrong, saving face contributes to overall harmony*

> —*developing consensus; individual comments or long speeches are acceptable in harmony cultures so long as the speaker ultimately accepts the group's choice and facilitates rather than takes away from the group; as the Japanese proverb goes, "the nail that sticks up gets hit"*

> —*cooperation as an expectation*

> —*truth as an organizing principle*

> —*appropriate ambiguity or silence used in a timely manner*

> —*avoid directness and confrontation*

> —*respect for tradition*

Mentoring relationship.   In recent years, research has highlighted interpersonal values toward role models or mentors. Research investigating the value that black professionals place on interpersonal helping roles indicates the race of the mentor is the best predictor of professional development.[31] It appears that a system that values role modeling and mentoring is vital and healthy for relationships.

In-groups and out-groups.   The distinction between in-groups (those valued usually because the source describing the perspective is a member) and out-groups (those devalued because the source describing the perspective is not a member) is a source of interpersonal value difference. For example, Broome reminds us that Greek in-group/out-group distinctions are significant, even historically meaningful organizing principles to a larger extent than in western societies. In this example, the entire culture's predominant interpersonal orientation revolves around this classification schema. In the broadest sense, then, cultural values toward others depend on group memberships and group loyalties surrounding those memberships. Successful interpersonal relationships are culturally bounded by a matrix of associations and one's personal reference group's acceptance or rejection of those associations.[32]

Inclusion and exclusion.   Cultural values also differ on the role of how much psychological distance to keep from others. How much emotional closeness or distance (called immediacy in communication literature) is appropriate and has enormous communication consequences arising from the value assigned by each culture. For instance, Gonzalez defined Mexican "otherness" and points out how Mexican Americans appear to push others away. In reality, the separation is a mask hiding the pain of oppression and exclusion from larger social processes. Just as important to many Mexican Americans is the value and drive toward inclusion. What Anglos perceive as ambivalence toward others is in reality a struggle beneath the psychological surface of dealing with identity and acculturation in a new culture, while facing the pain and grief over a conquered past, according to Gonzalez.[33]

Values Associated with Society

Another set of cultural values predisposes cultural members to respond in their activities with a sense of what the society as a whole expects. A brief introduction may be helpful before we continue with categories. Some of these values relate to personal behaviors, and some relate to group behaviors. Furthermore, individuals may experience negative consequences if they ignore or avoid societal value standards. In Singapore for instance, the national culture enjoys wealth and success, but these come at the expense of subjection of personal liberties. This dynamic relationship between society and self is understood by members in light of their culture, although foreign visitors may not understand or may reject perceived personal losses. Such a rank ordering of society over self, or in the case of North Americans, self over society, reflects this question of society values—their elements and diversity.

Morality and ethics.   Morality and ethics seem highly personal to North Americans. But for many people around the world, morality is a group matter. Inappropriate premarital activity can cause a family to lose a certain bride price otherwise gained for a daughter. Incorrect use of property can become a grave societal offense among some African cultures. Not using appropriate silence or disclosing too much can be seen as breaking the norms of silence or stealth among some Native American cultures.

Personal freedom.   Personal freedom is not only defined differently, but also not valued the same across cultures. In some cultures it is inappropriate to discuss personal choice in a way other than the individual's relationship to the group at large. One of the contrasting features that seems to surprise visitors from the United States to a host country is the sense of groupness. For instance, the Japanese sense of group relationship, loyalty, and hierarchy contrasts with the North Americans' sense of individuality. Conformity to social norms exists practically universally. Within the boundaries of social norms, some cultures stress groupness while others stress individualism. Of course, readers will recognize that harmony and its communication applications noted previously connect with the diversity of personal freedom indicated in this section.

Emotions. Some cultures value emotional expression, but other cultures prefer reservation. While there are exceptions, Asian cultures traditionally emphasize reserve and emotional restraint. The idea of extreme emotion, such as loud sobs during a funeral or boisterous laughter even at happier occasions, could be considered too emotional. To a lesser extent, some Scandinavian cultures appear publicly reserved. Britons and Germans appear more reserved than Italians, Greeks, and Czechs.

   The use of emotion in communication, therefore, varies according to culture. For example, the speech one makes in Lagos, Nigeria, should differ from a speech in Denmark in terms of emotional elements of communication style. Similarly, we should not be surprised to find our intercultural communication colored by a high emotional pitch in some cultures or affected by little enthusiasm in other cultures. To certain Europeans, North Americans appear pushy and too emotional; to Latin Americans, the same North American mannerisms appear cold and unfeeling.

Work and play. Many cultures separate work and play. In these cases, work demands diligence, concentration, even tedium. Since play is considered frivolous, combining work and play is unreasonable. Work and play do not mix! That view dominates some North American thought. In contrast, other cultures blend work and play. For the North American to insist on the divorce of work from frivolity and to judge others negatively is to invite estrangement.

Time. Time is valued more by some cultures than by others. To the U.S. businessperson, "Time is money." To the Ecuadorian storekeeper, time is relatively less important to one's friendships and other social obligations. The values that cultures place upon time, however, cause numerous misunderstandings, as you can imagine.

Tradition. If Tevia in the *Fiddler on the Roof* was right, then adhering to the past supersedes the present. Although as Tevia discovered, traditional values change. Cultures can be thought of as if on a continuum from relying on tradition at one end to embracing innovation on the other end. Individuals within a culture find themselves in consonance or dissonance with the mainstream values, as Tevia found about his children and their rejection of traditional ways.

Success. The idea behind getting ahead, winning, and generally being above average has deep roots as a North American value. Competition also is valued, since it purportedly stimulates success. However, this notion of success and failure lacks correspondence in many other cultures. In many cultures, cooperation is fundamental.

Individualism. Success in North American values is linked with personal achievement and rugged individualism. This individualism connects with personal freedom and choice in decision making. In contrast, some cultures do not value individualism. Again, some Asian cultures emphasize group cohesion and loyalty over individuals. Many African cultural members thwart personal goals for the sake of the family, village, or tribe. Some internationalists have likened the North American's view of freedom to an adolescent who lacks self-restraint. The point of view, of course, depends upon the values one holds toward individualism, freedom, and other related concepts.

Material well-being.   Many cultures value material accumulation of goods and wealth. Cattle herdsmen of East Africa, for example, prize their animals partially as a measure of status and wealth. In a similar way, North Americans accumulate goods as a measure of wealth and success. However, material well-being and accumulation of wealth can become ends valued in and of themselves—sometimes as the single most important value. The symbols of material well-being and wealth, obviously vary among cultures.

Values Concerning Land and Animals

How a culture views the totality of natural resources becomes an intriguing question. The narrower discussion of that issue, however strange it may seem to some readers, is to recognize the central value of land and space as well as the value of animals in the history and activities of a culture.[34]

Relationship with land.   First, consider the importance of *land as a cultural value.* For instance, farmland in China is related to a sense of security. It can be passed through generations; money may be used up, but not the land. Land values often center around kinship ties. This tie is reinforced by ancestor worship and creates a bond between a man and his land. It is not impossible for a man to sell his land but to sell breaks the bonds of filial piety. Because these bonds are so rarely broken, from childhood onward, a man develops a sense of personal identity with his land; it becomes a part of his very personality.

Like the Chinese, the Maoris of New Zealand feel quite strongly about the inheritance of the land to develop an ancestral continuity. These feelings have more immediate consequences for the Maoris than for the Chinese, according to Metge:

> It is a tangible link with the heroes and happenings of a storied past. Even more important, inherited rights in Maori land are bound up with rights of precedence in Maori community life and on the open space used as a gathering place. The older generation, in particular, recognize an almost mystical connection between land and personal standing. In each local district, Maoris give a special status to those they call tangata whenua (literally, people of the land). To qualify for this title and the privileges attached to it, a Maori must first of all be descended from a line of forbearers who lived and owned Maori land in the district continuously over many generations.[35]

With no ancestral connection to the Maori land, a person is considered an immigrant, frequently barred from public office and rarely listened to in public discussions.

Among traditional Navaho, a matrilineal kinship rule gives a woman her own plot of land, and the returns she reaps from it are strictly hers. The man does the same with his property. Even the children may be given designated pieces of land or a few animals and be expected to take care of these things as soon as the children are old enough.

However, the land and its productivity are not a status symbol to the Navaho, even when they bring in a considerable amount of money. They have a high regard for possessions but feel that anyone who becomes extremely wealthy must have come by the wealth dishonorably. Therefore, they advocate that the wealth must be distributed among the wealthy's less fortunate friends and relatives.[36]

The Plains Indians of North America were also hunters and gatherers, but their philosophy did not allow for a man's ownership of the land. To the Plains Indians, "All things are contained within the Medicine Wheel, and all things are equal within it. The Medicine Wheel is the Total Universe." A Blackfoot Chief explained the relation between the Indian and his earth as follows:

> Our land is more valuable than your money. It will last forever. It will not even perish by the flames of fire. As long as the sun shines and the waters flow, this land will be here to give life to men and animals. We cannot sell the lives of men and animals; therefore we cannot sell this land. You can count your money and burn it without the nod of a buffalo's head, but the Great Spirit can count the grains of sand and the blades of grass of these plains. As a present to you, we will give you anything we have that you can take with you; but the land, never.[37]

This concept of the land was not only related to the equality of all nature, but to the view of the earth as a mother. In Indian literature, the earth is referred to as the Earth Mother. Her daily power and influence on the lives of the Indians is reflected in the following passage by Chief Luther Standing Bear, chief of the Lakota, a western band of the Sioux Indian tribe:

> The Lakota was a true naturist—a lover of nature. He loved the earth and all things of the earth, the attachment growing with age. The old people came literally to love the soil, and they sat or reclined on the ground with a feeling of being close to a mothering power. It was good for the skin to touch the earth, and the old people liked to remove their moccasins and walk with bare feet on the sacred earth. Their tepees were built upon the earth, and their altars were made of earth. The birds that flew in the air came to rest upon the earth, and it was the final abiding place of all things that lived and grew. The soil was soothing, strengthening, cleansing, and healing.
>
> That is why the old Indian still sits upon the earth instead of propping himself up and away from its life-giving forces. For him, to sit or lie upon the ground is to be able to think more deeply and to feel more keenly; he can see more clearly into the mysteries of life and come closer in kinship to other lives about him. . . .
>
> The old Lakota was wise. He knew that man's heart away from nature becomes hard; he knew that lack of respect for growing things soon led to lack of respect for humans, too. So he kept his youth close to its softening influence.[38]

This love and respect for the earth is in opposition to the agrarian societies, who would often clear and plow the ground for agricultural purposes. One Wintu Indian woman expressed these beliefs:

> The White people plow up the ground, pull down the tree, kill everything. The tree says, "Don't. I am sore. Don't hurt me." But they chop it down and cut it up. The spirit of the land hates them. They blast out trees and stir it up to its depths.[39]

Relationship with animals.   Another set of values considers the *importance and roles of animals* in a culture. The sacredness of all life to the Hindu is well known. The cow, for instance, is highly symbolic of reincarnation. Jewish and

Islamic peoples condemn pigs and pork. Other societies revere the pig. The Maring, a remote tribe living in the Bismarck Mountains of New Guinea, hold a pig festival approximately every twelve years. During the festival, a massive number of pigs are sacrificed, and a battle is waged on enemy clans. Following the battle, a prayer is offered to assure the ancestors that the fighting is over and that the coming years will be spent replenishing the pig supply. The total concept of pig love is explained by Harris:

> Pig love includes raising pigs to be a member of the family, sleeping next to them, talking to them, stroking and fondling them, calling them by name, leading them on a leash to the fields, weeping when they fall sick or are injured, and feeding them with choice morsels from the family table. But unlike the Hindu love of cow, pig love also includes obligatory sacrificing and eating of pigs on special occasions. Because of ritual slaughter and sacred feasting, pig love provides a broader prospect for communion between man and beast than is true of the Hindu farmer and his cow. The climax of pig love is the incorporation of the pig as flesh into the flesh of the human host and of the pig as spirit into the spirit of the ancestors.[40]

Some cultures, such as the Balinese, do not regard animals as being on the same level as humans and carry a revulsion of animal-like behavior within the culture:

> Babies are not allowed to crawl for that reason. Incest, though hardly approved, is a much less horrifying crime than bestiality. (The appropriate punishment for the second is death by drowning, for the first being forced to live like an animal.) Most demons are represented—in sculpture, dance, ritual, myth—in some real or fantastic animal form. The main puberty rite consists in filing the child's teeth so they will not look like animal fangs. Not only defecation, but eating is regarded as a disgusting, almost obscene activity, to be conducted hurriedly and privately because of its association with animality. Even falling down or any form of clumsiness is considered to be bad for these reasons. Aside from cocks and a few domestic animals—oxen, ducks—of no emotional significance, the Balinese are aversive to animals and treat their large number of dogs not merely callously but with a phobic cruelty.[41]

The traditional Kwakiutl on Vancouver Island, on the other hand, claim animals as their ancestors, as Boas described:

> According to Indian theory, the ancestor of a numaya appeared at a specific locality by coming down from the sky, out of the sea, or from underground, generally in the form of an animal, took off his animal mask, and became a person. The Thunderbird or his brother the gull, the Killer Whale, a sea monster, a grizzly bear, and a ghost chief appear in this role.[42]

When the Kwakiutl hunted, an equality was established between the hunter and the actual and spiritual qualities of the animal they hunted. A certain ritual etiquette was observed by the hunters. The chiefs were the only real hunters of the tribe, because they embodied the spirits of the ancestors.

The Plains Indians of North America, because of their belief in the total harmony of the universe, also had a distinct respect for the animal. Any buffalo killed would have its heart left on the prairie as a sacrifice and as a symbol of the Indians' desire for the buffalo to prosper. Each person would receive a medicine animal at birth, a symbolic name of an animal that represented his or her character.[43]

Developing
Skills in
Encountering
Underlying
Dimensions of
Culture

1. *Do as others do.* Whenever you are visiting another culture, try to observe the methods of respect toward symbols within the new culture. For example, if you are visiting a special shrine or some holy place, try to practice respect for the feelings of culture members toward their symbols.

2. *Develop self-awareness.* The ability to know yourself is truly helpful. Puzzling, demanding situations are the norm in intercultural communication. Understanding world view can provide tremendous insight into your own cultural background and the background of the host culture.

3. *Try to understand missing social cues.* When we go to another culture, familiar social cues are missing. In their absence, we can become confused, a disorientation especially augmented by extreme differences in world view. Realizing this principle and striving to keep ourselves learning new cues can be helpful.

4. *Do not assume that you know a world view.* This chapter may leave you with the impression that, because you know some of the categories of world view, you now know all there is to know about a particular culture. Cultural belief systems are very complex, so do not assume that you have a handle on a new culture's belief system. Instead, keep asking questions, observing, and listening.

5. *Discover when to use formal and informal modes.* Almost every culture has cues that relate to those times when, according to the belief systems, you are supposed to behave formally. Other times, it seems everyone is a lot different, somehow more relaxed. The difference may be one of formality and informality. After a while, you will find yourself easily conforming to the role-switching situations.

This Chapter in Perspective

Underlying dimensions by which people perceive self and others and by which they process information represents a pioneering metaphor to explain intercultural processes. Monochronic-polychronic dimensions of culture involve singular or simultaneous time processing. High- and low-context cultures refer to expected information and meanings inherent in the situation or how much is expected to be articulated. Hofstede's work identifying four factors underlying culture explains a great deal of communication behavior. World view is a significant element of culture and represents the means by which cultures organize their world and their place in the universe. Cultural world view compels practices, rituals, attitudes, and communication behaviors.

This chapter contains data on elements of cultural world view. Those elements include shame and guilt, task and people, sacred and secular cultures, role of dead to living, nature of humankind, humans and nature, doing and being cultures, life cycle, and fatalism. The chapter also describes systems of cultural world view and the concept of personal communication world view.

Cultural values were discussed. Many values revolve around relationships with family, friends, and associates. Attitudes and values with respect to the elderly, parents, ancestors, others, society, land, and animals were examined.

Each dimension said to underlie culture has consequences for explaining inter-cultural communication. Sometimes these dimensions are useful for explaining the perception of difference in the first contact with a person or group. How the other person thinks or processes information becomes an assessment of similarity or difference, as our model indicates. A second consequence for intercultural communication is how underlying cultural dimensions explain communicator differences.

Exercises

1. Interview a person from an older generation. Ask for stories and examples of how culture has changed in their lifetime. What themes appear different today?

2. What cultural beliefs seem most related to behavior when it comes to dating? Friendship? Family? How do varying beliefs about these relationships influence communication? What themes do you see?

Endnotes

1. Richard Bandler, *Using Your Brain for a Change: Neurolinguistic Programming* (Moab, Utah: Real People Press, 1985).

2. Charles Phipps, "The Measurement of Monochronic and Polychronic Cognitions Among Hispanics and Anglos" (seniors honors thesis, Abilene Christian University, 1987).

3. E. T. Hall, *Beyond Culture* (New York: Anchor, 1976).

4. Stella Ting-Toomey, "Toward a Theory of Conflict and Culture," in *Communication, Culture, and Organizational Processes,* ed. William B. Gudykunst, Lea P. Stewart, and Stella Ting-Toomey (Newbury Park, Calif.: Sage, 1985); Stella Ting-Toomey, "Intercultural Conflict Styles: A Face Negotiation Theory," in *Theories in Intercultural Communication* (Newbury Park, Calif.: Sage, 1988).

5. Peter Ehrenhaus, "Culture and the Attribution Process: Barriers to Effective Communication," in *Intercultural Communication Theory: Current Perspectives,* ed. William B. Gudykunst (Beverly Hills, Calif.: Sage, 1983).

6. Min-Sun Kim, William Sharkey, and Theodore Singelis, "Explaining Individuals and Collectivist Communication—Focusing on the Perceived Importance of Interactive Constraints" (paper presented to the Speech Communication Association, Chicago, November, 1992).

7. Harry Triandis, "Cross-Cultural Psychology as the Scientific Foundation of Cross-Cultural Training," in *Intercultural Skills for Multicultural Societies,* ed. Carley Dodd and Frank Montalvo (Washington, D.C.: Sietar, 1987); Harry Triandis, "Individualism-Collectivism: Implications for Intercultural Communication" (paper presented to the Intercultural and International Communication Conference, Fullerton, California, March, 1990).

8. Sandra Sudweeks, "Taking Cultural Theory in the Classroom: A Review Essay," *Communication Education* 40 (1991): 294–302.

9. Sudweeks, 1991 (see note 8).

10. Michael Hecht, Peter Andersen, and Sidney Ribeau, "The Cultural Dimensions of Nonverbal Communication," in *Handbook of International and Intercultural Communication*, ed. Molefi Kete Asante and William B. Gudykunst (Newbury Park, Calif.: Sage, 1989).

11. Cecile Garmon and I have collaborated on several projects involving assessing personal and cultural world view over a number of years. I have been involved with some of these concepts from some early work I produced in 1977 in a book now out of print entitled *Perspectives on Cross-Cultural Communication.* Dr. Garmon, however, developed much of the resources indicated in this section. See Cecile Garmon, "Communication Correlates of World View" (masters thesis, Western Kentucky University, 1980); Cecile Garmon, "World View Differences Among College and University Administrators and Faculty in the South" (Ph.D. dissertation, Vanderbilt University, 1984).

12. Anthony Marsella, Michael Murray, and Charles Golden, "Ethnic Variations in the Phenomenology of 'Emotions,' " in *Intercultural Communication: A Reader,* 2d ed., ed. Larry Samovar and Richard Porter (Belmont, Calif.: Wadsworth, 1976).

13. Roberto Jimenez, "Mythology of Life and Mexican-American Acculturation," in *Intercultural Skills for Multicultural Societies,* ed. Carley Dodd and Frank Montalvo (Washington, D.C.: SIETAR, 1987).

14. Marshall Singer, *Intercultural Communication: A Perceptual Approach* (Englewood Cliffs, N. J.: Prentice-Hall, 1987).

15. Francis Shaeffer, *The God Who is There* (Downers Grove, Ill.: Intervarsity Press, 1968).

16. Philip Bock, *Modern Cultural Anthropology* (New York: Alfred A. Knopf, 1969).

17. Louis Faron, "On Ancestor Propitiation Among the Mapuche of Central Chile," *American Anthropologist* 64 (1962): 1151–63.

18. Florence Kluckhohn and Fred Strodtbeck, *Variations in Value Orientations* (Evanston, Ill.: Row and Petersen, 1961).

19. Larry Sarbaugh, *Intercultural Communication* (Rochelle Park, N.J.: Hayden, 1979).

20. Everett Rogers with Lynne Svenning, *Modernization Among Peasants: The Impact of Communication* (New York: Holt, Rinehart and Winston, 1969).

21. Carley Dodd and Cecile Garmon, "The Measurement of Personal Report of World View" (paper presented to the Speech Communication Association, Boston, November, 1987). These two authors have been working individually or together in this area of research for some 18 years. Their combined experience in other countries and their research experiences lead them to conclude that world view is a significant cultural variable experienced in such a way by individuals that communication outcomes are influenced by this concept of fatalism and its opposite. (See also note 11.)

22. Gale Auletta, "Response to Driskill and Nortons's Review of Research in Personal World View" (paper presented to the Speech Communication Association, San Francisco, November, 1989). See also, Gerald Driskill and M. Laurie Norton, "Dodd and Garmon's Personal World View and Communication Style in an Organizational Culture" (paper presented to the Speech Communication Association, San Francisco, November, 1989).

23. Driskill and Norton, 1989 (see note 22).

24. Larry Long, Manoocher Javidi, and Margaret Pryately, "Motives for Moves: A Cross-Cultural Examination of Communication Motives and Style Among Americans, Japanese, and Ukranians" (paper presented to the Southern and Central Communication Associations, Lexington, Kentucky, April, 1993).

25. See Garmon, 1984 (see note 11). Also, Joe Cardot, "A Comparison of Communication Social Style and World View Between Administrators and Faculty Members of Higher Education" (Ph.D. dissertation, Texas Tech University, 1990).

26. Cynthia Roper, "The Effects of Communication Apprehension, World View, Innovativeness, and Communication Style on Culture Shock" (masters thesis, Abilene Christian University, 1986).

27. Gerald Driskill and Carley Dodd, "Opinion Leadership, Personal World View, and Communication Style in an Organizational Culture" (paper presented to the Speech Communication Association, Chicago, November, 1988).

28. In this discussion, we are indebted to several sources influential in the theory and categories developed in this part of the book, including the following. John Condon and Fathi Yousef, *Introduction to Intercultural Communication* (New York: Bobbs-Merrill, 1975); Molefi Asante, "The Tradition of Advocacy in the Yoruba Courts," *The Southern Communication Journal* 55 (1990): 250–59; Pamela Kalbfleisch and Andrea B. Davies, "Minorities and Mentoring: Managing the Multicultural Institution," *Communication Education* 40 (1991): 266–71; Donald Klopf, *The Fundamentals of Intercultural Communication,* 3d ed. (Englewood, Colo.: Morton, 1995); H. Ned Seelye, *Teaching Culture*, 3d ed. (Lincolnwood, Ill.: National Textbook Company, 1993); David Lewis, Carley Dodd, and Darryl Tippens, *The Gospel According to Generation X* (Abilene, Tex.: Abilene Christian University Press, 1995).

29. M. Laurie Norton, "Adaptation Among the Elderly as Subculture" (Ph.D. dissertation, University of Oklahoma, 1991).

30. Richard Brislin, *Understanding Culture's Influence on Behavior* (Orlando: Harcourt Brace Jovanovich, 1993).

31. Pamela J. Kalbfleisch and Andrea B. Davies, "Minorities and Mentoring: Managing the Multicultural Institution," *Communication Education* 40 (1991): 266–71.

32. Benjamin J. Broome, "Pavelome: Foundations of Struggle and Conflict in Greek Interpersonal Communication," *The Southern Communication Journal* 55 (1990): 260–75.

33. Alberto Gonzalez, "Mexican Otherness in the Rhetoric of Mexican Americans," *The Southern Communication Journal*, 55 (1990): 276–91.

34. I am deeply indebted to graduate student Diane Schwalm's literature findings on the significance of values centered around land and animals.

35. Joan Metge, *The Maoris of New Zealand: Rautahi* (London: Routledge and Kegan Paul Ltd., 1976).

36. Alexander Leighton and Dorthea Leighton, *The Navajo Door* (New York: Russell and Russell, 1944).

37. Hyemeyohsts Storm, *Seven Arrows* (New York: Ballantine Books, 1972), 5.

38. T. C. McLuhan, ed., *Touch the Earth* (New York: Pocket Books, 1972), 6.

39. Ibid., 15.

40. Marvin Harris, *Cows, Pigs, Wars and Witches* (New York: Random House, 1974), 46.

41. Clifford Geertz, *The Interpretation of Cultures* (New York: Basic Books, 1973), 419–20.

42. Franz Boas, *Kwakiutl Ethnography* (Chicago: University of Chicago Press, 1966), 42.

43. Storm, 1972 (see note 37).

116 Part Two Perceiving the Nature of Cultural and Social Diversity

Part Three

Understanding Intercultural Language and Nonverbal Communication

Chapter 6

Linguistic Diversity and

Intercultural Communication

OBJECTIVES   *After completing this chapter, you should be able to*

1. Give examples of the significance of language for understanding culture and communication

2. Describe the reciprocal influence of language on culture and culture on language

3. Demonstrate the workings of the Whorf and Bernstein hypotheses

4. Describe perceptual differences and attitudes people hold toward individuals with accented speech

5. Identify theories of why certain dialects suggest prestige

6. Identify the relationship between speech and employability

7. Identify ethnolinguistic theories of identification

To study culture is also to study the language of a culture. Language shapes perceptions, actions, and thoughts. Language is part of the identity of a people. Individuals bring to the intercultural encounter not only their ethnographic categories, world view, values, cultural themes and so on but importantly their language—and its powerful shaping influence in the lives of cultural members. We do not focus on language in this chapter to examine only cultural differences but to understand more fully how even the fact that someone speaks another language or speaks your language with an accent influences social attitudes toward that speaker.

Differences Experienced Because of Language

Language and its Influence on Perception

We want to turn to several perceptual differences that we encounter because of language and its influence on perception, group relations, and meaning.

Many years ago, Benjamin Whorf wrote that language functions not only to report information but actually to shape our perceptions of reality, a point illustrated in figure 6.1. This idea revolutionized linguistic science—and intercultural communication specialists recognize today the continuing importance of language and culture on perceptions. Harry Hoijer wrote that:

> language plays a large and significant role in the totality of culture. Far from being a technique of communication, it is itself a way of directing the perceptions of its speakers and it provides for them habitual modes of analyzing experience into significant categories. And to the extent that languages differ markedly from each other, so should we expect to find significant and formidable barriers to cross-cultural communication and understanding.[1]

The term *linguistic relativity* applies to language as the shaper of reality (Whorf 1956). Since languages differ, linguistic communities could be expected to differ in their perceptual experiences of the world around them. Language acts like a filter, molding perception. An extension of this idea, according to Whorf, is *linguistic determinism* which refers to Whorf's assumption that language determines thought, which is to say that higher levels of thought hinge on language. Both ideas are not without criticism, but for the moment let us examine the idea that language shapes a perception of reality.

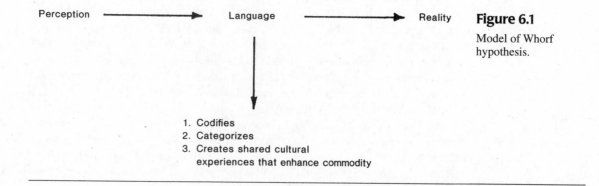

Figure 6.1

Model of Whorf hypothesis.

Figure 6.2

Color spectra for English, Shona, and Basa. (Gleason as noted.)

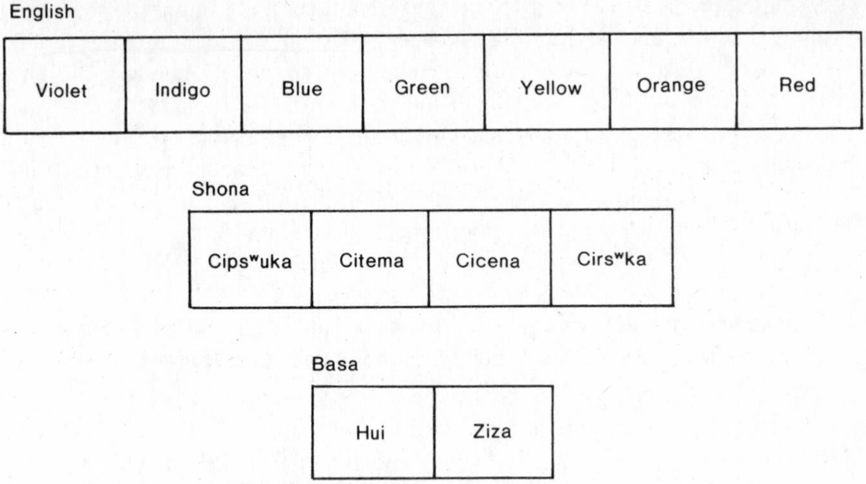

English

Violet	Indigo	Blue	Green	Yellow	Orange	Red

Shona

Cipsʷuka	Citema	Cicena	Cirsʷka

Basa

Hui	Ziza

In this sense, language categorizes our world. Just as a biologist uses a scientific taxonomy to classify organisms, so the normal speaker uses language to classify reality. But what if a word stands for an entire cluster of things in one language but only one unique element of the cluster in another language? Then even if the word is "translated" correctly the category systems the word symbolizes can be markedly different. For example, English contains seven basic colors on a type of color spectrum ranging from red on one end of the spectrum to violet at the other end. When this spectrum is laid end to end and compared linguistically with two tribal languages, the Shona and the Basa, the result is that the Shona and Basa languages have fewer words for the color spectrum, according to informed sources as illustrated in figure 6.2.[2] Undoubtedly, few people would argue that the Basa tribe sees nothing but "hui" (the bluish end) and "ziza" (the reddish end). Of course, they can see the physical color (language does not change the retina), but Whorf's theory suggests that the language classification forces a category that alters perceptual systems where the boundaries of difference may be relatively unimportant. Examples in support of the Whorfian theory do not imply unequivocally that people of one culture cannot think of objects for which another culture has plentiful vocabulary, like the camel parts. The fact is not that we cannot, but that we do not. That we do not think of such specificity may mean that such matters are unimportant or irrelevant to our lifestyles. Language categorizes our experiences, almost without our full awareness. So, we might sense things in our environments or in relationships because the culture reinforces the terms and meanings for those things. That is one reason why language is also a shaper in similar ways cultural members perceive things. In a recent article, Chesebro makes the case for a symbol system and a rhetoric changing throughout a culture's history that reflects key themes of the culture at that point in time.[3] For Whorf, the language that is then codified continues to reinforce the thoughts and perceptions of the culture's reality over time.

Language and the Perception of Concepts

Various sources underscore the idea that language influences perception and thought.

1. English has 1 word for snow; Norwegians have as many as 16. Do they perceive snow differently?
2. English has a limited vocabulary for coffee; Brazilians are supposed to have scores of words for coffee, the coffee bean, and the coffee process. How might their perceptions differ?
3. Arabic contains numerous words for a camel and its parts; English is limited. Do the cultural speakers differ in their thought structure or perceptions?[4]
4. The languages of certain Native Americans, such as the Sioux, do not have grammatical structure for past and future tenses. How would that affect perception of time with speakers whose language emphasizes time orientation?

It is obvious that humans usually adapt their speech to the social context. For instance, as you pass a friend in a corridor, the constraints of the social situation act selectively on your speech with the friend. This momentary social structure may cause you to speak to your friend in a code familiar to both of you: quips, phrases, single words, and interrupted sentences are understood because you know the other person and his/her meanings. An outsider listening to your conversation may not share your mutual experience and consequently may not understand this jargon. This common experience, though, has important scientific underpinnings, a relationship Basil Bernstein once described:

> Speech . . . is constrained by the circumstances of the moment, by the dictate of a local social relation, and so symbolizes not what can be done, but what *is* done with different degrees of frequency. Speech indicates which options at the structural and vocabulary level are taken up. Between language in the sense defined and speech is social structure.[5]

Bernstein's conceptual explanation of dyadic social relations expands to include a broader social structure. Once we think of social structure as not only momentary social context but as a meeting of in-group cultural members with out-group cultural members studied earlier, then speech, or linguistic code, results from the cultural contact. A graphic representation of Bernstein's hypothesis emphasizes the mediating nature of social structure. We actually convert a potential reservoir of language into speech behavior, or what is actually said, and the model that follows illustrates that principle:

The Code Switching of Language Based on Differences in In-group or Out-group Cultures

Language	*Social Structure*	*Communication Behavior*
1. Lexicon (vocabulary)	1. Social context	1. Restricted code
2. Syntax (word relations)	2. Culture, subculture, social system	2. Elaborated code

Whorf indicated that our linguistic categories influence our perception of reality.

In other words, what we say and how we say it comes directly from our perception of the cultural climate in which we find ourselves.

Given a closed group such as an in-group or a larger cultural context such as an out-group, speech is adapted into one of two codes: restricted or elaborated. The *restricted code* involves message transmission understood by the people in a net-working culture, highly predictable, and approaching redundancy. Both the vocabulary and the structure are drawn from a narrow range of common assumptions, shared interests, identity, and expectations. Everyone basically already understands the situation. To use the concept from an earlier chapter, restricted codes presuppose a high context culture. Speakers have no need to elaborate their meanings, according to Bernstein.

Restricted codes, then, are like jargon or "shorthand speech" in which the speaker is almost telegraphic. Close friends might make only brief references to something, and yet each is reminded of a wealth of experiences or concepts. An outsider would have difficulty understanding because of their shared experiences. Communication found among professional groups represents a type of restricted code, such as medical or engineering terminology. Bernstein observed that lower-working-class children in Britain tended to use only a restricted code, while middle-class children used both elaborated and restricted codes. Research continues to reinforce the principle that restricted code influences a culture's norms and self-image. Restricted code communication also provided common ground for members from divergent backgrounds so that they could talk about the same things in meaningful ways.

Elaborated codes are often used when communicating with out-groups. This use of language involves messages low in prediction. Hence, the speaker must employ verbal elaboration to communicate effectively. Since we cannot anticipate what is actually said, the verbal channel dominates. This dominance contrasts with restricted codes, where new information and uniqueness emerge primarily through nonverbal and paralinguistic channels.

This quite naturally leads to the question in current intercultural research of how to identify with out-groups. Interculturalists frequently invite us to use *communication accommodation* (the term linguistic convergence is sometimes used) which refers to adopting the restricted code of an in-group. This poses an interesting problem. Generally, communication accommodators who use restricted code find themselves appreciated by the group for whom the accommodation is intended. However, in-groups do not like out-group members to accommodate to restricted code communication (1) if the in-group is trying to maintain distinctiveness by use of the restricted code, or (2) if they perceive some malicious intent on the part of the out-group person communicating this way. If you find yourself accommodating in your communicating style, and it is perceived that convergence toward the other group has some hidden attempt or some hidden dimension, then you could be in trouble (see again chapter 4).

Some fascinating studies have indicated the influence that occurs when communication accommodation takes place. Gudykunst, Ting-Toomey, Hall, and Schmidt for instance, cite evidence that when salespeople accommodate to the language of their customers they are more successful. Customers in banks accommodate to the clerk's language usage and seem to be more comfortable in that situation.[6] When an individual perceives the situational norms—or the favorite way of talking for the in-group—interpersonal accommodation is more likely to take place. In the case of bilingual speakers, that accommodation takes place by speaking the more prestigious language for that situation. In the case of dialectical differences, speakers use the favored code for that particular situation. This process of using the code most appropriate for the situation is also called *code switching,* a frequent and usually successful process. Remember, people use communication accommodation for a number of reasons: personal agendas (such as social approval), maximizing information sharing, and heightening persuasion.

Language and meaning

The intercultural encounters we experience are not only influenced by language and perceptual differences, and language choice based on restricted and elaborated social situations, but also on language and how it is translated for members of a culture. For many reasons linguistic interpretation and semantics provide the source of numerous misunderstandings. For instance, an insurance company discovered that fires inadvertently occurred because warehouse employees acted carelessly around "empty" barrels of gasoline, although they previously had exercised great caution around "full" drums of gasoline. The terms *full* and *empty* seem to mask the real danger in working with gasoline drums—empty drums are extremely combustible, while full drums pose far less threat. The linguistic perception of the word *empty* in the general culture signified null or void, but in the work culture of volatile products like gasoline the semantic "interpretation" was disastrous. A story is told of a Christian Scientist who refused to take vitamins, since the recommender described them as "medicine." However, the same person gladly took the vitamins when he was told they were "food." Several years ago, Swedish

Slogans and the Importance of Language

Several years ago, a U.S. Commission on Foreign Languages and International Studies noted that, in some foreign markets, cars with the interiors labeled "Body by Fisher" were advertised as having "Corpses by Fisher." When Pepsi was first introduced in Taiwan, the slogan "Come Alive" was translated into Chinese as a rather sacrilegious message: "Pepsi brings your ancestors back from the grave." A number of years ago the Chevy Nova (a car from the 1960s and 70s) was marketed in Mexico. Sales were miserable, and only later did experts realize the linguistic reason: the name Nova when pronounced sounds like "no va" which translates "no go." How would you feel with a car whose very name defeats the purpose of owning a car? It is not difficult to see how meanings can vary radically even with good attempts at language translation.

citizens were embroiled in a controversy over the pronoun *ni*. This word was a term reserved for speaking to those of a lower social status. Apparently, some persons who were equal or superior in social status brought suit in court against those individuals who used *ni* toward them; the connotation of the word had evoked such strong images that it was almost literally a "fighting word"[7]

How the Sound of Linguistic Differences Affects Relationship Attitudes and Actions

Ethnic speakers, people from differing parts of the country, and speakers of a language as a second language represent examples of people who speak a language with *ethnolinguistic variation*. This term refers to language used by a group of persons, called a linguistic community, revealing unique features of pronunciation, vocabulary, or style usage. It includes dialect and accented speech. Many investigations have examined the existence and effect of dialectical differences. Many research efforts have concluded that:

▌ listeners form perceptions and attitudes toward speakers based on dialect and accent

▌ in a given language community some types of speech have more prestige than others[8]

Let us begin in reverse order with the question of prestige.

Why do some dialects or accents seem more prestigious than others?   One way to explain attitudinal differences concerning ethnolinguistic variability is to test the question of the inherent pleasantness of a particular dialect (such as its rate, melodic qualities, and other pronunciation characteristics). The details of research in this area are plentiful, but by and large they indicate that prestige or desirability is less a fact of inherent pleasantness of a particular accent and more the cultural conditioning connected with that accent. To put that theory to the test, one study of French Canadians rated speakers of European-style French as more intelligent, ambitious, and likable than speakers of Canadian-style French; they also regarded their own French dialect as less aesthetically pleasing than European French. However, when a sample of Welsh respondents, totally unfamiliar with the language, listened to the two French dialects, they did not attribute more prestige or favorability to the European-style French speakers. These neutral observers did not perceive inherently pleasing sounds between the dialects. Apparently, the linguistic cues provided in the two French dialects simply triggered perceptions of *status* differences based on cultural norms, not innate qualities of the dialects.[9]

Sociolinguists have proposed another explanation for the judgments people make about dialectical differences or accented speech. Prestige is best accounted for by *cultural norms* toward accented speech. We simply come to accept cultural norms advocating favorability toward a particular accented speech pattern. Furthermore, what we associate as status or prestige often is a by-product of historical development. Thus, prestige is linked to the social group status from which the dialect originated. For example, "had the English Court in the Middle Ages been established in another region of the country rather than the southeast, then it could be suggested that the national news would now be broadcast and televised in what is considered today a nonstandard, regional accent."[10]

How does language affect listeners' perceptions and social attitudes?   Considerable evidence indicates that speech patterns, dialect, and accent serve as a cue causing listeners to assign certain attitudes or characteristics to another person. For example, in studies that ask students to rate well-known public figures based on their speech accents, the research typically indicates that they judge stereotypically. So, northern audiences hearing a southern speaker often attribute stereotypical social attitudes toward that speaker, unless the speaker says something in the content to counter those social attitudes.[11] Or speakers with an accented speaking pattern from any part of the world may often be perceived as stereotypical of that part of the world. Thus, a person who sounds "foreign" may suffer from negative perceptions or benefit from positive perception associated with his or her home country, according to research on this topic.[12]

Several studies have assessed how teachers evaluate the speech of pupils. By and large the research on this topic is not flattering, since it appears that even trained professionals are sometimes guilty of attributing negative characteristics to children based solely on how "ethnic" the child sounds. There was clearly a bias against ethnic groups in favor of children who sounded less ethnic in their accented use of English.[13]

Research designed to test how employers assess job applicants indicated a similar trend to judge candidates by their accented speech rather than their qualifications. When the employers heard the different voices on tape they rated each "speaker" who sounded ethnic more negatively. Imagine their surprise to learn that the same speaker was an actor faking the "different" accented voices and there were not different people at all. Yet each was rated differently solely on accented speech.[14]

Collectively, all these studies devalued speech accents associated with English speakers with a Spanish accent, African American accent, and a southern U.S. accent. The individuals who used a "standard" English accent were considered among the highest rated.

We would like to think that many of the older studies in this area have given way to impressive changes of attitudes. Sadly, we cannot conclude that without much more evidence from sociolinguistic replications of these kinds of studies. Researchers continue to show that language relates to stereotyping of people associated with a particular language usage. Stereotypes create expectancies about others and how they conform to our expectations. We create self-fulfilling prophecies.

To put it another way, ethnolinguistic variations activate stereotypes. For example, Susan, a twenty-two-year-old student, met an international student from England. Her first reaction was that this person must be incredibly intelligent because of the way he talked. In other words, all of her biases concerning the elitism of British pronunciation flooded her thinking. Later she discovered that he was like any of her other friends in many respects. She had simply acted on her stereotypes.

Many of us let language lead us into avoidance or sensitivity, indifference or sincere caring. A number of judgments, from social class to social attitudes, are rooted in ethnolinguistic variation. The ethnolinguistic features promise bold implications for understanding, attribution, and intercultural listening. For example, researchers provide prolific evidence concerning groups where we really remain at risk as far as cultural misunderstanding.[15] Such groups include cancer patients, the bereaved, the physically challenged, the elderly, Native Americans, Hispanics, and African Americans.[16]

How Language Represents More than Sound, Syntax, and Semantics

A great wealth of evidence indicates that people use ethnolinguistic speech for identification. Scholars conclude that language is a vital aspect of any ethnic group's identity. As a result, one's self-concept derives from how one sees himself/herself as a member of a particular group. Indeed, there is emotional value attached to that particular membership.[17] Researchers label this property of the identity secured by emotional attachment to one's ethnic language *ethnolinguistic identity*.[18]

Expanding this notion, Ting-Toomey indicates how the amount of confidence people have about their ethnolinguistic identity predicts their confidence toward out-group members. If they are secure about their ethnolinguistic identity, intergroup confidence prevails. It also seems that members who feel secure in their identities are not afraid of losing the personal self. Rather, out of a sense of "Who I am" and "Where I fit in my group," there is strength that leads to positive motivation, an ability to accept different roles, rhetorical sensitivity, and increased self-monitoring.[19]

Ethnolinguistic identity also hinges on an assumption that one's linguistic community is acceptable in a number of ways. The degree of prestige, acceptability, and importance attached to a group's language is known as *ethnolinguistic vitality*. This term might sound unusual at first, but it makes sense. When I am faced with an ethnic or cultural group obviously different from my own, this encounter could be somewhat brief if I have the feeling that my ethnic or cultural group is being put down. Since my language is one of the most clear-cut surface ways that I am identified, it is quite easy to see how my confidence could suffer if my language is indeed somehow also disparaged.

I remember very well the story of Bill, who came from a rural coculture. On entering a rather large university, Bill was informed by his mass media professors that his rural accent was insufficient for radio and TV. No linguistic vitality here,

Bill was told, so like any intercultural communicator, Bill adapted to a new set of expectations and thus met the norms of the more prestigious general American patterns of speech. When Bill went home for Thanksgiving, his somewhat uneducated mother literally would not let Bill in the house because when he knocked and called out, she did not recognize his voice. Her response? "If that's you, Bill, you better start talkin' right, or you're not gettin' in this house." Even more tragic for Bill, is that he never finished college. The role expectations based on the two linguistic communities posed undue pressure. If he could somehow have learned to be bicultural, perhaps the problem would have been solved, but the roles were too much for Bill to take as he later indicated.

Ultimately, we need to use strategies by which we can be more effective in relating to out-groups and in-groups. One strategy, mentioned previously, is to use communication accommodation and thus to converge toward normative usage for any one situation. A second strategy comes from our review in chapter 5 of how intercultural communication misunderstanding occurs because of stereotypical thinking and poor attributions.

Relating to Language Differences

A third strategy is to explore the advantages of a second-language competence. A number of scholars make a fascinating case for expressing thoughts and feelings from a second-language perspective. For one thing, it seems obvious that we need to communicate in the "heart language" of the culture (heart language refers to the emotional attachments to one's native language). One Mexican American informant told me an important principle a few years ago on the topic of achievement phenomena among Mexican Americans:

> You must understand that Hispanics in Texas and throughout the Southwest fall into two groups. Those who want to adapt to the larger Anglo cultures, and their counterparts who choose not to have such motivation, have one major barrier. That barrier is that English does not convey the emotion and feeling level that we can feel in Spanish. The phrases in our language are too rich to be ignored. And so, if acculturation means we must lose our heart language, I choose not to acculturate.

These words were spoken by a person who was completing a master's degree, had an excellent executive job, and was a leader in the Hispanic community. She articulated a very important point: if we are to penetrate another culture and be effective, second-linguistic competence with that other culture is obviously important; otherwise, feelings, experiences, and subjective messages all are missed. Obviously, a person is disadvantaged without a second-language ability. In some ways it is tempting to think we can get by, especially since English is such a world language. However, people deeply appreciate the efforts we take to relate to their world—a world for them identified by their language.

A fourth strategy is to understand the pressure exerted on speakers of English as a second language to abandon their minority-language use. The point is well made by a number of scholars that when ethnic groups have low political, social, and economic status and low demographic representation, at least compared to other groups in a community, and when support for their ethnic language is low, the pressure to lose their ethnicity and assimilate the out-group language is intense.[20]

Verbal Style and the Culture of Language

Evidence indicates fundamental differences between groups concerning the "culture of language." That is, cultures hold beliefs about the nature of talk, nonverbal behavior, silence, and so on. Cultures can be compared regarding their expectations of verbal communication style. Verbal communication style means the choice of words as such, along with nonverbal messages and certain themes conveyed. Based on topics such as impression formation, assertiveness and control, tolerance for ambiguity, tolerance for silence, and high information expectations, a formidable list of themes expressed in verbal style stands out. Language in culture conveys dynamic messages beyond the words themselves as seen in verbal style usage.

We can illustrate samples of this "culture of language" in several ways by listing major categories experienced in many parts of the world.

1. *Verbal style to impress.* Some cultures are adept at using rhetorical and stylistic forms that convey extreme politeness or flattery. Examples include Arabic and Latin American cultures.

2. *Verbal styles to assert and control.* Some cultures use rhetorical forms and devices that emphasize standing up, controlling, asserting, or holding ground. Examples here might include Germans, Irish, Turkish, Palestian, Serbian, and Israeli.

3. *Verbal style that expresses tolerance for ambiguity.* In this case, the rhetorical and verbal devices emphasize patience, understanding, and empathy. Examples include Norwegian, Swedish, and some Asian.

4. *Verbal style that uses tolerance for silence.* Some cultures indicate adaptation within interaction by using long silence periods without discomfort. These periods serve as a time to save face and to negotiate in ways that are highly accommodating. Examples include Japanese and many other Asian cultures.

5. *Verbal style that expects high information.* Earlier in this text, we described these cultures as low-context cultures, since they expect information to be presented explicitly rather than indirectly or through the nuances of the situations participants are in. Examples of cultures with high information needs include the United States and other western countries that emphasize signage and informational qualities of organizations and relationships.

Developing Skills with Linguistic Diversity

1. *Listen for unintentional meanings.* In intercultural contacts, users of a second language in this interaction may read unintended meanings into the word usages.

2. *Listen for emotional meanings.* A word understood denotatively by both parties nevertheless may carry strong emotional feelings that are culturally conditioned for one person but not for the other person. Thus, a word that appears unequivocal to you may produce different images for the intercultural users of that word. We cannot assume that the word means the same thing to each person; we can only assume that words and phrases are culturally conditioned.

3. *Ask for clarification.* When someone speaks to you in a restricted code, ask for clarification. Invite the person to restate and amplify. The alternative, sometimes, is pretending you understood when, in fact, you did not.

4. *Offer clarification.* Our own cultural experiences make it unnecessary to elaborate in intracultural communication. Thus, we may unintentionally use a restricted code in intercultural contacts and produce confusion with conversational style and words that any of our intracultural friends might understand perfectly well. In intercultural communication, we should avoid slang, jargon, and personal references that exclude another person's experiences. Also, it may be helpful to avoid lavish words; try to be direct.

5. *Give others the benefit of a perceptual doubt.* Remember that not only our cultural experiences but our language can shape how we see things. The foreign national in our country or the host country national when we travel may categorize his or her world differently. Try to understand that world, and communicate as best you can within that person's framework.

6. *Meet people on their cognitive territory.* As the person who has studied intercultural communication, you must take the initiative in meeting people where they are cognitively. As you step into their cognitive territory, you will be more effective and broaden your self-insight.

7. *Learn greetings.* If you find yourself in a culture where the language difference suggests your learning a new language, then at least learn appropriate greetings. Of course, learn the entire language, but knowing how to greet others is imperative immediately.

8. *Realize that meanings are in people, not in words.* The dictionary does not really tell us everything about the meaning of words and phrases. The same word *bad* can mean something that is good or something that is awful, depending upon your cultural outlook and your use of language.

9. *Speak considerately.* If you are conversing with a person from another country, perhaps a visitor to this country, speak distinctly. Do not fall into the trap of compensating for the other person's broken English by speaking loudly. That only embarrasses you both.

10. *Do not give up.* When your attempts fail at language or at the larger considerations of intercultural communication, stay with the attempt.

11. *Learn when to be direct and indirect.* In Italy, you are expected to tell things to people in a straightforward manner; tell things as they seem to you. However, in Japan, people are concerned with saving face; you would rarely tell people something directly, especially if you know more than they about a particular matter. Rather, you would speak indirectly. In England or Scotland, one needs to be indirect also. One suggests but does not order or dictate.

This Chapter in Perspective

Obviously, intercultural communication involves language and its meanings. Meanings are highly conditioned by a number of cultural factors. The Whorf hypothesis suggests the mediating effect of language on reality. Implications of an adapted Bernstein hypothesis indicate that salient cultural features of a culture and social structure predict communication behavior. Communication behavior, or speech, is of two types: (1) restricted codes that involve narrow, jargonlike messages understood by other members of the subculture; (2) elaborated codes that include messages that necessitate verbal elaboration of meaning. Implications for intercultural communicators include feedback, clarification, renewed understanding, and initiative in encoding messages with the other person's cognitive framework in mind. Meanings are further eroded or heightened by the many semantic factors involved, especially illustrated in the case of poor translation and varying frameworks of interpretations.

In view of the literature, we can conclude that: (1) people judge others by their speech, (2) upward mobility and social aspirations influence whether people change their speech to the accepted norms, (3) general American speech is most accepted by the majority of the American culture, and (4) people should be aware of these prejudices and attempt to look beyond the surface.

In formal and informal speaking situations, we should not only realize our prejudices and try to understand more thoroughly various dialects, but also realize how our own dialect can affect others. This self-perception will help us to become better intercultural communicators. Also, through this knowledge of the effects of speech behavior, as teachers, researchers, or practitioners, our evaluations of others should become less narrow, and we should begin to see a total picture of others' communication behaviors. The chapter also offers a discussion of studies showing how dialect and accented speech affect social attitudes.

Finally the chapter notes several categories or themes between cultures that are conveyed from verbal style. A culture whose rhetorical style encourages a theme to impress or to assert and control may clash with cultures whose verbal style expresses the opposite qualities.

Exercises

1. Can you think of other examples of language differences between you and English speakers from other countries? Scan the newspaper for examples of how language seems to affect culture and how culture affects language.

2. Interview someone from another English-speaking country (Canada, Nigeria, India). Make a list of familiar concepts, and find the corresponding word in that person's use of English. Are different English words used for the same concept? Why?

3. Make a list of as many American English words for money as you can (for example, bread, greenbacks, change, skin, bucks). Do you think other cultures have as many words for money? Do Americans have many words for kinship, friendship, or other interpersonal relationships?

4. By talking to some of your professors and by looking at some relevant books in the library, try to ascertain which dialect or accent of English your region speaks. Try to find out what attitudes prevail toward that accented speech pattern. Why do such attitudes exist? How are those attitudes changed? Should those attitudes be changed?

5. Talk to several area employers—both in business and in universities. Are there any discernible attitudes toward employment that stem from linguistic usage? What about a person who uses bad grammar?

6. The chapter noted that sometimes teachers inadvertently rate their pupils on linguistic grounds rather than on competence. Discuss how this occurs and how this can be prevented.

Endnotes

1. Harry Hoijer, "The Sapir-Whorf Hypothesis," in *Intercultural Communication: A Reader,* 2d ed., ed. Larry A. Samovar and Richard E. Porter (Belmont, Calif.: Wadsworth, 1976), 116.

2. H. A. Gleason, *An Introduction to Descriptive Linguistics* (New York: Holt, Rinehart and Winston, 1961).

3. James Chesebro, "Distinguishing Cultural Systems: Change as a Variable Explaining and Predicting Cross-Cultural Communication," in *Handbook of International and Intercultural Communication,* ed. D. Tanno and A. Gonzalez (Newbury Park, Calif.: Sage, 1997).

4. Clyde Kluckhohn, "The Gift of Tongues," in *Intercultural Communication: A Reader,* ed. Larry A. Samovar and Richard E. Porter (Belmont, Calif.: Wadsworth, 1972).

5. Basil Bernstein, "Elaborated and Restricted Codes: Their Social Origins and Some Consequences," in *Communication and Culture,* ed. Alfred Smith (New York: Holt Rinehart and Winston, 1966), 428.

6. William B. Gudykunst, Stella Ting-Toomey, Bradford J. Hall, and Karen L. Schmidt, "Language and Intergroup Communication," in *Handbook of International and Intercultural Communication,* ed. Molefi Kete Asante and William B. Gudykunst (Newbury Park, Calif.: Sage, 1989).

7. Clyde Kluckhohn, "The Gift of Tongues," in *Intercultural Communication: A Reader,* ed. Larry A. Samovar and Richard E. Porter (Belmont, Calif.: Wadsworth, 1972).

8. Jack L. Whitehead, Frederick Williams, Jean Civikly, and Judith Algino, "Latitude of Attitude in Ratings of Dialect Variations," *Communication Monographs* 41 (1974): 387–407; Anthony Mulac and Mary Jo Rudd, "Effects of Selected American Regional Dialects upon Regional Audience Members," *Communication Monographs* 44 (1977): 185–95; Howard Giles, Richard Bourhis, Peter Trudgill, and Alan Lewis, "The Imposed Norm Hypothesis: A Validation," *Quarterly Journal of Speech* 60 (1974): 405–10.

9. Giles, Bourhis, Trudgill, and Lewis, 1974 (see note 8).

10. Giles, Bourhis, Trudgill, and Lewis, 1974, p. 406 (see note 8).

11. J. G. Delia, "Dialects and the Effects of Stereotypes on Interpersonal Attraction and Cognitive Processes in Impression Formation," *Quarterly Journal of Speech* 58 (1972): 285–97.

12. Dale T. Miller, "The Effect of Dialect and Ethnicity on Communicator Effectiveness," *Speech Monographs* 42 (1975): 69–74; Howard Giles, "Communicative Effectiveness as a Function of Accented Speech," *Speech Monographs* 40 (1973): 330–31.

13. Frederick Williams, Jack L. Whitehead, and Leslie M. Miller, "Ethnic Stereotyping and Judgments of Children's Speech," *Speech Monographs* 38 (1971): 166–70; Gene L. Piche, Michael Michlin, Donald Rubin, and Allan Sullivan, "Effects of Dialect-Ethnicity, Social Class, and Quality of Written Compositions on Teachers' Subjective Evaluations of Children," *Communication Monographs* 44 (1977): 60–62.

14. Robert Hopper and Frederick Williams, "Speech Characteristics and Employability," *Communication Monographs* 40 (1973): 296–302.

15. Howard Giles and Arlene Franklyn-Stokes, "Communication Characteristics," in *Handbook of International and Intercultural Communication,* ed. Molefi Kete Asante and William B. Gudykunst (Newbury Park, Calif.: Sage, 1989).

16. Robert Emry and Richard Wiseman, "An Intercultural Understanding of Ablebodied and Disabled Persons' Communication," *International Journal of Intercultural Relations* 11 (1987): 7–27.

17. Gudykunst, Ting-Toomey, Hall, and Schmidt, 1989 (see note 6).

18. The label was first applied by L. M. Beebe and Howard Giles, "Speech Accommodation Theories: Discussion of Terms of Second-Language Acquisition," *International Journal of the Sociology of Language* 46 (1984): 5–32.

19. Stella Ting-Toomey, "Identity and Interpersonal Bonding," in *Handbook of International and Intercultural Communication,* ed. Molefi Kete Asante and William B. Gudykunst (Newbury Park, Calif.: Sage, 1989).

20. Giles and Franklyn-Stokes, 1989 (see note 15).

Chapter 7

Intercultural Communication

and Nonverbal Messages

OBJECTIVES   *After completing this chapter, you should be able to*

1. Define nonverbal communication and its functions

2. Identify significance of nonverbal communication for intercultural communication

3. Describe categories of body movement

4. Identify eye movement and facial movement as indicators of emotion

5. Discuss greeting behaviors most often associated with nonverbal communication and their relation to cultures

6. Identify nonverbal differences among cultures

7. Describe particular touching behaviors and their implication for intercultural communication

8. Identify the role of paralanguage in structuring meaning and interpersonal understanding.

At a health clinic in downtown Los Angeles, a thin, stoop-shouldered, expectant mother made her way through the crowded waiting room to find the one remaining chair. Her obvious nervousness made the sound of her dropping a paper cup of coffee resound more like a cannon than a whoosh—at least to her overanxious ears—as the coffee blackened the tile floor. One of the other patients merely sighed and rolled her eyes, another mumbled something gruff under her breath, while a nurse standing by the counter released a rather loud "umph." Still others showed looks of disgust, amidst a mass of skewed mouths and arched eyebrows. Such scenes illustrate how actions can produce silent messages of approval or disapproval. The meanings we interpret from nonverbal behaviors are culturally conditioned—and significant. Our behavior often speaks louder than our words.

Overview to Nonverbal Intercultural Communication

Adapting to cultures is not merely using the right verbal language and following procedures from the cultural system. Intercultural communication modifies nonverbal behavior in order to manage the perceptions interpreted by another person. Since how we interpret nonverbal behaviors varies culturally, this area provides a rich and fertile topic for intercultural communication.

Significance of Nonverbal Communication

Nonverbal behavior is a significant area of communication study for at least three reasons.[1] First, nonverbal behavior *accounts for much of the meaning* we derive from conversations. One level of meaning is the actual stated message. Label this the *cognitive content.* It is the part we consciously process. We also have a feeling about another person and the conversation we just had. This feeling is called the *affective content.* For instance, your roommate is lying in bed as you enter the room. Your roommate says something about his day and mentions he is feeling fine. Later you may find that he was really depressed because of an earlier test and because of dating problems. The cognitive content of this encounter consists of what was said openly. The affective content is the conveyance of feeling. In any case, Mehrabian indicates that 93 percent of meaning in a conversation is conveyed nonverbally—38 percent through the voice and 55 percent through the face.[2] Even conservative figures suggest 70 percent of meaning stems from nonverbal components.

Second, nonverbal behavior is significant because it spontaneously *reflects the subconscious.* We normally attempt control over the words we say. Occasionally we may slip up, lose control over our words, and have to apologize, but usually some degree of control is there. However, with nonverbal behavior, we may "leak" our true feelings in other, more subtle, behaviors. In fact, even accomplished liars can be detected by subtle nonverbal cues they unknowingly emit. Hence, because we assume that nonverbal behavior is spontaneous and not easily manipulated, we tend to believe it, even if it contradicts the verbal.[3]

A third reason that nonverbal communication is significant is that we *cannot not communicate.* Even if we choose silence, the nonverbal dimension of our communication is always present. Even if we remove ourselves *bodily* from the scene of interaction, our absence may speak loudly.

Unfortunately, the phrase nonverbal communication can be open to many interpretations. Do we mean the behavior or signal produced, or do we mean the interpretation of actions? Should nonverbal signals be isolated from the verbal? As Mark Knapp states, "Generally, when people refer to nonverbal behavior they are talking about the signal(s) to which meaning will be attributed—not the process of attributing meaning. . . . The term nonverbal is commonly used to describe all human communication events that transcend spoken or written words. At the same time we should realize that these nonverbal events and behaviors can be interpreted through verbal symbols."[4] Thus, nonverbal communication involves not only the actions but the cultural interpretation of those actions in relation to the verbal communication uttered simultaneously.

Nonverbal communication serves several functions. First, nonverbal communication may *complement* a verbal message. If you smile and say, "Hi, how are you?" these behaviors complement each other.

Second, nonverbal behavior may *contradict* other messages. Breaking eye contact while saying, "Nice talking to you," contradicts a speaker's positive verbal message. Shrinking back and frowning while saying, "I love you" is another example of a nonverbal message contradicting a verbal message.

Third, a nonverbal message can *repeat* a verbal one. For example, a librarian says, "Let's be quiet" and places a finger to the lips. In U.S. culture, the index finger to the lips is a nonverbal symbol of the need to be quiet. It will send a clear message without verbal utterance.

Fourth, nonverbal communication serves to *regulate* communication. It is the major means of controlling the flow of conversation between interactants. By head nods, eye contact, vocal inflection, and body leans, we can tell if it is our turn to enter a conversation.

A fifth function of nonverbal communication is to *substitute*. Nonverbal messages may substitute for verbal ones in certain settings. A small child may point to a toy instead of saying, "I want that." In your classroom, you may wave to a friend and point to a meeting place instead of yelling across a crowded room.

Overall, nonverbal behavior functions as a culturally rule-governed communication system. Rules dictate all of our communication behaviors, but rules are especially evident in nonverbal communication. The examples are countless but include greeting, leaving, politeness, entering a room, friendship expectation, and classroom behavior. Furthermore, the rules are governed by culture, and the rules and nonverbal behavior differ among cultures.

By looking at categories of nonverbal behavior we come to a better understanding of the many ways intercultural meanings are inferred. The first of these is kinesics.

Kinesics: Body Language

The term *kinesics* refers to gestures, facial expressions, eye contact, body positions, body movement, and forms of greeting and their relation to communication. Certain kinds of body movements are physiological, such as yawning, stretching, and relaxing. Other kinesic patterns—staring, walking slumped over, raising a clenched fist, showing a victory sign—are personally and culturally conditioned. For instance, when you say, "Hello," you may use a greeting gesture such as the palm of your hand extended outward with the fingers pointed upward, in the manner of waving, moving the palm from side to side. As they say goodbye, North Americans place the palm of the right hand down, extend the fingers, and move the fingers up and down. In India, West Africa, and Central America, such a gesture would imply beckoning, as if we were calling a cab or asking someone to move toward us. The way we fold our arms, the direction of our body orientation (toward or away from the other person), the direction and manner of our eye contact, and our manner of walking and sitting in the presence of others are significant kinesic behaviors that differ culturally. Other people can quickly decide if we are angry or pleased with them, if they are members of our culture and share our nonverbal code.

In the intercultural setting, kinesic behaviors can trigger totally unintended responses. In Indonesia, for instance, it is common to enjoy conversation with a person in his or her house while sitting on the floor. As you sit, however, great care must be taken not to point the soles of your shoes or feet toward the other person. Such a behavior is offensive, for the gesture, no matter how innocently intended, indicates that you consider that person beneath you. In certain parts of India, one does not point the toes or the soles of the shoes in the direction of hanging wall pictures of certain deities. This behavior is taboo in that culture. One of the first objectives in intercultural communication is to understand and observe the other culture's kinesics.

Misuse or misunderstanding of kinesic communication behavior has enormous consequences. In a well-known example, during the cold war between the United States and the former Soviet Union, Nikita Khrushchev visited the United States, and as he emerged from the airplane, officials, news reporters, and other visitors greeted him cordially. In response, Khrushchev clasped his hands together and raised them above his shoulder. To television viewers and U.S. observers, the gesture appeared like a boxer raising clasped hands signaling victory. However, Khrushchev intended the gesture to represent a clasping of hands in friendship.

Consider the sometimes deleterious effects of unguarded kinesic behavior illustrated in the following example:

> Several years ago, a popular American politician took a trip to Latin America. Upon his arrival at the airport, he emerged from the airplane, stood at the top of the loading ramp, and waved to the people awaiting his arrival. Someone shouted out, asking him how his trip was. He responded by flashing the common "OK" gesture. Shortly thereafter, he left the airplane and engaged in a short visit with a local political leader. Following that visit, he went to the major university in the area and delivered an address on behalf of the American people. During his talk, he emphasized that the United States was most interested in helping this neighboring country through economic aid that would help develop the economy and relieve the difficult economic surroundings of the poor. His speech, in fact his entire visit, was a disaster.
>
> Why? Everything this gentleman did verbally was quite acceptable. But nearly everything he did nonverbally was wrong. To begin with, a photographer took a picture of our visitor just as he flashed the "OK" sign to the person who asked how his trip went. That picture appeared on the front page of the local newspaper. You may wonder, "What is so bad about that?" The gesture, which we use in the United States to signal "OK," is a most obscene gesture in this particular Latin American country.
>
> After this "excellent start," our representative went to the university to give his speech, apparently unaware of the fact that this university had recently been a scene of violent protest against that government's policies. His choice of that place to speak

was interpreted by the government as showing sympathy for the rioting students, but perceived by the students as an invasion of their territory by a friend of the government. Further, while our representative was presenting an excellent speech in English, concerning our interest in helping the poor people of that country, the speech was being translated for the audience by an interpreter in full military uniform. The interpreter was a clear symbol of the military dictatorship that was in control of the country at that time.

It is certainly not surprising that the intended goodwill visit of our representative had a contrary effect. This is an excellent example of what can happen when people are unaware of, or unconcerned with, their nonverbal behavior.[5]

Gestures

Gestures are one category of kinesics which fall into several sub-categories. As you study these, remember the purpose is to understand not only your own culture's rules and expectations but also the interactional rules when encountering another culture.

Adaptors.   Some of our gesturing behavior occurs primarily out of a physical bodily activity we must perform at the moment. For example, holding our hand over our mouth as we cough or sneeze is a North American cultural response to that bodily need. Shading our eyes with our hand in bright sunlight also represents an adapting type of gesture. Our hand and arm movements in opening a door also represent gestures that of necessity involve a set of arm and hand movements. In some ways, even these physiological responses are traced to cultural influence. For instance, several cultures do not cover the mouth when coughing.

Emblems.   Nonverbal emblems are gestures that have a clear referent and thus are culturally assigned some meaning. For instance, holding your index and middle fingers upward in a "V" represented the victory emblem during World War II. During the peace movement in the United States during the 1960s, the "V" sign became culturally accepted as a peace symbol. During the 1976 Olympics, the black civil rights movement used the raised fist as an emblematic symbol of the black power movement.

Illustrators.   Illustrative gestures serve to complement spoken words. In pointing directions to someone, we are illustrating the verbal message with a gesture, using perhaps the index finger to emphasize the direction. Sometimes a person's hand slashes through the air to accent some word or phrase. A speaker who uses the hands to "draw" a picture in the air also applies an illustrator. A number of sub-categories of illustrators include:

Illustrative gestures of regulation, such as:

1. *Batons.* Illustrators that emphasize or accent a word or phrase (Example: bringing hand down on a key word)

2. *Regulators.* Illustrators that depict pacing. Also, regulators such as eye contact and silence can indicate turn-taking (Example: snapping your fingers to coincide with a musical beat or the gesture "stop," thus regulating)

Illustrative gestures indicating pictures-type representation:

3. *Directors.* Illustrators that point (Example: pointing with a finger)

4. *Ideographs.* Illustrators that sketch a direction of thought (Example: a speaker says, "I want to pursue this line of thought" and offers a sweeping arm gesture or raises a finger for a first point, second point, and so on)

5. *Kinetographs.* Illustrators that depict bodily action (Example: moving both arms as if you were jogging, thus depicting the idea of running as you converse)

6. *Pictograph.* Illustrators that "draw" a literal picture in the air (Example: using your fingers, hands, and arms to illustrate the shape of a football)

Gestures become especially revealing in ongoing conversation. For instance, illustrators tend to increase with a speaker's increasing enthusiasm, and they also increase if it seems the listener does not understand. How many times have you observed people talking with a foreign national resorting to using illustrators when language barriers appear?

Also, some studies show that, among North Americans, gestures reveal discrepancies in a speaker's words. When someone is lying, the hands and feet sometimes leak a message that tells us that something may be concealed. That mismatch between words and action also is evident in eye movement and facial expression in what Ekman and Friesen have called "nonverbal leakage."[6]

Posture

Like gestures, posture is a significant aspect of kinesic behavior. Although many people can describe posture when asked, it is not by any means universal, since posture varies culturally. When comparing across cultures, three basic behaviors in posture typically occur (1) inclusive postures, (2) interpersonal postures, and (3) reflective postures.

Inclusive postures involve using the body to block off or separate groups or individuals. One type is the "bookend" gesture, in which group members form a circle, or extend their legs or arms, to close off their group from outsiders. For example, while someone may extend his or her legs "simply to stretch," that person often will extend the legs in such a way that they form a barrier to any people outside the group. Another type of inclusiveness is intervention, in which someone intervenes between individuals who are disputing or being distractive.

Interpersonal postures involve seating arrangements where two people sit face to face. If two people sit side by side to view a common object, their interpersonal posture is parallel and focused away from the other person. Sometimes, a person can be both interpersonal and parallel by splitting the body in half (the upper torso turned parallel, the lower torso turned interpersonal) and in this way include more members in a group.

Reflective postures involve repetition of one's posture by another. For example, often when two people sit across from each other in a group, one person will begin to reflect the posture of the person opposite. Also, when one person in a group shifts postures, others often follow this shift.

Body movement can also be used to detect the beginning and end of conversation. In American culture group members express several behaviors when they want to change topics, to speak, or to end the conversation:

Kinesics Regulating Conversation

1. Leaning forward 40 degrees
2. Breaking eye contact
3. Smiling
4. Major nodding movements
5. Change of posture (trunk or legs or both)
6. Foot contact with the floor

These cues can be effective, though subtly, in altering communication. Consider the person who stands with arms crossed, looks constantly at a clock, taps the foot repeatedly, and breaks eye contact frequently. These signals usually mean it is time to go. Of course, each culture has its own interpretation of rules for various behaviors; it is important to establish the baseline of meaning.

Another aspect of kinesics that affects intercultural communication is oculesics, or eye behavior, which accounts for meaning in communication. Like all these aspects of nonverbal behavior, eye contact varies culturally as well as with personality and gender. The actual eye actions and their interpretations can affect areas of communication like perception of social poise, anxiety, submission, confidence, and credibility.

Oculesics

Cultural differences in oculesics become a major source of misunderstanding and ineffective intercultural communication.[7] If a white teacher reprimands a young black male, for instance, and the student responds by maintaining a downward glance, which to him signifies respect, rather than looking directly at the teacher, which is the expected behavior for respect for many white teachers. Navaho Indians ascribe personal eye contact as a harsh way of indicating disapproval; thus, one does not meet the eyes except under those conditions.[8]

Other eye movements also hold culturally distinct meanings. For example, eye winking among North Americans means, "I'm teasing about this," or may convey flirting. When Nigerians wink at their children, this eye behavior signals the child to leave the room. A "friendly" wink may be perceived as an insult in Thailand.[9]

Like other kinesic signals, oculesic behaviors are culturally dependent for their meaning. To illustrate, consider the various meanings of a widening of the eyes, according to Condon:[10]

Significance	Intention	Culture
Really!	Surprise, wonder	Dominant Anglo
I resent this	Anger	Chinese
I don't believe you	Challenge	French
I don't understand	Call for help	Hispanic
I'm innocent	Persuasion	African American

We can easily mistake a Hispanic child's plea for assistance, for example, as some other emotion, unless we understand cultural kinesics.

Greetings

Cultures have unique greeting kinesic activities that are rich in diversity. The American handshake, or the hug and a pat for more intimate acquaintances, finds parallels in various other cultural systems. Several examples from LaBarre's work illustrate the diversity of greetings. For instance, Polynesian men greet each other by rubbing one another's back while embracing. An Ainu man, greeting his sister, "grasped her hands in his for a few seconds, suddenly released his hold, grasped her by both ears and gave the peculiar Ainu greeting cry; then they stroked one another down the face and shoulders." In Matavai, a formal greeting after a long separation involves abrasively scratching the head and temples of the other person with a shark's tooth, to the point of bleeding.[11]

Handshaking represents a common greeting in North America, although shaking hands is inappropriate as a greeting in some cultures. Many Asians bow the head slightly and put the hands in front of the chest to show respect. Vietnamese men, for instance, do not shake hands with women or with older people, unless the old people or women offer their hands first. Also, two Vietnamese women do not shake hands.

The practice of waving to someone as a greeting is insulting as is slapping someone on the back to signify friendship, at least to the Vietnamese. In the first place, waving motions are used by adults to call little children, but little children do not call adults in this fashion. Similarly, backslapping is considered rude and especially insulting to women.

One must also consider the relationship of the person one greets. In many parts of Asia, for example, bowing occurs at more precipitous levels, depending on the relationship and the status of the other person—in general, the more status, the lower the bow. The same type of principle holds true for the order of greeting. In North America, one greets persons in a group by convenience and proximity to each person. However, in many parts of Africa and Asia, one must greet the head of a family or older persons first, then the younger ones.[12]

Clearly, greetings involve intricate behaviors, for misusing them creates a negative intercultural first impression. Perhaps these examples will remind you to observe, ask, and even experiment to learn this important element of kinesics—the nonverbal greeting.

Facial Expressions

Another important principle about body language as it applies to intercultural communication is the inference of "meaning" based on facial expressions. As we noted earlier, Mehrabian claimed that 55 percent of our meanings come from facial expression. In fact, several research studies have documented six universal emotions based primarily in facial expression: sadness, happiness, disgust, anger, surprise, and fear. Researchers typically examine facial expressions captured by hidden cameras of people from different cultures who are watching stress-inducing films. Since the film watchers are unaware of being watched, their nonverbal reactions are spontaneous and uncensored. The mask is off. Most experts agree that different cultures exhibit the same basic facial responses. These studies offer cross-cultural comparisons to help us better understand the response patterns of individuals in different cultures.[13]

Through facial expressions we convey our emotions, such as happiness and surprise. © Ira Kirschenbaum/ Stock Boston.

However, when scientists are present as respondents watch these stress-inducing films a second time, some cultures more than others mask their true emotions. Ekman and Friesen first described this phenomenon as *display rules* when they observed Japanese hiding their negative expressions with a smile during the emotion-packed films.[14] Cultures simply do not perceive emotions alike. For instance, Leathers describes how Germans are far more sensitive than Americans to facial disgust (distaste, disdain, and repugnance), but insensitive to sadness and specialized anger (rage, hate, annoyance).[15] Many emotions are neurophysiological—for example, fear—and thus are universally and biologically shared. But as we stated, people learn display rules and how to manage emotions in culturally appropriate ways.

Some emotions are more universally conveyed by facial expressions than others, according to St. Martin: sadness, happiness, and disgust.[16] However, a second group of emotions have more diversity in their interpretation: anger, surprise, and fear.[17]

Proxemics: The Use of Space

Proxemics refers to the study of spatial relations. The study of proxemics includes three aspects of space: (1) fixed features of space (such as architecture and spacing of buildings), (2) semifixed features (such as seating arrangements and furniture arrangements), and (3) personal space.

Fixed Features of Space

Visitors from parts of the southwestern United States, who are used to wide open spaces, seem amazed at the closeness of residences in the northeast. In the southwestern and western United States, for instance, a person can drive on a highway for miles and never see a sign of people or dwellings, a rare occurrence in more populated sections of the United States. North Americans from the United States visiting a foreign country sometimes express surprise about the proximity of individual dwellings and the narrow roads. There is probably some truth to the observation that Americans use more space than nationals of many other countries. Intercultural communicators need to realize that cultures have alternative approaches to space and ways of using it.

The shapes and sizes of buildings affect individuals. An elaborately structured building may, in a sense, communicate modernity because of its architectural uniqueness. Other buildings may give a perception of power and strength. Obviously, values, economic factors, and even religion play roles in determining architecture, but a culture's values (or the architect's values) determine the use of space.

The size of rooms is also a subject of psychological impact. A large office may communicates status and power. The smaller the office, the less status appears connected with the office occupant. In an office complex, office staff who share space are perceived to have less status, higher status employees have their own corner or partitioned area, and the highest employees enjoy the most private, largest, plushest offices. This arrangement of status by space is expected in North America, but different cultures use and perceive room size differently. In some countries, important province government officials may share an office with six or eight other employees in a small room. This unspoken language of space is so strong that employment problems may arise when one person gets a larger office than someone else.

The origin of fixed features of space began with cultural needs over territoriality. That concern sometimes translates into geographical and political boundary questions between cultures and also converts to the ways cultures use buildings and fixed features of space in screening behavior. Screening refers to our structuring of our territory. For example, a fence marks a territory in much the same way we use hedges or survey posts. The message in these cases is clear, revealing private ownership and covertly saying, "Respect this boundary—this is mine."

The Vietnam Peace Talks

In 1968, the majority of the American people were very concerned with getting peace talks started in Paris to seek a solution to the Vietnam war, but it seemed that it would take forever before the talks could begin. The problem centered around the seating of the various delegations for the peace conference and the shape of the table. The United States and South Vietnam each wanted two sides at the table; North Vietnam and the Viet Cong each wanted four sides. Four sides would put the Viet Cong on an equal status with the other three parties in the talks, something the North Vietnamese and Viet Cong insisted on, but that the United States and the South Vietnamese were unwilling to accept. After eight months and literally thousands of deaths and injuries on both sides, a compromise was reached whereby the North Vietnamese and the Viet Cong could interpret the table settled upon as four-sided while the United States and South Vietnam could interpret it as two-sided. Almost anyone not directly involved in those negotiations would agree that the behavior of these parties was absurd. Nevertheless, this extreme sensitivity to the nonverbal communication of the shape of the table resulted in months of delay and thousands of deaths. The importance of nonverbal communication in this setting could hardly be overestimated. (Note: The table selected was round.)

Source: from James McCroskey, 1972 noted earlier in this text.

Semifixed Features of Space

Semifixed features of space refer to spatial arrangements of movable objects within a room, such as furniture, accessories, and file cabinets. In the United States, a small, cluttered desk implies low status; a larger desk usually indicates higher status. However, the position of the desk and the arrangement of the chairs in a business office are of communicative importance as well. If the chairs in an office are directly in front of the occupant's desk and if the occupant does not come from behind the desk, a nonverbal tone of impersonal behavior may be perceived. As we might expect, again, the use of space and material objects is culture bound. For example, among Germans where privacy often is valued, a closed door in an office is the expected behavior. In North America, a closed door can indicate something else, for many managers attempt to maintain an aura of openness by leaving the door or curtains open. When an employee enters the office and closes the door, other employees receive a message that something is secretive, depending upon how long the conference lasts and the facial expressions after the conference.

Semifixed features of space can be arranged to encourage face-to-face participation, called *sociopetal* arrangement according to E.T. Hall. Living areas in personal dwellings in North America and meeting rooms of various sorts normally encourage interpersonal communication because of the furniture arrangement. *Sociofugal* arrangements tend to diffuse communication since the arrangements lead conversation away from interpersonal relations to impersonal relations. Many lecture arrangements, waiting rooms, and libraries are sociofugal.[18]

Semifixed features of space differ interculturally. For example, in the evenings, Syrian men converse sitting across a room from each other, with the furniture arranged to facilitate this pattern. Certain cultural groups, like the Chinese, seem to prefer furniture located in side-by-side seating arrangements for personal communication, rather than sitting with direct eye contact.

Personal Space

Use of space often focuses on the dynamic and variable space between people. This personal space refers to an individual's unconsciously structuring the microspace immediately surrounding the physical body. This space is not only culturally determined but results from varying relationships. That is, among North Americans, friends usually stand closer than strangers. Furthermore, Hall observed that space communicates and thus affects our intercultural relationships:

> The flow and shift of distance between people as they interact with each other is part and parcel of the communication process. The normal conversational distance between strangers illustrates how important are the dynamics of space interaction. If a person gets too close, the reaction is instantaneous and automatic—the other person backs up. And if he gets too close again, back we go again. I have observed an American backing up the entire length of a long corridor while a foreigner whom he considers pushy tries to catch up with him. This scene has been enacted thousands and thousands of times—one person trying to increase the distance in order to be at ease, while the other tries to decrease it for the same reason; neither one being aware of what was going on.[19]

By and large Middle Eastern, southern European, African, and some Latin American countries emphasize closer personal space than Western cultures or Asians. Many travelers and field workers return from host cultures and often their biggest complaints center around the mismatch of expectation regarding interpersonal distances normally maintained in these cultures.

We can better understand these missed expectations when we compare cultures to attempt to understand their rules about personal space. But we also need to understand the rules concerning relationships regarding variable space within a culture. To not understand is to incur discomfort or uncooperativeness when people enter our body space.

Examples of personal space related to intercultural communication are numerous. For example, North Americans tend to prefer greater distances between themselves and others than do Latin Americans, Arabs, and Greeks. When these proxemic expectations are violated, embarrassment or even hostility can result. Comparing intraethnic proxemic stability with interethnic stability, Erickson concluded that, at least among the African Americans and Polish Americans whom he studied, intracultural communication produced far more proxemic stability (African American with AA, Polish American with PA) than in interethnic communication (African American with Polish American).[20] In a study of seven countries, reports indicated that the English use more space than the French or Italians. French and Italians in turn use significantly more space than the Irish and Scottish. It seems, therefore, that a comfort level exists intraculturally that lends itself to stability. When two persons with different ethnicity interact, they experience discomfort because they do not know the proxemic rules of the other person's culture.[21]

Personal space varies interculturally. Misunderstanding of personal zones creates a source of intercultural conflict. © Michael Weisbrot/ Stock Boston.

Hall described these variances as four comfort zones of personal space. Each zone differs with respect to the culture and with regard to the nature of the relationship. The *intimate* zone encompasses touching and a very close distance of up to eighteen inches for North Americans and is a zone reserved only for close, intimate relationships. The *personal* zone ranges from 18 to 36 inches and is used for friendship and confidentiality. The *social* zone is the normal conversational space for North Americans and includes space from about three feet up to twelve feet. The *public* zone is used for talking across a room and for public speaking and includes distances of twelve feet and greater.

Our difficulty in intercultural communication comes from conversing in unexpected and different zones. For instance, North Americans usually converse in the personal and social zones. Many Middle Eastern and Latin American individuals, however, converse in North American intimate but Latin American personal zones. As a result, North Americans are perceived as distant and cold, and these other cultures are perceived as pushy. These unexpected spatial violations are expressed in a model of interaction between personal space zones, as indicated in figure 7.1. When a culture A person expects to communicate within the social zone, then appropriate distance and action is initiated. In response, that person expects social distance to be reciprocated. However, if a culture B person expects to communicate within, say, an intimate zone, then this second person in actual response moves closer to establish what he or she now considers the proper distance for communication. What we see is a striving for the expected zones to convey parallelism or consonance in the relationship and an adjustment and nonverbal negotiation when people do not act as expected.

Figure 7.1

Model of interaction between parallel and unparallel personal-space zones.

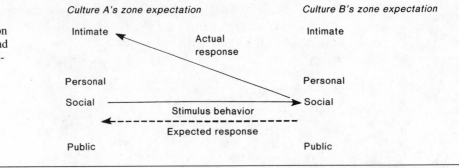

Chronemics: Our Use of Time

Our understanding of time falls under a class of nonverbal communication called chronemics and is influenced by culture. Time is a potent force, communicating as powerfully as verbal language. In North America, for instance, lateness for a business appointment communicates lack of interest. A recent news report indicated that certain U.S. workers can be docked half a day's wages for being as little as one minute late, according to one labor contract.

In intercultural communication encounters, ours and the other person's concepts of time may influence our communication behavior. Many village meetings in Africa begin when everyone is ready. A forty-five minute wait may not be unusual for a business appointment in Latin America, even though such a period seems insulting to a North American. The ensuing conversation between the Latin American and the United States businessperson is likely to be evaluated negatively because of misunderstanding between the two cultural clocks.

North Americans tend to think of time as a road or long ribbon stretched out in a progressive linear path, having a beginning and an end. They also believe that this road has compartments, or segments, that should be kept discrete from one another. This compartmentalization of time is so distinct that the term *monochronic time* applies to many North Americans, a concept meaning that cultural members prefer doing one thing at a time. In contrast, many other cultures prefer operating with several people, ideas, or projects simultaneously, illustrating the concept of *polychronic time*. Observers sometimes condition us to mark Latin American differences with North Americans in terms of these categories, with the Latin Americans falling into the polychronic time category. Other observations lead us to believe that monochronic or polychronic time is not only cultural, but based on training, occupation, personality, and right- or left-brain orientation. The implications of M-P culture are discussed earlier in this text.

Time can also be viewed in terms of cultural *synchrony*.[22] Cultural synchrony refers to the rhythms, movement, and timing of a culture. For instance, when walking on the streets of New York, a faster-paced movement than we would in a rural town in Montana is expected. East Africans move with a methodology quite apart from Germans. The rhythms themselves have a time dimension to them. Part of effective intercultural communication involves "being in sync" with those timed rhythms.

In general, North Americans feel that time is a commodity, something to be used, bought, wasted, saved, spent, and in other ways manipulated. By contrast, many cultures, including African, Latin American, and Southeast Asian, view time more flexibly. A number of Southeast Asian cultures view time cyclically rather than linearly, a contrast that may explain the North Vietnamese attitude during the war in Vietnam of, "We will wear you down." The Americans were used to a quick end to war because of their history and their attitudes toward time, but the enemy was accustomed to waiting scores of years, even centuries, for desired results.

One reason for these differing views of time is the difference that cultures maintain concerning *types* of times.[23] *Informal* time refers to loose calculations of time, such as "after a while," "later," and "some time ago." *Formal* time refers to exact points in time, such as "by 2:00 today," and "yesterday at 5:00"; in other words, more of a clock time. *Scientific* time refers to ultra-precise designations of time, such as laboratory timing of experiments. One of the most frequent intercultural communication breakdowns occurs when one cultural member operates on formal time and a member of a different culture operates from an informal time orientation. The one person shows up for a meeting at 2:00 P.M., and the other person arrives sometime in the afternoon. Our understanding of these different perceptual expectations can enormously reduce our stress level in intercultural communication.

Sensorics indicate the communicative and perceptual functions of the human senses. Our senses can be considered instruments of functional nonverbal communication. For example, some people are often turned off to another culture because of the *smell* of foreign situations; one cultural group thinks the other has a somewhat obnoxious odor. Highlanders of New Guinea saturate their bodies with mud and pig grease and hardly ever bathe. Compare that situation with a Ghanaian, who typically bathes once or twice a day, and imagine the intercultural barriers between these two engendered by the one variable, smell. Scholars such as E. T. Hall increasingly consider the olfactory sense a highly significant feature of cultural transactions.

The sense of *taste* differs culturally, as any international traveler knows. *Color* and *texture* preferences are likewise visual features that are culturally appreciated. *Auditory* preferences are also culturally influenced. Consider, for instance, widely divergent musical preferences among and within various countries. The notion of *thermal* sensory communication, in which we perceive others' body heat, may also be considered sensory perception. Some people actually seem to radiate more heat than others, and Hall in his writings has suggested that this factor may account for our descriptions of others as warm or cold personalities.

Our sensoric perceptions work together, interacting with the cultural context, to shape a total view of a culture and our intercultural contacts. One way to describe our intercultural reactions comes from the following formula:

$$\text{Degree of sensory difference} = \frac{\text{Disliked sensory experiences}}{\text{Like sensory experiences}}$$

This formula illustrates that, if our disliked sensory experiences outweigh the liked ones, then the ratio of our feelings, weighted and added according to their importance, is high. The resulting ratio is the sense ratio difference. The higher the number, the greater the degree of sense ratio differences.

Sensorics

All of these contrasting differences bombard the senses simultaneously and account for some of the reasons that people experience culture shock. Overcoming sensoric nonverbal differences is an important part of intercultural adjustment.

Haptics: Touching Behavior

Intercultural communication also involves cultural touching and its effects. The nature and importance of our use of touch is called haptics.

A number of factors have been linked with haptic behavior, most notably culture and gender. Intraculturally there are rules about touch governed by the culture and the gender of the interactants.

To illustrate intracultural haptics, observations of touching during North American communication show that males avoid touching other males, but females express themselves in touching other females during conversation. If there is a link between haptic behavior and gender of the communicators, its roots lie in cultural roles. Males are inhibited from touching other males because of cultural taboos, although females are allowed flexibility in touching other females. However, cultural roles restrict females touching males, although males traditionally were often permitted greater flexibility in male-female communication. However, those general findings are mediated by age, situation, and culture.

From an intercultural perspective, research suggests that some cultures are highly touch oriented, while others are nontouching. Hecht, Andersen, and Ribeau refer to these as *contact* cultures and *distance* cultures. The contact cultures using more touch and less space include Latin America, Middle Eastern, southern and eastern Europe. They prefer sensory involvement. In contrast, North Americans, Asians, and northern Europeans are considered low-contact cultures and express more of a distancing style, although Asians typically use a little more of this style than the other two.[24] Also, Arab, Jewish, eastern European, and Mediterranean cultures have been characterized as touching cultures, while Germans, English, and other white Anglo-Saxons are characterized as infrequent touchers.[25] In a field study comparing German, Italian, and North American haptics, Shuter confirmed that national stereotypes about contact and noncontact cultures partly depend on personality and gender. For instance, males interacted farther apart and touched less in both Germany and the United States than in Italy. Italian males, however, stood closer and touched significantly more than Italian females. It also appears that Italian males interact nonverbally in ways considered appropriate only for German and American women. However, German females were more tactile than Italian women and that U.S. women showed as much tactility as Italian women.[26]

Overall, when you find yourself in a contrasting culture, we suggest that you initially observe, ask, and probe—and avoid operating on stereotypical information only. It is imperative that we become observers of nonverbal behaviors in a host country to avoid the barriers that only nonverbal behaviors can erect.

Paralanguage

Paralanguage is that set of audible sounds that accompany oral language to augment its meaning. In other words, speech carries symbolic cues, not only through verbal and nonverbal cues, but also through vocal qualities to which various linguistic systems ascribe meaning. You may again recall Mehrabian's report that

Level of touch and use of space are fundamental, universal needs by which we communicate many of our interpersonal feelings and attitudes. © Frank Siteman/Stock Boston.

when Americans communicated feelings, words accounted for 7 percent of the messages, paralanguage for 38 percent, and facial expressions for 55 percent of the total feelings communicated.

One way to illustrate paralanguage is to consider a phrase and with different vocalic emphasis, completely change the meaning. The following examples will illustrate:

1. John, you love Mary. (declarative statement of fact)
2. John, you love *Mary?* (question; I thought you loved someone else)
3. John, you love Mary! (excitement)
4. John, *you* love Mary? (I thought Bill loved her)
5. John, you *love* Mary. (I thought it was just liking)

Clearly, the words alone do not carry the meaning. Rather, we interpret the feelings and emotions of the speaker by perceiving the variations of vocal quality. Furthermore, a number of variations in vocal quality, intensity, tone, and pitch height can alter otherwise simple statements or questions.

In another way, perceptions we create about ourselves to listeners clearly develop from paralanguage. Dynamism in credibility largely stems from vocal expressiveness. Many people understand our emotional involvement and sensitivity from vocal and facial cues. In this way, our vocalics may reveal our feelings to others. For example, Thai people use silence to show respect, agreement, or even disagreement, depending upon how the silence is used. Also, speaking softly shows good manners and education. Consequently, many Thais feel that the people in the United States are angry because Americans speak more loudly than Thais.[27]

The Meaning of Nonverbal Communication in Culture

How does one make sense of nonverbal messages in another culture? How do we interpret them? Overall, nonverbal messages may complement, contradict, repeat or accentuate, regulate, or substitute, the verbal message. But more specifically, how does an interpretation of nonverbal behaviors (kinesics, proxemics, chronemics, sensorics, haptics, and paralinguistics) work? How do we organize codes into behaviors with meanings? Each culture perceives nonverbal behaviors, converting them for communication value, along several dimensions—clusters of how we usually organize nonverbal messages.

First, messages of *immediacy* refer to those nonverbal aspects of approach, accessibility, and openness at one end of a continuum and avoidance and distance at the other end. For example, high-immediacy behaviors in the United States include smiling, touching, eye contact, open body position, closer distances, and vocal animation. Along with these behaviors, immediacy also includes how we regulate privacy. As you might expect, high-contact cultures, by their very definition, also evaluate people as similar and more credible if they engage in immediacy behaviors.[28]

Second, evidence also points to *status* and *power* as part of an interpretive cluster. That is, we use and interpret nonverbal messages to indicate status or power. A primary example is furniture arrangement and size in a large office—or even the large office itself. Consider the way we attempt to control others by leaning over people, touching in dominant ways, or taking up more space. Furthermore, we often interpret nonverbal messages around the dimension of *responsiveness*. Scholars such as Mehrabian use this term to indicate the way we react to people, things, and events. For instance, if we speed up our own speech rate, others interpret us as more responsive to a special need or even to the people around us. If we were to increase gestures or use more eye contact, these too would make us appear more responsive to our environment. Up to a point, this change in activity level makes a person appear more attractive and in some ways more credible.

A third and final interpretative aspect of nonverbal behavior is *metacommunication,* meaning a message about a message. Nonverbally, we communicate a message about a message, like the perceived message of empathy as we lean forward and touch while verbally giving bad news. During negative performance appraisals, for example, our tone of voice and use of eye contact may say, "You're OK; you'll make it." More than just a function of reinforcement, people look for the hidden messages, or the metacommunication, which serves as an important category for interpreting nonverbal meaning.

Developing Intercultural Skills for Nonverbal Communication

You may find some of the following skill suggestions helpful in improving nonverbal communication.

1. *Observe and discover specific kinesic behaviors for any one culture.* When people do things that puzzle you, ask them why they are acting in that manner.

2. *Avoid letting your emotions get the best of you.* In many cultures, people will touch you and bump you, and you may feel emotionally insecure or angry. Remember, some cultures simply do not think of private, personal body space.

Sometimes, fifty Africans can crowd into the same amount of space that holds only twenty North Americans. The reason is that the Africans' personal space suffers no intrusion from crowding and touching.

3. *Notice spatial positions.* To figure out the appropriate interpersonal distance in an intercultural contact, plant yourself and avoid backing away. The other person will then stop at the culturally relevant distance.

4. *In practicing eye contact, observe what is appropriate within different contexts.* In some cultures, you may observe males maintaining eye contact, but a male and a female avoiding eye contact. Thus, you can learn how to respond.

5. *If you think you acted incorrectly, ask people, if it seems appropriate, what you did wrong.* Only by asking will you learn, because a host national normally will not volunteer information.

6. *Certain sensoric differences can be frustrating because our old social cues are removed.* To counteract this tendency, remind yourself that differences do not have a wrongness about them. By enthusiastically trying new foods and enjoying new sounds, for instance, you can create a pleasant feeling for yourself. In two words, be positive!

This Chapter in Perspective

Clearly, a significant element of intercultural communication is the silent language of nonverbal communication. Kinesics refers to gestures, posture, body movement, eye contact, facial expression, and greeting behaviors and their effects on communication.

After a discussion of fixed and semifixed space, dimensions of personal space emit silent messages, especially as cultural members structure their interpersonal body space according to cultural norms. The study of proxemic behavior, particularly because of its obviousness and frequency, may be one of the most significant aspects of nonverbal communication.

Another element of nonverbal communication involves chronemics—our understanding of and use of time. Perceptual misunderstandings with regard to time create frequent intercultural communication breakdowns.

Understanding the relationship of familiar senses to unfamiliar sights, sounds, tastes, smells, and touches of a host culture (the study of sensorics) leads the intercultural communicator to try to avoid overreaction and to probe deeper meanings of a new culture. The most evident way that the effects of a large sense ratio can be overcome is by further understanding of predictable stages of psychological intercultural distress in the process of culture shock.

This chapter also discusses cultural touching behaviors and their effects. Finally, the chapter briefly describes the nature of paralanguage.

In reality, nonverbal communication operates under incredibly complex rules. It is hoped that the basic concepts introduced in this chapter will be enough to prepare you for the meanings of nonverbal communication.

Exercises

1. Spend some time in the student center or some public place and make a list of the nonverbal communication behaviors you observe. What do these behaviors mean? When are they used?

2. With your list of nonverbal behaviors from exercise 1, go back another time and look at nonverbal communication in terms of interpersonal relationships. What type of oculesic patterns do you observe? What kind of relationships produce what types of proxemic behavior? What is the role of gender on nonverbal behaviors that you observe?

3. Interview some international students about haptics in their culture. What cultural practices differ from your own cultural practices? Ask the international students to describe their feelings when they first came to the United States and attempted to interact meaningfully in nonverbal ways. What did they do to adapt to the new culture? What principles does this suggest for you in adapting to intercultural acculturation?

Endnotes

1. Pat Garner, "Nonverbal Communication," in Carley Dodd and Michael Lewis, *Introduction to Human Communication,* 2d ed. (Dubuque, Iowa: Kendall/Hunt, 1992).

2. Albert Mehrabian, *Silent Messages,* 2d. ed. (Belmont, Calif.: Wadsworth, 1981).

3. Garner, 1989 (see note 1); Mark Hickson and Don Stacks, *Nonverbal Communication Studies and Applications* (Dubuque, Iowa: William C. Brown Publishers, 1985).

4. Mark Knapp, *Essentials of Nonverbal Communication* (New York: Holt, Rinehart, and Winston, 1980), 3, 21.

5. James C. McCroskey, *Introduction to Rhetorical Communication* (Englewood Cliffs, N.J.: Prentice-Hall, 1972).

6. Paul Ekman and Wallace V. Friesen, "Hand Movements," *Journal of Communication* 22 (1972): 353–74.

7. Molefi Kete Asante and Alice Davis, "Encounters in the Interracial Workplace," in *Handbook of International and Intercultural Communication,* ed. Molefi Kete Asante and William B. Gudykunst (Newbury Park, Calif.: Sage, 1989).

8. Fathi Yousef, "Nonverbal Communication: Some Intricate and Diverse Dimensions in Intercultural Communication," in *Intercultural Communication: A Reader,* 2d ed., ed. Larry A. Samovar and Richard E. Porter (Belmont, Calif.: Wadsworth, 1976).

9. Suriya Smutkupt and La Ray Barna, "Impact of Nonverbal Communication in an Intercultural Setting: Thailand," *International and Intercultural Communication Annual* 3 (1976): 130–38.

10. E. C. Condon, "Cross-Cultural Interferences Affecting Teacher-Pupil Communication in American Schools," *International and Intercultural Communication Annual* 3 (1976): 108–20.

11. Weston LaBarre, "Paralinguistics, Kinesics, and Cultural Anthropology," in *Intercultural Communication: A Reader,* 2d ed., ed. Larry A. Samovar and Richard E. Porter (Belmont, Calif.: Wadsworth, 1976).

12. Nguyen Kim Hong, "Vietnamese Themes" (paper presented to the Regional Indochinese Task Force Workshop for the New York City Board of Education, New York, January 1976).

13. David Matsumoto, Harald G. Wallbott, and Klaus R. Scherer, "Emotions in Intercultural Communication," in *Handbook of International and Intercultural Communication,* ed. Molefi Kete Asante and William B. Gudykunst (Newbury Park, Calif.: Sage, 1989).

14. Ekman and Friesen, 1972 (see note 6).

15. D. G. Leathers, *Successful Nonverbal Communication: Principles and Applications* (New York: Macmillan, 1986).

16. Gail M. St. Martin, "Intercultural Differential Decoding of Nonverbal Affective Communication," *International and Intercultural Communication Annual* 3 (1976): 44–57.

17. Mark L. Knapp, *Essentials of Nonverbal Communication* (New York: Holt, Rinehart and Winston, 1980).

18. E. T. Hall, *The Silent Language* (Garden City, N.Y.: Anchor, 1973).

19. Ibid., 180.

20. Frederick Erickson, "One Function of Proxemic Shifts in Face-to-Face Interaction," in *Organization of Behavior in Face-to-Face Interaction,* ed. Adam Kendon, Richard M. Harris, and Mary R. Key (Paris: Mouton, 1975).

21. Martin S. Remland, Tricia S. Jones, and Heidi Brinkman, "Interpersonal Distance, Body Orientation, and Touch in the Dyadic Interactions of Northern and Southern Europeans" (paper presented to the Speech Communication Association, Chicago, October 1992); Robert Shuter, "The Centrality of Culture," *The Southern Communication Journal* 55 (1990): 237–49, also calls for an increased understanding of intracultural patterns, a point made clear in the many examples of nonverbal differences.

22. E. T. Hall, *The Hidden Dimension* (Garden City, N.Y.: Doubleday, 1966).

23. Hall, 1973 (see note 18).

24. Michael L. Hecht, Peter A. Andersen, and Sidney A. Ribeau, "The Cultural Dimensions of Nonverbal Communication," in *Handbook of International and Intercultural Communication,* ed. Molefi Kete Asante and William B. Gudykunst (Newbury Park, Calif.: Sage, 1989).

25. Mehrabian, 1981 (see note 2); M. F. A. Montagu, *Touching: The Human Significance of Skin* (New York: Columbia University Press,1971).

26. Robert Shuter, "A Field Study of Nonverbal Communication in Germany, Italy, and the United States," *Communication Monographs* 44 (1977): 298–305.

27. Smutkupt and Barna, 1976 (see note 9).

28. Hecht, Andersen, and Ribeau, 1989 (see note 24).

Part Four

Cultural Adaptation
and Communication
Effectiveness

Applying Intercultural Competencies

Chapter 8

Adapting to Culture

OBJECTIVES   *After completing this chapter, you should be able to*

1. Cope with anxiety upon entering a new culture

2. Adjust in a new culture more effectively through understanding adjustment models and strategies presented in the chapter

3. Inform others of the acculturation and adaptation processes

4. Identify the negative effects of poor intercultural adaptation

5. Describe reverse culture shock

6. Develop skills for cultural reentry

We begin a new unit in the text by examining our communication and adaptation to culture. As the central text model reveals, in the heat of uncertainty or anxiety when confronted with perceived differences we strive to find a dissonance reducing solution. We develop a third culture C. Out of the third culture context, we develop competent communication accommodation, largely involving adaptation. However, we might adapt well or poorly, depending on how functional our intercultural competencies and accommodating strategies leading to effective intercultural outcomes, or how dysfunctional we might be leaning on past stereotypes, engaging in ethnocentrism, withdrawing, ignoring, and a host of other behaviors. This chapter synthesizes the processes of how people reduce their uncertainty and anxiety upon entering a new culture. There are many transitional experiences and shocks we face: job shock with a new position, role shock when changing relationships, life transition shock when going through a family or personal epoch. In this material, we deal with culture shock and identify the larger concerns of communication adaptation.

When one enters a different culture, a natural anxiety emerges. This normal tendency to feel somewhat worried about the new culture and your response to it, however, can become an overwhelming fear, turn to inordinate mistrust, and lead to an eventual return from the culture earlier than we expected. We do not have to leave the United States to enter a second culture—sometimes another culture is only a few miles away. This chapter focuses on the process of adapting to the new culture and the related process of learning its ways.

INTERCULTURAL INSIGHT

Cultural Adaptation

The problem of cultural adaptation is well illustrated by the following statements from people who entered a new culture:

"At first, I felt as if this country was the best place in the world. But after a while, I began to feel as if they were all crooks."

"I don't know what happened to me. I hadn't been in this place for more than three months when I had a compelling urge to return home. It wasn't just homesickness, which I expected to feel, but it was a kind of compulsion."

"My anxiety about the country did not really have to do with the food. I developed what I now guess was a phobia about the place and my interaction with people. Back home, I was always outgoing, but in the new country, I hardly felt like leaving the compound. I was almost scared to death."

These statements typify people's feelings, which fall rather predictably into a pattern we call *culture shock*, or the early adaptation phase of transitioning into a new culture. Culture shock refers to the transition period and the accompanying feelings of stress and anxiety a person experiences during the early period upon

The Early Adaptation Experience: Culture Shock

Culture shock can leave a person entering a new culture with a feeling of alienation and decreased contact. © D. Young Wolff/ PhotoEdit.

entering a new culture. Several terms apply to this concept including culture stress, adaptation, transition shock, adjustment, socialization, and so on.

There is no right or wrong to experiencing culture shock—it happens to almost everyone, although it occurs in varying degrees. After all, your nervous system is working overtime, and your surroundings are very new. It is normal to experience some level of culture shock. However, just like anxiety in your own culture, culture shock can become overwhelming. Knowing what to expect and knowing how to cope with culture shock should assist you in handling these feelings.

Any number of symptoms can occur during cycles of culture shock. These symptoms can be (1) physiological such as a constant headache, an upset stomach, and sleeplessness. The symptoms accompanying cycles of culture shock can be (2) emotionally based such as anxiety, irritability, paranoia, extreme homesickness, loneliness, excessive concern over health and safety, and feelings of powerlessness and helplessness. The symptoms can also be (3) communication based such as withdrawal from relationship and conversation, excessive complaining, frustration, and defensive communication.[1]

Because of its disorienting qualities, adapting to a new culture presents some unusual blocks to effective intercultural communication. To put it in perspective, again, adapting to a culture has analogies to many transitions, such as entering college, moving to a new house, taking a new job, moving to another city, or losing a loved one. For those reasons, we can experience transition shock, job shock, role shock, and, according to Alvin Toffler, shock related to rapid cultural and technological change, called future shock.

The good news is that we can understand and develop skills in adapting to new cultures that reduce the negative qualities. We begin with a model that explains the normal cycles or stages of early adaptation and culture shock. This model presented in figure 8.1 shows how most of us enter a new culture feeling

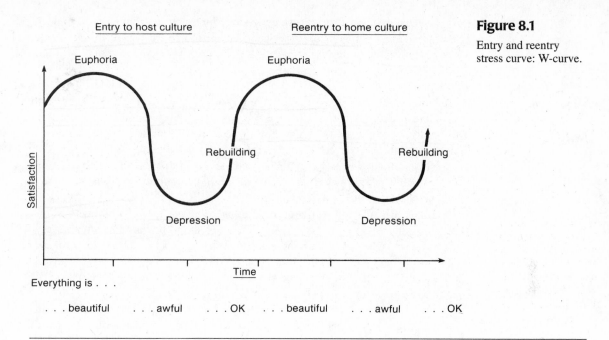

Figure 8.1

Entry and reentry stress curve: W-curve.

Entry to host culture   Reentry to home culture

Euphoria   Euphoria

Satisfaction

Rebuilding   Rebuilding

Depression   Depression

Time

Everything is . . .

. . . beautiful   . . . awful   . . . OK   . . . beautiful   . . . awful   . . . OK

rather positive. Following this "honeymoon" experience, many experience a down side to being in the new culture and express their feelings in one of several typical styles. Finally, most of us emerge back into a level of higher satisfaction having learned from the pain of dissatisfaction how to see the good and the bad in the new culture and therefore how to adjust. We turn now to the predeparture stage which is a prelude to the three major stages of adjustment in the new culture.[2]

Predeparture Stage

In this stage, you plan to enter the host culture. The planning and development of the trip and the purposes of the entry make you simultaneously excited and wary. You may be looking forward to new food and yet remain apprehensive. You may be enjoying the new language and yet remain concerned about using it properly. You anticipate how new people will respond to you and yet worry that they might reject you. However, you face the future with optimism, and the planning continues.

Stage One: Everything Is Beautiful

When you arrive in the new culture, you feel a sense of excitement, pleasure, and self-satisfaction for making the decision to come to this beautiful place. During this phase, nearly everything appears wonderful. The food is exciting; the people seem friendly. Although you may experience some of the symptoms mentioned earlier, such as sleeplessness and mild anxiety, your enthusiasm and curiosity quickly overcome these minor discomforts. The sense of euphoria is so great that some writers call this stage the honeymoon stage. You should have come long ago—you think to yourself—to this piece of heaven. The people are polite and gracious, unlike some people you know back home, and so you may come to feel that you have discovered utopia.

Studies indicate that this stage varies significantly from a short time to months. However, this stage of ecstasy is lost to a second stage of frustration, anger, depression, or denial.

Stage Two: Everything is Awful

The honeymoon is over! Now, things have gone sour. After a while, you begin to feel more anxious, restless, impatient, and disappointed. It seems you have a more difficult time saying what you mean. You are meeting more people who do not speak English, and yet your foreign language knowledge has not improved dramatically. Perhaps you begin to realize that the eager expectations were just a fantasy, colored by the honeymoon stage, reinforced by your euphoria when you first arrived. Now you feel that you were wrong.

There is increasing difficulty with transportation. Shopping seems to come too often, and you are getting a little tired of having to bargain for almost everything you purchase. Even with these surrounding problems, no one seems to care. The host country seems indifferent. Today, you learn that devaluation of the dollar has shrunk your purchasing power in the new culture. Besides that, your wallet or purse was stolen.

This period of adaptation is marked by a loss of social cues and a time of inconvenience that you had not experienced earlier. The confusion heightens with the unfamiliar smells, sounds, food, and cultural customs. Not only do some of the physical symptoms set in at this stage, but depression, loneliness, and fear pervade your attitudes and feelings. The reaction is predictable.

The "everything is awful" stage can last from a few weeks up to several months. Some people never experience this stage at all, though others experience it more seriously. The goal, of course, is to work toward a balanced view of the people, the customs, and yourself.

Most people in the "everything is awful" stage cope with the frustration in one of the ways that follow, as indicated by research conducted for the U.S. Navy.[3] Typically, individuals express their feelings in one of these following patterns of communication. While anyone can feel angry, depressed, or in denial anytime and anywhere, the importance of these communication patterns is their intensity during the second stage of culture shock.

Fight. Some people in the "everything is awful" stage of culture shock scoff at the host country. They may also reject the nationals of that country, thinking that the people in that culture have inferior ways—in short, they look down on the culture of the host country and act ethnocentrically. Other people in this situation actually destroy property, which only fuels the guilt and makes the situation worse. For example, one teenage boy, whose father served as a change agent in a foreign country, reacted not only with insolence to his classmates at the international school but also destroyed personal property of some of his father's friends in the new culture. To say the least, the fight reaction during the "everything is awful" stage can lead to legal difficulty in the host culture. Symptoms include excessive irritation, angry outbursts, defensiveness, and frustration over minor things.

Flight.   Other people in the "everything is awful" stage of culture shock remove themselves from the culture. The most obvious examples are the people who leave for home shortly after arriving in the host culture. Even if these people do not leave, other symptoms accompany this coping behavior. For example, they may withdraw from all contact with the new culture. Not only do they avoid speaking or trying to learn the new language, but they avoid contact with the host nationals. During this episode, they may develop nervousness, depression, alcoholism, mental debilitation, excessive homesickness, loneliness, disorientation, and general withdrawal.

Filter.   Some people in the "everything is awful" stage of culture shock can experience three kinds of filtering behavior. The filtering behavior refers to a denial of reality, and it occurs in several ways.

1. First, people can *deny differences* between themselves and people in the host culture or between their hometown and a city in the new culture. Some people in this condition go to great lengths to argue about the harmony and similarity between home and host cultures. One international student in a North American university, for example, spent a great deal of time in his conversations with North Americans trying to convince them of how few differences he had noticed and "how wonderful America is." He, like all of us at times, was denying differences.

2. A second way people filter is by *glorifying their home* culture. For example, a North American from the United States may forget all about the problems back home and remember only the good things. This process is something like the old statement about looking at things through rose-colored glasses. Only in this case, the tinted glasses are framed by a need for security. This distortion of perceptions extends into views toward the host culture. One underlying reason for glorifying home is a disgust, contempt, or ethnocentric attitude toward people in the new host culture.

3. A third reaction within this filtering behavior is to *go native*. Sometimes, people totally reject their old culture and enthusiastically adopt the host culture. Of course, the problem is that these people are never accepted in the new culture for anything but what they actually are, so this behavior really does not work.

Flex.   A final behavior within the "everything is awful" stage is flexing. In this more positive phase, the visitors or new residents observe, try new things, and reflect on events, trying to sort out the frustrations and understand them. During this situation, they begin to look at life in the new culture, to reflect on why the people act in a certain way. Then, they go out and try some new food, habits, and customs. Eventually, this process leads into the final stage of culture shock—the "everything is OK" stage.

Stage Three: Everything Is OK

After several months in the new culture, you may find that you view both the negative and the positive in a balanced manner. You finally have learned a lot more about the culture, and while you still do not like some things, you now like more things than a few months ago. Not everyone is a crook, you think to yourself, and, in fact, there are some good folks along with some bad. By now, you have become more accustomed to the foods, sights, sounds, smells, and nonverbal behaviors of the new culture. Also, you have fewer headaches and upset stomach problems and less confusion, uncertainty, and loneliness. Your physical health and mental health have improved. Normal contacts with host nationals are increasing, and you do not feel that you must defend yourself. You can accept yourself and others around you. Congratulations! You have just made it through the worst of culture shock.

As previously mentioned, some people experience culture shock in varying degrees. Also, because culture shock occurs over a period of time, you may not always realize that its stages are temporary. The best thing to do is to admit that you are experiencing culture shock, try to identify your stage of culture shock, and work toward becoming more familiar with the new culture. Feeling good about yourself before you go into the new culture is important. A positive self-concept alleviates self-doubt and allows you to experience new things with less stress.[4]

Furthermore, these features apply to any diverse context, domestic or international. People can experience just as much adaptation difficulty moving to a new city as moving to a new country.

The process just described has been referred to as the U-curve for entry and the W-curve referring to the entry-reentry cycle. The model in figure 8.1 refers to the stages in the W-curve. Other graphs can explain the early adaptation process, but for several reasons this model is presented as the best for this kind of process explanation.[5]

Long-Term Cultural Adaptation

How would you feel if you moved to a new town, changed schools, or undertook a new job? As you can guess from the previous discussion, there would probably be some degree of culture shock. What if you were an immigrant coming to a new country, an international student entering the United States, or a Native American moving from a reservation to Chicago? The process would be more difficult. Beyond the early adaptation experience of culture shock lies the process of long-term cultural adaptation. This idea refers to the long-term acculturation or adapting to new cultural behaviors that are different from one's primary learned culture. Although a number of observers are interested especially in how long-term adaptation or acculturation works with relatively new immigrants, such as the influx of Cubans, Vietnamese, and Koreans into the United States, the principles apply broadly to moving to a new location, changing jobs, and adapting to ethnic diversity in education and in the workplace. To understand acculturation is to discover interpersonal relations, the effects of prolonged culture contact, and how well individuals adjust to change especially to an entirely new culture. All this involves a learning, socialization process—it is not easy and takes time.

People living in a new culture for a short time, or sojourners, do not necessarily have to rely on the host culture as much as long-term adapters. Many investigations, such as Young Kim's research in this area, illuminate the variables involved.

Growth and Adaptation

What happens when a person lives a short or long-term in another culture? We believe some important factors contribute to the adaptation process.

Adaptation involves survival skills.   Part of the process of acculturation is learning survival skills—how to cook, eat, work, rest, do banking, seek transportation, and the scores of other things that bombard the new person who plans to live permanently in the new culture. The daily press of living becomes the dominant concern. From an understanding of Maslow's hierarchy of needs we can learn that once these physiological needs are met, a person seeks more psychological assurances, such as security, self-esteem, and acceptance. If the survival skills are not adequately dealt with, a person may suffer lessened adaptation.

Adaptation and change.   Culture adaptation assumes attitudes and behaviors will ultimately change. Without an understanding of positive conditions bringing about the changes, ethnic people can remain trapped, victims of negative experiences that prevent acculturation. In the long run, growth results from stretching and experiencing the inevitable stresses.

Kim explained the growth process in her stress-adaptation-growth model.[6] Kim's research proposes that adaptation is an accumulation but progressive series of positive and negative experiences. There may be two steps forward and one step back as we move toward adaptation only to be pulled into stress. We do not always adapt in a smooth, continuous process. Pictured as a coiled spring, which stretches and grows but is pulled back by its own tension, the stress-adaptation-growth dynamic ultimately depicts adaptation in the new culture (figure 8.2).

A number of variables have been examined in an attempt to identify the communication and participation activities when arriving to live permanently in a new culture. Although many studies are very specific, dealing with particular ethnic groups, the following principles emerging from these studies apply to our discussion of adaptation.

Factors Contributing to Long-Term Adaptation

Ethnic identification.   Whenever a minority culture is faced with learning the new ways of a contrast culture and surviving in that culture, there is a strong ethnic identification. By that we mean that the minority person or immigrant seeks identification with familiar people, customs, and language. In recent years within the United States, these groups have been encouraged to maintain their ethnic ties in what is termed *cultural pluralism*. Young Kim's earlier study of Korean immigrants in Chicago indicates that ethnic identification is high, especially in the early years of acculturation.[7] Interpersonal and organizational involvement among this group remains stronger than ties with the host nation, although the number of intercultural contacts increases over a period of time. However, too strong a network of ethnic relationships can reduce adaptation[8]

Intercultural friendships.   Although ethnic identification remains higher than intercultural identification, studies of successful adaptation indicate that, as time passes, intercultural friendships develop. For example, turning to a study cited above by Kim, she reported that among her Korean respondents the number of casual friends who are Americans increases significantly after the Korean immigrant has been in the United States about five years. After a few more years, the number of Korean casual friends decreases but always remains greater than the number of American friends.

Figure 8.2

Stress-adaptation-growth dynamic (Young Y. Kim as noted in text).

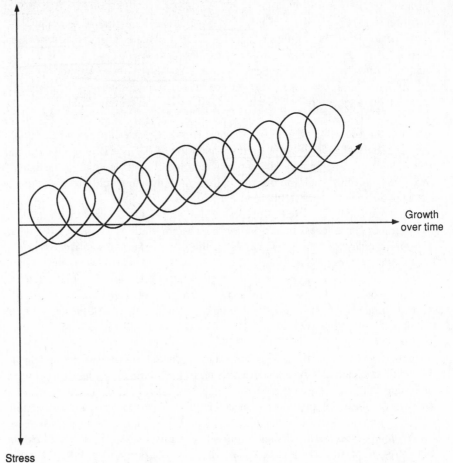

The same principle works for intimate friends: the number of American friends rises dramatically, and the number of Korean friends decreases somewhat. In other words, as the immigrants begin in the new country, they attach themselves to friends within their ethnic group. Although they maintain these ties, the new immigrants branch out and develop interethnic friends after a number of years.

Cultural involvement. The longer a person lives in a new culture, the more that person tends to become more culturally involved, at least under the following conditions.[9]

1. *Acculturation motivation.* If a person is highly motivated to be acculturated, he or she usually becomes more culturally involved with group memberships in the host culture than a person who is not motivated to acculturate.

2. *Linguistic competence.* English competence is important for explaining why some Koreans acculturate faster and better than others in the United States.

Working through cultural adaptation involves stress, but accompanying growth by making new friends, developing positive attitudes, and trying new things.
© Jean-Claude Lejeune/ Stock Boston.

3. *Education.* Education also affects acculturation and cultural involvement, since more highly educated persons entering the host culture seem to develop more friendships and join more groups than less educated people.

4. *Dual membership.* People involved in the ethnic culture, through group memberships and friendships, also tend to be involved in the host culture. Exposure to one medium is highly related to exposure to another medium. This dual cultural involvement effect can be called the *centripetal acculturation effect.* In this case, acculturation and involvement in one's own culture predict involvement in a host culture—involvement generates more involvement, up to a point.

5. *Occupational status.* Data also indicate that occupational status facilitates the acculturation process. The more one is expected to interact and the higher the status of the occupation, the greater the adaptation.[10]

6. *Uncertainty reduction.* Research indicates that uncertainty-reduction skills facilitate increased adaptation.[11] Furthermore, reduced anxiety heightens the adaptation process. If Pearce and Kang are correct, too wide a variety of interacting with individual differences and significant diversity of communication experiences of immigrants with the host culture confuses the ethnic sojourner. In this case, uncertainty not only remains unresolved, it could go up or increase anxiety.

7. *Mass media usage.* As Kim's model indicates, mass media involvement stimulates processing and adaptation to some extent. The media become a source of language trial-and-error as well as a source of humor and general cultural features.

8. *Communication skills.* Without appropriate communication skills in place, research shows that various communication difficulties can emerge that detract

Figure 8.3

Adaptation of Kim's multidimensional model of intercultural adaptation (Young Y. Kim as noted in text).

from cultural adaptation. In research with Thai students studying in the United States, Lakey demonstrated significant findings in his survey of communication difficulty. He found the following communication factors to be the most important for adaptation:

a. Managing and regulation

b. Interpersonal relationships

c. Learning rules of social behavior

d. Mismatch between home-culture skills and host-culture skills

e. Inadequate stereotype and picture of host culture because of incomplete information

f. Differences in interpretive functions—thinking and interpretation about American thought and logic that are inaccurate, leading to less adaptation

g. Too low a level of enmeshment; that is, low internalization and contact

Lakey describes the problem with many international students as communication and social-skill deficits.[12]

Overall, the adaptation process can be viewed, as Kim indicates, as a model predicting adaptation (figure 8.3). She links a person's adaptation predisposition (acculturation motivation, change orientation, personal resistance) and the host culture's receptivity. These two influence the immigrant's communication competence and social participation in interpersonal and mass communication. These communication factors, in turn, activate adaptation outcomes (including stress, intercultural identity, and functional abilities). In sum, the idea is that one's personal motivation and the host culture's facilitation opens up windows of possibility for immigrants to communicate interpersonally and be exposed to mass communication. Communication with the host culture and, to a lesser extent, with members of the ethnic culture, leads to adaptation.[13]

In sum, long-term adaptation or acculturation does not occur in everyone's life in the same way. Some people are motivated to acculturate, while others are not. At least for first-generation immigrants and for immediate culture contact, total integration is gradual and depends upon several factors. Even then, however, perhaps we are recognizing the reality that cultural pluralism is a fact for the future. The challenge for intercultural communicators is to recognize the dynamics of the cultural adaptation and acculturation factors and apply these principles, along with personal competencies and communication accommodation, to meaningful relationships.

A body of literature has been evolving that documents the process of reentry into one's home culture after a stay in another culture. The research in this area reveals staggering information about what Austin cited as a "conspiracy of silence."[14] No one wants to admit that he or she is having difficulty readjusting to the home culture, so the reentry process has often involved people suffering quietly with stress. Austin, a leading researcher in reentry, having surveyed and counseled in his psychological practice hundreds of returned government, missionary, and business personnel, noted that a slight majority of people returning face stress in reentry and that in some cases the need for counseling is severe.[15] Among children, 10 percent are reported to need psychological counseling. Data also suggest that returning children may experience a delayed adolescence by as much as ten years.[16] There is lot at stake in understanding the factors associated with intercultural reentry.

Adaptation and Reentry

The cycle of reentry stress is similar to the cycle of entry stress experienced upon first arrival in a new culture. Thus, a W-curve best represents a model for understanding the entry/reentry cycle (see figure 8.1). Upon first returning home, there is a sense of relief and excitement about being in familiar surroundings, seeing old friends, and so on. However, to the surprise of everyone, especially the returning expatriate, a sense of depression and negative outlook follows the initial reentry cycle. Symptoms described earlier in the chapter may result. Research in reentry has revealed some unique factors that contribute to a negative spiral during the downturn phase of the reentry cycle.

1. First, *self-concept decreases.* There is a feeling of nonacceptance of the self and a general search for identity.[17] In fact, evidence suggests that returning Vietnam veterans especially experienced this loss of self because they came home to a U.S. culture that rejected their role.

2. A second factor that can lead to reentry depression is a *homesickness and nostalgia* for the country the person just left.[18] The home culture looks so negative at times that the reentering person longs for the "good old days" in the country where he or she lived for the past several years.

3. A third unique factor associated with reentry depression is that persons facing reentry may experience a *value change.* One of the most obvious areas of value change is a kind of disgust with American materialism and feeling an embarrassment of riches.

4. Fourth, a change that contributes to a depression stage following reentry includes the returned person's dissatisfaction with the *fast-paced way of life* and a desire for a simpler life.

5. Fifth, a desire for *deeper friendships* and relationships accompanies reentry. In the host culture, great effort was expended to make friends and all that has to happen again, but it does not seem as automatic as the returnee expected.

6. Sixth, a heightened *concern over ecology and politics* is a change of many repatriates' way of thinking. The overseas experience often leads one to see waste and conservation in new ways.

7. Seventh, many repatriates return with a heightened *awareness over minority issues and racial prejudice.*[19]

Practically speaking, reverse culture shock, or cultural reentry, is a cultural vertigo because of the dizzy feeling people experience when returning from overseas to find that the home culture is no longer the same. The mental snapshot they took when leaving is now blurred. Reactions to cultural vertigo have been documented by Schmidt's[20] interview research and include the following observations:

1. You're not the same person upon returning, and you have a new outlook on the country.

2. It's difficult to use your experience from overseas, and people can't deal with you—it's hard to fit in.

3. You find that you're two years behind the times in clothing, slang, and other things.

4. You don't have a network to help you, as you had overseas, which makes it difficult to break in and hard to make friends.

5. Preparing for reentry is a little like preparing for old age. It doesn't begin at age seventy.

6. Find a friend or mentor before going overseas who can keep you abreast of things at home and see that your name is brought into conversations.

7. Keep in communication with people back home, and keep them up-to-date with you but also ask what changes they're going through. Don't flaunt your foreign experience. Some suggest writing two letters a week—one to work associates and another to family/friends.

8. Indicate new skills being developed and how they might be used back home.

9. Make preparations (information gathering) before returning and be prepared for changes—home will be new.

10. Distill the essence of your overseas experience because people won't want to sit for hours listening to you and watching slides. Don't assume that you are the person who has had the exciting time—listen to others.

Developing Skills in Intercultural Communication and Adaptation to a New Culture

Overall, adapting to new cultures involves first working through culture shock. The following suggestions should assist you not only in culture shock but also in longer-range adaptation.

1. *Do not become over-reactionary.* This advice stems from the tendency to become overly frustrated during various stages of culture shock. Patience goes a long way; if you control your emotions, you can more easily see yourself and others.

2. *Meet new people.* Force yourself to go out of your way to meet others. By engaging in these new friendships, you gradually gain personal confidence and ul-

timately learn a lot more about the culture than by your sheer determination. A new friend can tell you things that you may spend months learning otherwise.

3. *Try new things.* Being creative and trying new foods, clothes, and so on can assist you in meeting the stress of the new culture. Trying new things is not easy, but if you can try them gradually yet persistently, you will enjoy the new culture quickly.

4. *Give yourself periods of rest and thought.* Adapting to a new culture is like being in school for several hours a day—it is hard, mental work. Like any other serious learning endeavor, you need time to rest properly. Also, you need time to reflect and put your thoughts together. Do not be a recluse, but a little time to yourself can prove beneficial.

5. *Work on your self-concept.* The mind can be directed toward positive or negative thoughts. While this idea may seem oversimplified at first, try feeding yourself a diet of positive thoughts. Of course, you can go overboard and distort reality, but positive thinking can help you. Tell yourself that you are really not so bad and that most other people go through the same experiences that you face during culture shock.

6. *Write.* Sometimes writing in a diary or some other medium can release tension and frustration. Also, reflecting at a later time on what you have written can prove insightful to personal growth.

7. *Observe body language.* As stated in chapter 7, body language and nonverbal communication in general are subtle but persuasive. Part of the frustration of culture shock is not knowing the culture's system of body language. People bump into you without apology, and people may not smile at you the way they do back home, and so you miss the cues once so familiar. By learning the nonverbal rules, you may discover that the behavior of the people of the new culture does not indicate anger or any other dissatisfaction with you personally.

8. *Learn the verbal language.* Take time to learn as much of the host culture's language as possible. Not only does using the native language compliment people in the host culture, but it obviously aids your survival skills.

This Chapter in Perspective

This chapter describes physical and psychological symptoms of transition into a new culture, called cultural adaptation. Some of those symptoms include physiological, emotional, and communication-based factors associated with culture shock.

The chapter also outlines three stages of culture shock following a predeparture anticipation stage: (1) the "everything is beautiful" stage involves a sense of euphoria and pleasure with the new culture; (2) the "everything is awful" stage is typified by a flurry of negativism in which one fights, flees, filters, or flexes; and (3) the "everything is OK" stage characterized by a balanced view of the new culture.

During and after culture shock, however, people who plan to be permanent residents of a host culture face the stress of long-term stress adaptation to new people and customs. An obvious part of acculturation is first learning survival skills. We typically change our attitudes toward host nationals following culture contact, but only under a number of conditions. Long-term adaptation or acculturation includes the stress-growth-adaptation dynamic. The chapter discussion of adaptation also highlights the importance of communication factors in facilitating adaptation.

This chapter also documents processes and suggestions for meeting the demands of cultural reentry. The psychological stress underlying reentry can be understood and dealt with. A number of useful suggestions are provided.

Exercises

1. Interview a business or professional person who has been working overseas for a while. Ask for impressions of his or her psychological states during the earlier and then during the later period of this person's stay in the host country. What patterns emerge? Why?

2. Discuss with some ethnic leaders in your community the problems of acculturation of minorities in your locale. Ask them for their advice as to how ethnic groups or other minorities can acculturate in ways mutually beneficial to ethnic group members and the dominant culture.

3. Do some research in the library or in some of your other university or college courses about the theory of cognitive dissonance. What parallels do you see between that theory and the patterns of culture shock discussed in this chapter? How can dissonance theory reduction techniques be used in reducing culture shock?

Endnotes

1. Calvero Oberg, "Culture Shock: Adjustment to New Cultural Environments," *Practical Anthropology* 7 (1960): 170–79; Peter S. Adler, "The Transitional Experience: An Alternative View of Culture Shock," *Journal of Humanistic Psychology* 15 (1975): 10–14; Janet Bennett, "Transition Shock: Putting Culture Shock into Perspective," *International and Intercultural Communication Annual* 4 (1977): 45–52.

2. A number of writers have explored the causes and symptoms of culture shock and have outlined the phases that people enter and leave throughout the transition process. Oberg, 1960 (see note 1); Adler 1975 (see note 1); Bennett 1977 (see note 1); Edward C. Stewart, "The Survival Stage of Intercultural Communication," *International and Intercultural Communication Annual* 4 (1977): 17–31. In addition to these works, the United States Navy manual *Overseas Diplomacy*, U.S. Navy, Bureau of Navy Personnel, 1973, outlines a number of phases and subphases that commonly occur. These include eager expectation, everything is beautiful, everything is awful, and everything is OK.

3. *Overseas Diplomacy*, 1973 (see note 2).

4. Stewart, 1977 (see note 2); Bennett, 1977 (see note 1).

5. Other graphs can explain the early adaptation process, including straight lines starting high and continuing in satisfaction, straight lines starting low and continuing to stay low in satisfaction, graphs that start low and go high linearly, and graphs that start high and go low in a straight linear line. For a variety of reasons, I choose to impress the W-curve because of its modeling consistency with other life cycle models and what I believe after hundreds of interviews with students over the years to be an ac-

curate representation of the cycles we experience. I would also stress, however, Young Kim's stress-adaptation-growth model as an accurate representation, especially for long-term adaptation which is why that model appears in the next section of the chapter. Young Yun Kim, *Communication and Cross-Cultural Adaptation: An Integrative Theory* (Avon, England: Multilingual Matters, 1988).

6. Young Yun Kim, 1988 (see note 5).

7. Young Yun Kim, "Inter-Ethnic and Intra-Ethnic Communication: A Study of Korean Immigrants in Chicago," *International and Intercultural Communication Annual* (1977): 53–68.

8. Jin K. Kim, "Explaining Acculturation in a Communication Framework: An Empirical Test," *Communication Monographs* 47 (1980): 155–79.

9. Kim, 1977 (see note 7); Kim, 1988 (see note 6).

10. Young Yun Kim, "Toward an Interactive Theory of Communication—Acculturation," *Communication Yearbook* 3 (1979): 436–53; Margaret Inglis and William B. Gudykunst, "Institutional Completeness and Communication—Acculturation," *International Journal of Intercultural Relations* 6 (1982): 251–72; Jose G. Baldassini and Vincent F. Flaherty, "Acculturation Process of Colombian Immigrants into the American Culture in Bergen County, New Jersey," *International Journal of Intercultural Relations* 6 (1982): 127–35.

11. William B. Gudykunst and Mitchell Hammer, "Strangers and Hosts: An Uncertainty Reduction Theory of Intercultural Adaptation," in *Cross-Cultural Adaptation: Current Approaches,* ed. Young Y. Kim and William B. Gudykunst (Newbury Park, Calif.: Sage, 1988). For effects of uncertainty reduction on adaptation, see also Young Yun Kim, "Intercultural Adaptation," in *Handbook of International and Intercultural Communication,* ed. Molefi Kete Asante and William B. Gudykunst (Newbury Park, Calif.: Sage, 1989); W. Barnett Pearce and K. W. Kang, "Acculturation and Communication Competence," in *Communication Theory from Eastern and Western Perspectives,* ed. D. L. Kincaid (New York: Academic Press, 1987).

12. Paul Lakey, "Communication/Social Difficulty of Thai Students in the Process of Cultural Adaptation" (Ph.D. dissertation, University of Oklahoma, 1988).

13. Kim, 1988 (see note 6).

14. Clyde N. Austin, "Cross-Cultural Reentry," in *Intercultural Skills for Multicultural Societies,* ed. Carley Dodd and Frank Montalvo (Washington, D.C.: SIETAR, 1987a).

15. Clyde N. Austin, ed., *Readings in Cross-Cultural Reentry* (Abilene, Tex.: Abilene Christian University Press, 1987b).

16. Cheryl Davis, "The Relationship of Family and Peer Communication to Third Culture Kids" (master's thesis, Abilene Christian University, Abilene, Texas, 1990).

17. Austin, 1987a (see note 14).

18. Leslie Moore, "A Study of Reentry Stress of Returned Missionaries from Churches of Christ" (master's thesis, Abilene Christian University, Abilene, Texas, 1981).

19. Austin, 1987b, (see note 15).

20. Wallace Schmidt, letter to author, 1986.

Chapter 9

Intercultural Communication Competencies Associated with Intercultural Effectiveness

OBJECTIVES *After completing this chapter, you should be able to*

1. Define effectiveness and its dimensions

2. List factors of intercultural competency associated with intercultural effectiveness outcomes

3. Apply criteria from models of intercultural effectiveness toward intercultural selection

4. Identify effectiveness issues in a model

5. Develop steps for intercultural personnel selection

This chapter deals with the competencies necessary for effective intercultural communication outcomes. Our central text model stresses that in the context of the third culture C, we adapt to culture and develop communication accommodation strategies in ways that are functional leading to effective outcomes or dysfunctional leading to ineffective outcomes. The overall intercultural model along with the original models presented in this chapter linking competency to intercultural effectiveness will clarify this area of intercultural effectiveness research that previously lacked clear models, principles, and application for intercultural competency. The connection to personnel selection makes this material practical as well as theoretically insightful.

The theme of this chapter is that intercultural competencies lead to intercultural effectiveness. Before learning what is involved in effective outcomes, we need to learn what is meant by intercultural effectiveness. Experts agree that some form of *outcome success* is expected. Not all agree exactly on the nature of the outcome, but the results of intercultural effectiveness fall into the general area of ability to function within a culture. Of course, how well you function is a matter of degree, but the critical question is what is central to outcomes. Once we have defined what is the expected outcome, then we are in a position to know how to get there.

What Is Intercultural Effectiveness?

Numerous articles, papers, and lectures are available on the topic of competency and effectiveness, although researchers and practitioners sometimes mix these two concepts. The main point and our central theme in this chapter is that intercultural competency factors lead to intercultural effectiveness. Intercultural competency factors are the skills and qualities associated with successful outcomes in an intercultural context. You have to know, do, or feel certain qualities usually before successful outcomes occur. And, even though communication contributes to the ultimate success of intercultural experiences, there are other social and personal factors in addition to but related to communication concepts.

There is a large body of research regarding this topic of intercultural outcomes and competencies leading to successful outcomes. In this chapter, we have selected three of the most common and central outcomes for related to effectiveness: *task performance, ability to adapt to the new culture,* and *the ability to establish healthy interpersonal relationships.*[1]

First, task performance is doing well at your job. While significant, however, professional performance alone does not qualify for success. Second, successful adaptation to the culture is necessary (as discussed in the last chapter). Third, successful interpersonal relationships signal effectiveness outcomes. You cannot be defined as ultimately successful if you do not accomplish your job, adjust poorly in the new culture, and interpersonally communicate so poorly that you have no friends. Overall, these three outcomes set the standards. Fortunately, these are outcomes for which one can prepare. This trio of factors is not always accepted as a "package," as in some corporate cultures where task success is a primary measure.

When all these considerations are factored, research and insight have led researchers and intercultural trainers to conceive of the predictive variables that most likely contribute to intercultural effectiveness. That is, researchers have sought to link competence-related qualities leading to effectiveness outcomes.

A Case Study of Intercultural Ineffectiveness

I will resist the temptation to tell a hundred stories here from intercultural consulting experiences and briefly describe just one. Bill and Susan (not their real names) are an American expatriate couple working in an overseas environment. Their communication and psychological assessments revealed significant communication barriers between them as a couple as well as between them and their projected host culture. They were advised by their psychological consultant and by their communication consultant to avoid leaving until help was secured. They rejected the advice, only to experience severe difficulties not only in adjusting to the new culture, but in forming adequate relationships, and in getting the job done that the husband was hired to accomplish. All this and many more negative experiences occurred despite excelling in task-related professional training! In other words, one's professional competency can be obliterated by poor people skills and competencies. Within time they returned to the U.S., suffered emotional and relationship problems, and are now divorced.

With major team work and insight from several others noted in our references, we have gone the next step and attempted to (1) distill the most salient predictive competency factors associated with intercultural effectiveness outcomes, and (2) produce two models that might help us visually understand this process. Figures 9.1 and 9.2 reveal the first model called the "cube model." It demonstrates social/psychological competency predictors and cultural/situational competency predictors associated with the three effectiveness outcomes.[2]

The second model is called the E-Model, with the E standing for "effectiveness." The three outcomes defining effectiveness are pictured on the right as arms of the letter E. The notion of intercultural competencies associated with effectiveness is pictured on the left as contributing to effectiveness. Figure 9.3 portrays the model and identifies operational definitions of each effectiveness outcome.[3] A scale was developed to accompany the E-model and is presented in the appendix.

Intercultural Competency Factors Associated with Intercultural Effectiveness

Cognitive Style Variables

The models presented in this chapter underscore numerous competencies associated with and predictive of the three effectiveness outcomes. Next, an extensive set of cognitive style, communication behaviors, and situational variables is shown to correlate with positive intercultural effectiveness outcomes.[4]

Ethnocentrism. The deleterious effects of judgmental attitudes and a feeling of being superior to others from another cultural group are well documented. In a series of investigations correlating a scale to measure ethnocentrism with culture stress, significant correlations indicated that highly ethnocentric individuals are less likely to adjust well during a transitional experience.[5] As you might expect prejudice and ethnocentrism are difficult bar-

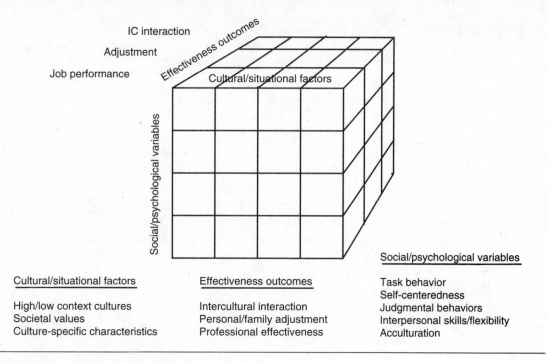

IC interaction
Adjustment
Job performance

Effectiveness outcomes

Cultural/situational factors

Social/psychological variables

Social/psychological variables

Cultural/situational factors	Effectiveness outcomes	Social/psychological variables
High/low context cultures	Intercultural interaction	Task behavior
Societal values	Personal/family adjustment	Self-centeredness
Culture-specific characteristics	Professional effectiveness	Judgmental behaviors
		Interpersonal skills/flexibility
		Acculturation

Figure 9.1

Cube model for intercultural effectiveness. (Source: Kise, Phipps, and Sufferlein as noted in text.)

riers and often block adequate cultural adjustment and relationship formation in the host culture. Even in the middle of the down stage of culture shock it is important to keep your criticism of the culture and negative attitudes toward host country foreigners to a minimum.[6]

Tolerance for ambiguity.   The ability to react to new but ambiguous situations with little difficulty is a significant skill in intercultural effectiveness.[7] In other words, if you can handle situations you do not immediately understand, then you probably have a high tolerance for ambiguity. Intercultural communication by nature poses ambiguities; other people, institutions, organizations, and even your attitude toward yourself just do not seem to make any sense. General confusion and disorientation may result just from being in another culture. Fluidity and flexibility are very important for building relationships in intercultural climates.

Cognitive complexity: perceiving wide categories about people.   Cognitive complexity refers to the ability of a person to perceive a wide variety of things about another person and to make finer interpersonal discriminations than cognitively simple individuals. Using a sample of Americans working in five countries of South America, Norton found that cognitively complex individuals

Figure 9.2

Enlarged example of
cube model.

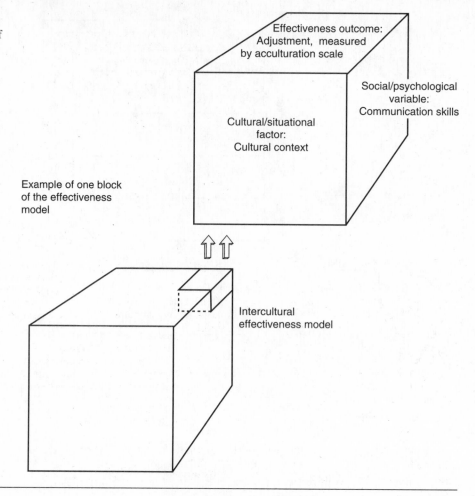

Effectiveness outcome:
Adjustment, measured
by acculturation scale

Social/psychological
variable:
Communication skills

Cultural/situational
factor:
Cultural context

Example of one block
of the effectiveness
model

Intercultural
effectiveness model

Figure 9.3

E-model of
intercultural
effectiveness. (Source:
Walter, Choonjaroen,
Bartosh, and Dodd as
noted in text.)

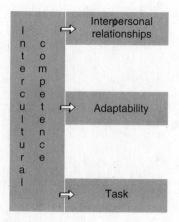

Intercultural competence

Interpersonal
relationships

Adaptability

Task

Task

- Technical and/or professional performance
- Resourcefulness
- Imagination/creativity
- Ability to innovate

- Performance evaluation
- Organizational communication
- Goal development
- Management of task

**Figure 9.3–
continued**

Operational outcomes
of intercultural
effectiveness
categories for E-
model.

Adaptability

- Flexibility
- Maturity
- Knowledge of host culture
- Language skills
- Nonjudgmental attitude

- Patience
- Respect for culture
- Open-mindedness
- Tolerance for ambiguity
- Appropriate social behavior

Interpersonal relationships

- Friendship
- Emotional control
- Sense of humor
- Sensitivity towards others' needs
- Empathy
- Consideration towards others

- Trust others
- Leadership
- Positive relations with strangers
- Ability to get along with co-workers
- Family relations
- Lack of ethnocentrism/prejudice

---

scored significantly lower on measures of culture stress than cognitively simple individuals.[8] This means that people who have enough category width to see a variety of things about another person in contrast to seeing only limited details experience greater intercultural effectiveness. In general, cognitively complex individuals make better and more accurate judgments in developing impressions about others. They see more possibilities about people and situations.

Self-esteem and confidence.   Clearly, our self-esteem predicts intercultural effectiveness. A negative self-esteem can shake the foundations of our personal outlook thus inhibiting effectiveness. Also, self-confidence and initiative directly correlate with personal adjustment and performance.[9] Everyone has self-doubts once in a while, and even those occasional negatives can chip away at intercultural effectiveness. As Shakespeare said, "Our doubts are traitors and cause us to lose the good we oft might win by fearing to attempt." Fear can freeze our emotions and our spirits. At the root of some fear is low self-esteem. Beyond those momentary losses of confidence, however, most of us can really perform beyond our expectations.

One of the needs discovered in intercultural counseling is that some individuals need genuine, self-confidence building programs before they go overseas. That need is also present for an entire family in many cases as they plan an intercultural assignment.

Innovativeness. Innovativeness refers to our ability to try new things, to engage in some social risk taking, particularly where new information and developing social relationships are concerned. Evidence suggests that our ability to try new things is linked with intercultural effectiveness.[10] Being a risk taker does not mean advocating social deviancy or taboo-breaking behavior. On the contrary, innovativeness means the ability to make significant strides in developing and accepting new ideas within a context of social acceptance. A willingness to experiment with new approaches and especially a willingness to learn are highly linked with intercultural communication success.

Trust in people. Researchers have correlated trust in people with intercultural effectiveness and found this variable to be an important predictor.[11]

Acculturation motivation. The desire to learn language, become knowledgeable about the culture, and adapt within a new culture is correlated with successful acculturation.[12]

Communication Behaviors

Task insistence. Insistence on getting the job done can lead to ineffectiveness, at least for tasks such as skills transfer and development.[13] This role behavior is likely to become even more dysfunctional in cultures where occupational roles and expectations are at odds with cultural norms. A person who works for an organization that exhibits an intensive communication style is likely to experience failure within a culture that appreciates a more leisurely pace of work and task behavior.

Self-focused communication. Self-centered communication is less functional for effectiveness.[14] Examples include calling attention to oneself, bragging, and showing disinterest in the ideas of the group. In Japan, making excuses for why something did not work out does not work as well as a simple apology. In general, excessive self-praise or self-blame usually are ineffective in intercultural interactions.

Empathetic communication. A number of researchers report that the ability to put ourselves in the shoes of others is a significant relationship skill. That same ability is helpful in intercultural effectiveness. To understand things from another's point of view is critical in a number of circumstances, including communicating innovative ideas and performing up to our potential in intercultural communication. Active listening and accurate perceiving are significant extensions of empathy.[15]

Communication openness. Many researchers in the field of interpersonal communication observe the importance of openness and flexibility for maximum interpersonal relationships to develop and to be maintained. The opposite is dogmatic or defensive communication which has been significantly correlated with lack of adjustment by linking measures of flexibility with intercultural adjustment and performance.[16] While it is good to share how we feel about things, we become obnoxious when we communicate in a way that puts people down or that leaves no room for disagreement or further dialogue.

Interpersonal comfort.   Research also shows that our ability to feel comfortable interpersonally is significantly correlated with maximum intercultural adjustment. Other research indicates that interpersonal trust, interpersonal interest, interpersonal harmony and interaction are correlated with effectiveness.[17] Thus, if you do not feel comfortable with your interpersonal relationships in your home culture, you may not feel any more comfortable in a host culture.

Control in communication world view.   The amount of immediate and personal control we sense about our communication environment has been significantly correlated with intercultural effectiveness. Researchers have identified a significant connection between personal control in one's communication contexts and ease of intercultural adjustment.[18] These findings suggest that taking charge of (but not dominating) your communication climate impacts adaptation in a new culture and your ultimate success in being interpersonally effective.

Communication anxiety.   Studies have revealed that our personal anxiety about communication affects intercultural adjustment and intercultural effectiveness. Research shows that the higher the communication apprehension, the lower the intercultural effectiveness.[19]

Conversation management.   This area refers to social skills such as interpersonal harmony, responsiveness in conversation, self-monitoring, and self-disclosure appropriate to the culture.[20] These imply turn-taking and the ability to adapt interaction goals and behaviors to others. Also keeping cultural rules and practicing etiquette are conversational skills.[21]

Rhetorical competence.   Astute perception about the rhetorical rules and procedures in a culture can be significant as well as appropriate content material in speech and interaction.[22] This category could include media appropriateness where extremes have been linked to lack of adjustment and obsessive-compulsive behavior.[23]

Rigidity of the host culture.   All the positive personal and social characteristics imaginable do not lessen difficulty in a new culture if the host culture is hostile to outsiders or if the host culture is rigid.[24]

Situational and Systems Factors Related to Competency

Similarity to host culture.   Gudykunst and Kim identified the importance of closeness to the host culture as a predictor of successful outcomes.[25] The amount of prior knowledge, experience, and familiarity with the potentially new culture is also important.

Intercultural training.   Intercultural training plays a vital role in developing competencies for effectiveness.[26]

Family system.   Researchers and practitioners realize that intercultural communication and cultural experiences touch everyone in a family. This system's approach stresses family life as a competency skill antecedent to successful overseas expatriation.[27]

Organizational culture.   The nature of the organizational culture of the sending agency can influence success in the new culture. Factors associated with the organizational culture are personal commitment to the organization, personal compatibility with the organization, longevity with the organization, and supportiveness of the organization toward intercultural projects and personnel.

Selection for Intercultural Effectiveness

Briefly stated, administrators involved in personnel selection have a number of important considerations: personality, communication skills, family, professional competency, and so on. The decision maker must bear in mind that effectiveness is not a single but a multiple construct involving the major outcomes identified above: job performance, cultural adaptation, and interpersonal/family/significant other relations.

How does one choose? The model in figure 9.4 provides a stepwise approach to making intercultural selection and allows us to put all this research into perspective.

1. Describe projected outcomes defining intercultural success. For example, job performance, interpersonal communication success, and positive adaptation.

2. Choose the most professionally competent person who is also the most relationally competent. Keep in mind who adjusted successfully in previous transfers. Interviews, peer reviews, and performance records are useful. The best should be chosen, for the consequences are severe otherwise. Entire overseas operations have been shut down because of poor selection. This first level examines technical and professional competence. (Can the person do the job expected? One AT&T human resources executive with an extensive training budget and himself a veteran of working in the Middle East once told me that job performance was the best predictor for overseas job performance.)

3. Choose a person who wants to go. Personal desire and motivation are highly significant building blocks.

4. Screen for psychological barriers or mental maladjustments that could prevent cultural adjustment or relationship building. Psychological testing (MMPI, 16 PF, Myers-Briggs, Taylor-Johnson Temperament Analysis, etc.) are used by many organizations to determine emotional disorders. This is not to suggest that a person cannot receive help and be prepared at a later time, but experienced practitioners in this area insist that unresolved emotional disorders invite numerous problems connected with field work.

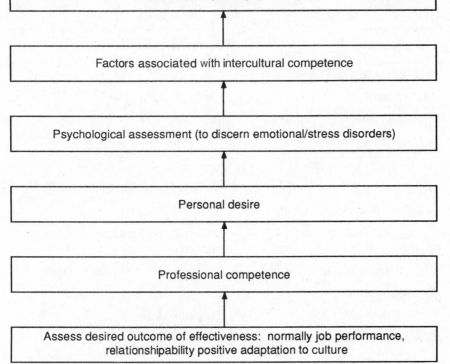

Figure 9.4

A model for intercultural selection.

Cultural adaptability for family

Factors associated with intercultural competence

Psychological assessment (to discern emotional/stress disorders)

Personal desire

Professional competence

Assess desired outcome of effectiveness: normally job performance, relationshipability positive adaptation to culture

5. Does the candidate meet intercultural competencies predicted to be associated with successful intercultural effectiveness outcomes noted earlier and in table 9.1?

6. Does the candidate's family relationship and motivation pose a barrier? Can training be developed for the family? Is the marriage experiencing difficulty?

Selection is complicated, but training must accompany intercultural deployment. Unfortunately, most training is minimal in many organizations, even though experts agree that expatriates should receive at least 40 hours of intercultural training plus 150 hours of language training.

The broadest view of intercultural effectiveness outcome is viewed in figure 9.5, which explores the broader picture among antecedent, process, and consequent conditions. Beyond merely exploring variables that predict intercultural effectiveness, we recognize the intercultural climates that intervene and affect the ultimate effectiveness outcomes.

In the long run, intercultural communication skills are not "push button" substitutes for understanding. Communication strategies are never mechanistic, artificial ways around loving, warm, personal involvement with people and the

Table 9.1 Summary Predictors of Intercultural Communication Effectiveness

Effectiveness	Ineffectiveness
High people, less task emphasis	High task, less people emphasis
Few self-statements	Many self-statements
Low ethnocentrism	High ethnocentrism
High tolerance for ambiguity	Low tolerance for ambiguity
High empathy, good listening	Low empathy, poor listening
High openness, low dogmatism	Low openness, high dogmatism
Cognitive complexity	Cognitive simplicity
Comfort with interpersonal relations, trust	Discomfort with interpersonal relations, mistrust
High personal control, low fatalism	Low personal control, high fatalism
High innovativeness	Low innovativeness
High self-esteem	Low self-esteem
Low communication apprehension	High communication apprehension
Positive conversational management skills	Poor conversational management skills
Positive family communication	Negative family communication
Friendly, warm	Unfriendly, cold
Extroverted	Introverted
Rhetorical sensitivity	Lack of rhetorical sensitivity
High acculturation motivation	Low acculturation motivation
Familiarity and knowledge of host culture	Little knowledge of host culture
Openness to strangers of host culture	Rigidity of host culture
Great amount of intercultural training	Low amount of intercultural training

hard work required to make relationships work. Understanding what skills link with positive intercultural outcomes begins a positive journey. In that way, intercultural skills are really the application of an eclectic awareness of factors contributing to effectiveness and a personal motivation to make these work in our relationships.

Mediated by intercultural climate

Antecedent conditions		Effectiveness outcomes
Personal style and cultural knowledge	Personality system	Task effectiveness
	Interpersonal systems	Positive interpersonal relations
Variables contributing to intercultural effectiveness	Social systems	
	Organizational cultural systems	Cultural adaptation and positive stress
	Macrocultural systems	

Figure 9.5

A model for intercultural skills.

How can you perform better in intercultural contexts? Perhaps the strategies that follow will add more skills to your understanding of the principles already introduced in this chapter.

Developing Skills in Intercultural Effectiveness

1. *Work to emphasize areas of similarity with others.* To the extent you can underscore commonality, generally the better the interpersonal relationship.

2. *Try to accept differing opinions.* In this way, you can remain open and receptive. Dogmatism has a way of blocking intercultural communication.

3. *Make your verbal messages consistent with your nonverbal messages.* Listen to yourself, and try to see yourself talk. Discrepancies between the verbal and nonverbal send a mixed message that in the long run discredits you.

4. *Avoid dominating conversations.* Listen to how much time you spend communicating while in a group. You may be dominating others in the group, and it may not be long before they find you a bore. Listening to others, inviting their explanations, and showing genuine interest are communication suggestions.

5. *Avoid being submissive in conversations.* Although domination can prove to be harmful, if you are overly submissive, people may decide that you have nothing to contribute, a condition that leads to intercultural relationship demise.

6. *Be an affirmer.* You do not have to be a backslapper or act obsequiously to be confirming in your communication behavior. Your intercultural counterparts will appreciate your attempts at being understanding rather than critical.

This Chapter in Perspective

This chapter highlights the notion of intercultural effectiveness defined as the desired outcomes typically expected in an intercultural experience. Most experts agree that task performance, cultural adaptation, and formation of interpersonal relationships are basic. Models were presented to illustrate these areas. Second, the chapter focused on cognitive style, communication behavior, and situational/system variables that are predictive competencies associated with intercultural effectiveness. A model of personnel selection and a summary of predictive factors was presented.

Exercises

1. Observe children at play. List mediating variables that you observe in their communication, and give examples. Are racial differences noticed by children? If not, why not? Report these findings to your class and exchange observations with other class members. How do children reflect and foreshadow adult intercultural communication?

2. Do a field study in which you observe dyads, or pairs, of people. Keep records. Compare nonverbal communication between friends with nonverbal communication between strangers.

3. Read a news magazine account of an intercultural contact. After reading the story, list at least five ways in which most people display poor interpersonal-intercultural communication.

Endnotes

1. Mitchell R. Hammer, "Intercultural Communication Competence," in *Handbook of International and Intercultural Communication,* ed. Molefi Kete Asante and William B. Gudykunst (Newbury Park, Calif.: Sage, 1989); F. Hawes and Daniel Kealey, "An Empirical Study of Canadian Technical Assistance," *International Journal of Intercultural Relations* 5 (1981): 239–56; Mitchell R. Hammer, "Behavioral Dimensions of Intercultural Effectiveness: A Replication and Extension," *International Journal of Intercultural Relations* 11 (1987): 65–88; Judith Martin and Mitchell R. Hammer, "Behavioral Categories of Intercultural Communication Competence: Everyday Communicators' Perceptions," *International Journal of Intercultural Relations* 13 (1989): 303–32. Philip R. Harris and Robert T. Moran, *Managing Cultural Differences,* 4th ed. (Houston: Gulf, 1995); William B. Gudykunst, Richard I. Wiseman, and Mitch R. Hammer, "Determinants of a Sojourner's Attitudinal Satisfaction," in *Communication Yearbook* 1, ed. Brent Ruben (New Brunswick, N.J.: Transaction, 1977); Daniel Kealey, "A Study of Cross-Cultural Effectiveness: Theoretical Issues, Practical Applications," *International Journal of Intercultural Relations* 13 (1989): 387–428.

2. Kaoru Kise, Charles Phipps, and Terry Sufferlein, "Cube Model for Intercultural Effectiveness" (presented originally for this text, Abilene Christian University, Abilene, Texas, 1995). This model is based on the behavioral categories indicated by Brent D. Ruben, "Human Communication and Cross-Cultural Effectiveness," *International and Intercultural Communication Annual* 4 (1977): 95–105; and the cultural factors of E. T. Hall, *Beyond Culture* (Garden City, N.Y.: Anchor, 1976).

3. Michael Walter, Nanmanas Choonjaroen, Kimberly Bartosh, and Carley Dodd, "E-Model of Intercultural Communication Effectiveness" (presented originally in this text, 1995). The model is built on research and papers primarily from Mitchell R. Hammer and Clifford Clarke, "Predictors of Japanese and American Manager's Job Success, Personal Adjustment, and Intercultural Effectiveness" (paper presented to SIETAR Annual Congress, Montreal, Canada, May 1987); Philip R. Harris and

Robert T. Moran, 1995 (see note 1); Daniel Kealey and Brent Ruben, "Cross-Cultural Personnel Selection Criteria, Issues, and Methods," in *Handbook for Intercultural Training,* ed. Dan Landis and Richard Brislin (New York: Pergamon, 1983); Michael F. Tucker and Vicki E. Baier, "Research Background for the Overseas Assignment Inventory" (paper presented to the SIETAR International Conference, San Antonio, Texas, May 1985).

4. Mitchell R. Hammer, "Intercultural Communication Competence," in *Handbook of International and Intercultural Communication,* ed. Molefi Kete Asante and William B. Gudykunst (Newbury Park, Calif.: Sage, 1989); Brent D. Ruben, "Human Communication and Cross-Cultural Effectiveness," *International and Intercultural Communication Annual* 4 (1977): 95–105; Margaret Olebe and Jolene Koester, "Exploring the Cross-Cultural Equivalence of the Behavioral Assessment Scale for Intercultural Perceptions," *International Journal of Intercultural Relations* 13 (1989): 333–47; Richard Wiseman, Mitchell Hammer, and Hiroko Nishida, "Predictors of Intercultural Communication Competence," *International Journal of Intercultural Relations* 13 (1989): 349–70; Norman Dinges and Deborah Lieberman, "Intercultural Communication Competence: Coping with Stressful Work Conditions," *International Journal of Intercultural Relations* 13 (1989): 371–85; Daniel Kealey, "A Study of Cross-Cultural Effectiveness: Theoretical Issues, Practical Applications," *International Journal of Intercultural Relations* 13 (1989): 387–428.

5. Carley H. Dodd, "An Introduction to Intercultural Effectiveness Skills," in *Multicultural Skills for Multicultural Societies,* ed. Carley H. Dodd and Frank F. Montalvo (Washington, D.C.: SIETAR, 1987). The ethnocentrism scale was developed by Kregg Hood, "Correlation of Ethnocentrism and World View" (manuscript, Abilene Christian University, Abilene, Texas, 1982).

6. William B. Gudykunst and Young Yun Kim, *Communicating with Strangers* (New York: Random House, 1984); Michael F. Tucker and Vicki E. Baier, 1985 (see note 3).

7. Brent D. Ruben, 1977 (see note 2); Michael F. Tucker and Vicki E. Baier, 1985 (see note 3); Gudykunst and Kim, 1984 (see note 6); *Overseas Diplomacy* (U.S. Navy, Bureau of Navy Personnel, 1973); Cornelius L. Grove and Ingemar Torbiorn, "A New Conceptualization of Intercultural Adjustment and the Goals of Training," *International Journal of Intercultural Relations* 9 (1985): 205–33.

8. M. Laurie Norton, "The Effects of Communication Effectiveness and Cognitive Complexity on Culture Shock" (master's thesis, Abilene Christian University, Abilene, Texas, 1984).

9. Janet Bennett, "Transition Shock: Putting Culture Shock into Perspective," *International and Intercultural Communication Annual* 4 (1977): 45–52; Tucker and Baier, 1985 (see note 7); *Overseas Diplomacy,* 1973 (see note 7).

10. *Overseas Diplomacy,* 1973 (see note 7).

11. Tucker and Baier, 1985 (see note 3).

12. Young Y. Kim, *Communication and Cross-Cultural Adaptation: An Integrative Theory* (Avon, England: Multilingual Matters, 1988).

13. Brent D. Ruben, 1977 (see note 2).

14. Ruben, 1977 (see note 2).

15. Mitchell R. Hammer, "Intercultural Communication Competence," in *Handbook of International and Intercultural Communication,* ed. Molefi Kete Asante and William B. Gudykunst (Newbury Park, Calif.: Sage, 1989); Everett M. Rogers, *Diffusion of Innovations,* 4th ed. (New York: Free Press, 1995).

16. Tucker and Baier, 1985 (see note 7).

17. M. Laurie Norton and Carley H. Dodd, "The Relationship of Self-Report Communication Effectiveness to Culture Shock" (paper presented to the Speech Communication Association, Chicago, November 1984); Tucker and Baier 1985 (see note 7).

18. Tucker and Baier, 1985 (see note 7); Carley H. Dodd, "An Introduction to Intercultural Effectiveness Skills," in *Multicultural Skills for Multicultural Societies,* ed. Carley H. Dodd and Frank

F. Montalvo (Washington, D.C.: SIETAR, 1987); Larry W. Long, Manoocher Javidi, and Margaret Pryately, "Motives for Moves: A Cross-Cultural Examination of Communication Motives and Style Among Americans, Japanese, and Ukranians" (paper presented to the Southern and Central Communication Associations, Lexington, Kentucky, April 1993).

19. Carley H. Dodd, "An Introduction to Intercultural Effectiveness Skills," in *Multicultural Skills for Multicultural Societies,* ed. Carley H. Dodd and Frank F. Montalvo (Washington, D.C.: SIETAR, 1987). Communication apprehension has an enormous impact on confidence in communication and relationship development. See James C. McCroskey, "Oral Communication Apprehension: A Reconceptualization" (paper presented to the Speech Communication Association, Louisville, Kentucky, 1982).

20. Margaret Olebe and Jolene Koester, "Exploring the Cross-Cultural Equivalence of the Behavioral Assessment Scale for Intercultural Perceptions," *International Journal of Intercultural Relations* 113 (1989): 333–47; Byron Myers, "Predictions of Intercultural Effectiveness" (master's thesis, Abilene Christian University, Abilene, Texas, 1990); Mitchell R. Hammer, "Intercultural Communication Competence," in *Handbook of International and Intercultural Communication,* ed. Molefi Kete Asante and William B. Gudykunst (Newbury Park, Calif.: Sage, 1989).

21. Larry Sarbaugh, *Intercultural Communication* (Rochelle Park, N.J.: Hayden, 1979).

22. Jolene Koester and Carl Holmberg, "Returning to Rhetoric," in *Intercultural Communication Theory: Current Perspectives,* ed. William B. Gudykunst (Beverly Hills, Calif.: Sage, 1983).

23. David Lewis, Carley Dodd, and Darryl Tippens, *Shattering the Silence* (Nashville, Tenn.: Christian Communication, 1989).

24. Gudykunst and Kim, 1984 (see note 6).

25. Gudykunst and Kim, 1984 (see note 6).

26. Grove and Torbiorn, 1985 (see note 7).

27. Tucker and Baier, 1985 (see note 3); Harris and Moran, 1995 (see note 3).

Chapter 10

Intercultural Communication and Conflict

OBJECTIVES   *After completing this chapter, you should be able to*

1. Identify the importance of interpersonal relationships in intercultural communication effectiveness and conflict

2. Understand and identify personality characteristics that mediate and influence intercultural communication conflict

3. Describe how perceived relationships and certain verbal behaviors, such as self-disclosure, affect communication conflict

4. Cope with interpersonal conflict and gain personal awareness of intrapersonal conflicts

5. Improve intercultural interaction skills

Intercultural communication is the study of the influence of cultural variability in the communication process between people. International and cross-cultural communication also deal with culture, but they focus less on the interaction between people and more on the global, political, and economic systems issues that affect cultures. In studying conflict, we are not analyzing historical, economic, and geopolitical factors as such. Our purpose for discussing the "interface" and the "interaction" or communication between people and groups, is to focus on the interpersonal-intercultural aspects associated with conflict.

Consider the case of a mid-size city in the mid-south portion of the United States that received a number of Cambodian, Laotian, and Vietnamese refugees. Some of these people were once "boat people," and the community was sincerely interested in the refugees and their plight. Religious, civic, and governmental groups combined their efforts with the local mass media to encourage participation in various relocation efforts. Despite the encouragement and dedicated efforts of many people, a number of minor frustrations gradually arose among the townspeople and various individual encounters with the boat people. Finally, a seminar was conducted to assist not only community personnel, but educators and other interested persons. During the seminar, it became clear that one of the struggles in working with the refugee group was the many misunderstandings regarding intercultural differences. These ranged across areas like language, nonverbal messages, customs, rules, cultural adaptation issues, and more. Minor frustrations evolved and numerous conflicts resulted.

This particular situation is not unique, for it has been enacted thousands of times where a presenting set of issues between people from two cultures is conflictual in nature. Beyond language, cultural, and interpersonal differences, there are numerous conflict related factors that enter into intercultural relationships. This chapter explores these factors and offers orientations that should facilitate managing intercultural conflict.

Examples abound every day concerning intercultural conflict. A news story, for example, revealed that the Italian actress Sophia Loren was negotiating with legal advisors about staying in her home country. We also may learn that a Middle Eastern culture has heavy investments in land holdings in the midwestern section of the United States and that negotiations are underway for more property acquisition. A new international student may become a classmate. In the student center, we can observe and talk with other American students whose racial backgrounds differ from ours. The tremendous changes in global relationships and the advances in travel and communication render the potential for intercultural conflict certain— part of our understanding of intercultural communication involves exploring the reasons why intercultural conflict can occur in our relationships. In turn, how can we practice conflict management competencies facilitating intercultural success?

Missed Interpersonal Expectations as Source of Intercultural Communication Conflict

Conflict comes from a number of origins. Most experts agree with the fundamental principle that *misunderstanding cultural expectations* lies behind many conflict circumstances. By identifying cultural conflict areas, we can improve our awareness and skills for communication accommodation. This chapter identifies a number of communication-based competencies associated with conflict. Understanding the principles behind these communication competencies and adaptation

Conflict over intercultural expectations accounts for much of the conflict between diverse cultures. © Jean-Claude Lejeune/Stock Boston

to address expectations and issues concerning intercultural conflict is the goal of this chapter. By converting these concepts into skill competencies we should increase the intercultural "relationship" aspect of effectiveness as we discussed in the last chapter.

Self-disclosure is revealing personal and somewhat intimate information about oneself. Since this kind of information is not normally conveyed in most communication, self-disclosure is viewed as guarded information about oneself not obtained normally except under close relationships. Research in American culture reveals a strong relationship between self-disclosure and trust, liking, and reciprocal self-disclosure.[1] With these ingredients at the heart of open communication, it is easy to see why expectations can be missed. If understood or performed well, openness and self-disclosure can build trust and liking; if expectations are violated, trust and liking can be torpedoed. Therefore, it is vital to understand just how different cultures value this topic of communication and to know its strengths and limits.

First, self-disclosure and expectations to be "open" and "share" with others varies interculturally. In high-context cultures information is gathered from means other than the message. Individuals, consequently, are thus expected to engage in more small talk and use indirect communication patterns.[2] An overall review of intercultural self-disclosure and friendship concluded that high- and low-context cultures account for differences: the high-context cultures are predicted to account for less disclosure. That concept explains why in one study comparing Americans, Japanese, British, Germans, Australians, and Koreans, the authors reported that the Japanese disclose significantly less.[3]

Second, self-disclosure and openness mismatches occur for a variety of interpersonal reasons in relation to each cultures' expectations. First, when *reciprocity*

Self-disclosure and Openness in Communication

Without self-disclosure on some level, communication and personal growth remain static. © Laima Druskis/Stock Boston

is not met, expectations are not met. In intimacy, one usually is expected to match the other person. If you under-disclose in a culture that expects you to reveal more, violation of communication norms has occurred; similarly over-disclosure creates cultural conflict. Second, when disclosure occurs with the *wrong person or at an inappropriate stage of the relationship,* conflict occurs. Status and hierarchy are very important in many cultures, such as high power-distance cultures we discussed earlier in this book. Perhaps silence or small talk are more appropriate in some cultures with a high status person. Sometimes, too, a person is in a changing role relationship and mismatched with the stage of the relationship. For instance, an acquaintance now becomes a dating partner thus changing the amount of disclosure that can be expected in that relationship. In fact overall once friendships reach a certain stage, culture has less influence on communication patterns and disclosiveness would likely follow that trend.[4]

Hierarchical Communication

Another conflict source surrounds hierarchy in relationships. For instance, when talking with a close friend, what are your feelings? More than likely, the dominance-submission variable is not operating. How would you feel visiting a foreign ambassador in his or her office? Perhaps you would feel a bit more submissive. The same feeling can occur in various role relationships, such as employer-employee, officer-enlisted person, nurse-patient, parent-child, and teacher-student.

Hierarchy and power. In the case of intercultural communication, hierarchy and power are often products of group norms and expectations. The resultant communication in these cases is less culturally sensitive and often conflictual. Power-distance cultures, identified and discussed earlier, remain potential sources of hierarchy leading to intercultural conflict. If person A from a high power-distance culture operates from cultural norms with person B from a low power-distance culture, we would expect differences in decision making, rules, submission, cooperation, turn-taking, conversation equality, and a number of communication qualities important in building positive, healthy relationships.

Hierarchy and roles. Roles are behaviors performed because of attitudes or expectations of position. A person may communicate and behave in a certain way because his or her role demands such behavior. A law enforcement officer who seems hard and unbending in his or her work role may be highly sympathetic and jovial with family or friends.

Hierarchy and status. Status differences are potential sources of conflict related to hierarchy. For instance, a cultural role in the Middle East indicates that the higher status person pays the check in a restaurant. If you are the higher status person, you may be confused, especially if the other person dramatically insists on paying. However, this insistence is a way of saving face when the higher status person wins the battle of the check and pays—usually to the relief of the lower status person, who insisted in the first place to maintain his or her pride.[5] In Asian, African, and Middle Eastern cultures, age is an indicator of status. Many cultures revere their elderly, showing honor and respect. If you were working as a manager in an international situation, you can imagine the personnel implications if you passed over an older employee for a younger worker.

Another potential intercultural conflict source occurs with misplaced formality in various relationships. With some people, little formality is necessary, while for other relationships, formality is expected. For instance, there is probably little formality between you and your roommate or between you and a good friend. Perhaps, however, your formality level increases with a professor or whenever you enter a situation where you cannot predict the degree of formality expected.

This concept of formality and informality is not merely a matter of etiquette, but a question of intercultural relationship. For example, you may approach a conversation informally, using first-person pronouns and using the other person's first name. The other person, approaching the relationship formally, may refer to titles and make frequent references to one's position in life. Naturally, this conflict over appropriateness of formality can cause embarrassment and extreme discomfort.

To his discussion of formality in relationships, Sarbaugh added that the more differences between two interacting parties—or heterogeneity, to use his term—the more difficult it is to predict the social roles and norms expected. This inability to sense what is expected creates a great deal of frustration.[6] Thus, part of intercultural communication effectiveness involves some attempt to assess just what level of formality is expected. For instance, in the United States, if you are talking with

Formality in Relationships and Communication

an older person, what terms of address are appropriate? There are a number of older people who prefer formal methods of address and others who prefer that you call them by their first name. Before embarking on one level of formality or another, try to determine what the other person prefers; often, that person's conversation reveals a preference. In the same way, many cultural norms dictate formality—so, listen for any cues that can help you set the tone appropriate for a conversation.

Communication in the Workplace

Many of our perspectives on management cannot always be applied on the job in intercultural situations. Effective managers who work internationally usually alter their organizational structure and their personal management styles to conform to unique cultural needs. Failure to adapt to the cultural differences in the workplace can lead to conflict, as the following categories illustrate.

Speed and efficiency.   Some cultures work at slower rates than others. The job gets done in these cases, not because someone is insisting on speed and efficiency, but because of interaction and trust in relationships. Adapting to a culture's time orientation is one of the simplest, yet most helpful, changes we can make when living in a second culture. For example, one U.S. firm waited two years in Japan for an important decision. The American executives were surprised to learn that that time was necessary for the indispensable preliminary of establishing relationships before negotiating.

Cultural rules of employment.   Because of status and equality norms, cultural rules toward employment differ. For example, in Iran, a worker who has become ill may send his brother in his place to work that day. Loyalty is a frequent theme in many parts of Latin America and the Middle East, so much so that a worker who changes jobs too often is viewed as shiftless and disloyal. A story is told how a promotion of a manual laborer to foreman by a U.S. mining operation in the South Pacific led to his murder. In that culture, advancement above one's peers violates tribal rules of equality—hence, the death.[7]

Nonverbal communication.   In parts of Africa, Latin America, Asia, North America, Japan, and the Middle East, an indication of "yes" can also mean "I hear you" but may not necessarily be an agreement. The context and tone of voice convey the intended meaning nonverbally. In Asia, pointing the soles of your feet or your toes is offensive, just as standing too close or too far can be offensive. In some cultures, a handshake implies welcome; in others, it implies distance.

Work and friendship.   In some cultures, work and friendship are distinct. In the U.S. work culture the standard is to work eight hours and then leave for some form of social life. In many cultures, such as Japan, the Middle East, and Latin America, work, play, and friendship are blended. A Japanese employee may work until 6:00 or 7:00 P.M. and then be expected to go to a restaurant or bar to engage socially with business associates. In these contexts, the after-hours work is a source of the company getting to know and trust someone. Also, many cultures expect several visits before doing business.

Meaning of friendships.   Friendships are long term in a number of cultures. The friendship opens commitments to hospitality, gift giving, and, in Latin America, godparenting. The North American concept of friendship is casual, with upward and social mobility overriding long friendships in favor of friendships that come and go. This difference makes a friendly North American vulnerable to being criticized as hypocritical because the person does not follow through with the friendship.

Role expectations of a manager.   Some cultures expect managers to assume responsibility for the total life of the employee, including sickness, personal problems, and children's welfare.[8]

Direct and indirect communication.   Communication styles of directness or indirectness vary culturally. North Americans are expected to come to the point. Phrases like "get to the point" and "small talk before the main point" indicate that some Americans do not like wasting time by including time in their conversational and speech patterns. However, in parts of the Middle East and Latin America, people are considered rude if they come to the point too quickly, before appropriate timing and relationships are built. They talk around the point.

Acceptance and Empathetic Communication

Expressing acceptance and practicing empathy to the needs of others is often an important element in building a positive communication context for intercultural communication. The implication of that principle calls into question one's personal communication style: sarcasm, fear, appeal, condescending messages, controlling messages, usually are not perceived as empathetic nor expressing acceptance. Thus, one's use of such messages can have a negative effect from a contrast culture not accustomed to such treatment.

Empathy usually expresses positive relationships in ways helpful for intercultural effectiveness. Broome identifies this model by calling for relational empathy in the creation of a third culture. Rather than empathy being seen as a product, intercultural empathy involves a reproductive, creative approach where several things happen in creating a third culture. Broome explains these as: (1) shared meaning; (2) developing an open process of understanding; (3) developing an understanding during discourse approximating the other's point of view; (4) continual adjustment of the other's point of view during interaction. In this sense, empathy is a growing, dynamic, change-sensitive approach rather than a static, recipe view.[9]

Communication Avoidance

Have you noticed how some people stick with a point of discussion and solve problems while other people avoid working toward solutions? Communication *avoiders* are those individuals who usually are either unable, or do not want, to seek solutions to issues. While everyone at times may choose to ignore problems and even flee various issues instead of maintaining an open line of communication, avoiders do so consistently. Getting angry, hiding behind a newspaper in the cafeteria, pretending not to see another, giving the silent treatment, or acting pompously and dictatorially are manifestations of avoidance behavior. An avoider can experience more frustration during various stages of culture shock.

Of course, cultural behaviors can include avoiding or coping. The Japanese man who sits silently or quietly exits during a confrontation may be responding culturally, not personally avoiding. He may choose another time or place to resolve a question. The American who seems intent on pressing for a contract with an Italian businessman may not be personally coping but insisting on a cultural pattern of efficiency or time management.

Using Communication to Manage Intercultural Conflict

The first section of this chapter focused more on how individuals develop missed expectations that lead to intercultural conflict. This section turns toward a solution-focus and offers theory and principles designed to lead us toward creative applications once we understand the principles involved.

Using Communication to Reduce Disagreement in Conflict

Inevitably, even our best efforts at establishing and maintaining intercultural relationships are sometimes shattered by our discovery that others like what we dislike or dislike what we like. The resulting communication and attitudes have implications for personal styles of resolving conflict in what researchers refer to as "balance theory."

In its extended form, the notion of balanced relationships suggests that if you and another person like the same thing and like each other, a balanced relationship exists. However, the relationship is unbalanced when people who like each other do not like the same thing or when two people who like the same thing do not like each other. The first component in this description of interpersonal relationships is A's orientation toward a topic X, which includes A's attitude toward Y (approach or avoidance) and various beliefs about X (cognitive attributes). The second component is A's orientation toward person B. A and B can have positive or negative attractions toward each other while holding favorable or unfavorable attitudes toward topic X. When there is an unbalanced state (A and B like each other, but A feels positively about topic X while B feels negatively about X), there is a tension to restore balance through communication.[10]

Balance can be restored in several ways. For example, suppose a Mexican American named Roberto (A) and an African American named Shaun (B) like each other (they have been friends for two years and work as department heads in the same department store in San Antonio). Roberto likes a new accounting system recently installed (X), but Shaun hates it and speaks negatively about the new system. In this obviously unbalanced situation (potentially producing some degree of conflict), several possibilities exist for change. To restore balance, (1) Roberto may convince Shaun to change his attitude toward the new system (or Shaun may convince Roberto); (2) Roberto may change his feelings about Shaun or Shaun about Roberto; (3) they may agree to tolerate the inconsistency and remain friends; or (4) each may work elsewhere.

These outcomes are augmented by some possible cultural differences. For example, both Roberto and Shaun may unwittingly sift their perceptions of the other through some cultural stereotypes. Thus, Shaun may think that Roberto is trying to win points with their store manager, also a Mexican American, and, for a moment, falls prey to his stereotype that Mexican Americans always stick together in groups. Roberto lets himself believe that Shaun dislikes the system because

Conclict can occur for a variety of reasons, including task or role misunderstandings. In this photo each person has an expected task or role, to which he or she tacitly agrees. (Photo by Mike Moore, Kenya.)

Shaun, according to Roberto's personal stereotype of other African Americans, is not very innovative and prefers tried-and-true methods over change that might be uncertain. Such misunderstandings occur frequently. By analyzing such topical likes or dislikes into their components, suggested by balance theorists, we can anticipate interpersonal outcomes.

Sometimes interpersonal conflict develops between person A and person B and leads to topical conflict. For instance, Larry was a flight instructor who disliked his student Abdul from Iraq. Abdul assumed that he could bargain with Larry for free flight time and also waited to read the flight instruction manual until after Larry's personal instructions rather than before. Larry, however, had a set fee and expected Abdul to read the manual well in advance of any personal instruction. This constant difference further fueled Larry's dislike toward Abdul. Later, attempts to reconcile topical disagreements were thwarted by interpersonal conflict. Since Larry disliked Abdul, there was little motivation for him to work through their differences.

When the relationships between person A, person B, and a topic are variable, balance theory provides one way of analyzing and predicting interpersonal outcomes. By examining the personal attitudes between two or more people and their respective attitudes toward salient topics, we can better understand why we are motivated to change or why we choose to ignore development of some interpersonal relationships. Understanding these balance dynamics gives important background to use the skills question presented in table 10.1 and to apply several of the skills listed toward the end of the chapter.

Using Leadership Style and Communication to Manage Conflict

An understanding of leadership styles within systems offers a way to present solutions over conflict. An adaptation of Quinn and McGrath's leadership style model in figure 10.1 reveals that styles of open versus authoritarian can be crossed

Do You Check Contextual Variables?

1. With whom are lines of communication (networks) open or closed in various groups?

2. Why are these networks open or closed? Are you turned off by someone's personality?

3. What is the frequency of communication among various group members? Do clique groups deny access to the group to others who could benefit from group participation?

4. Are hierarchical lines of communication within a formal group, such as an organization, open? How can those communication links be improved?

What Intercultural Relationships Are Operating in Any Given Interpersonal Contact?

1. Do you emphasize overlap of experience in communicating with others?

2. Do you emphasize areas that will build credibility?

3. Are you open in reception of information?

4. Is your verbal message consistent with your nonverbal message? Do your actions match your words?

5. Do you look for the what and the why of a message—what a person says and why that person is saying it?

6. Do you find yourself dominating most conversations? Do you only make statements, or do you periodically ask questions in conversation?

7. Do threatening or nonstatus quo messages that affect you cause you to screen out such messages?

Are You Aware of the Listener as You Engage in Communication?

1. Do you consider the knowledge, education, and background of the listener and speak in terms the listener understands? Do you use jargon and slang?

2. Is it easy for others to tell you what is on their minds? Why?

3. Do you work considerately with others who fear rejection? Do you provide reassuring and positive feedback in your communication?

4. Do you stay with problems and work toward solutions, or do you avoid working through problems?

5. Do you periodically compliment others? Do you separate an issue under consideration from the person?

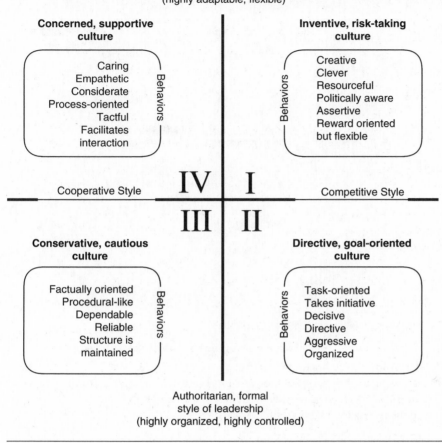

Open, participatory
style of leadership
(highly adaptable, flexible)

**Concerned, supportive
culture**

Caring
Empathetic
Considerate
Process-oriented
Tactful
Facilitates
interaction

Behaviors

**Inventive, risk-taking
culture**

Creative
Clever
Resourceful
Politically aware
Assertive
Reward oriented
but flexible

Behaviors

Cooperative Style   IV | I   Competitive Style

III | II

**Conservative, cautious
culture**

Factually oriented
Procedural-like
Dependable
Reliable
Structure is
maintained

Behaviors

**Directive, goal-oriented
culture**

Task-oriented
Takes initiative
Decisive
Directive
Aggressive
Organized

Behaviors

Authoritarian, formal
style of leadership
(highly organized, highly controlled)

Figure 10.1

Leadership style and
potential organizational
conflict. (Adapted from
Quinn and McGrath as
noted in text.)

with cooperative versus competitive styles.[11] The resultant quadrants produce cultures that are inventive and risk-taking (I), directive and goal-oriented (II), conservative and cautious (III), and concerned and supportive (IV). This model illustrates the potential conflict because of differences in expectations within cultures emphasizing one style or quadrant over another. In essence, by "matching" the expected cultural quadrant, participants reduce differences, engage in expected messages that fit the quadrant, and thus build a common third culture. We could then expect conflict to be reduced during this process.

This model is similar to a frequently cited model called the Thomas-Kilmann conflict style model also resulting in four quadrants: collaborating, competing, avoiding, and accommodating along with a middle style, compromising (figure 10.2). Like the Quinn and McGrath system presented above, it is easy to see how mismatches between styles (for instance you use competitive style, I use accommodating style) account for conflict, and how engaging the participants to use similar styles with expected and appropriate rhetorical style and devises within

Figure 10.2

Thomas-Kilmann
conflict styles.

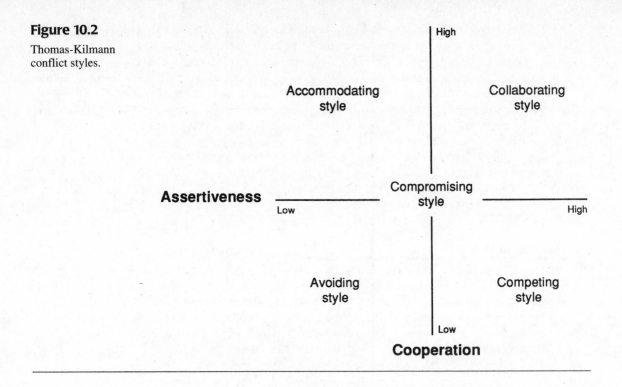

each quadrant would help the conflict communication efforts. In fact, in research to accomplish this very solution, that is to match quadrants, the results were promising. Individual leaders in organizations in an intercultural environment altered their decision making, time, trust, and power.[12]

Applying Metaphors to Prevent Intercultural Conflict

Ting-Toomey reminds us of fundamental metaphors in Japanese culture that describe the gentle nature of working through conflict. One of those is *nemawashi,* which means "root binding," or carefully binding the roots of a plant before pulling it out. The metaphor is rich, explaining to us the interpersonal smoothing process that occurs before actually taking action concerning a decision within a system. Through the broadly based consultation approach, differences are worked out and a consensus is achieved. Disagreements are resolved privately before they become causes of public stress.[13] Her example clearly helps us see how metaphors of cooperation, teamwork, win-win scenarios and the like become rhetorical devices in conversation and in documents that facilitate an attitude of conflict reduction.

Applying Systems to Proactively Preventing Conflict

We can identify conflict preventative communication strategies. While some of these are culturally based, their application can extend beyond their cultural origins.

Assuring group ownership system. One conflict-prevention strategy used in Japanese culture is the *ringi system* (often called by other names as well). This refers to the wide circulation of a document containing relevant proposals to which people up and down the organizational hierarchy affix their seals as a sign of approval. In this way, consensus is achieved and individuals feel ownership of the project. It has been said of the ringi system that it may take six months for a decision to be made, but once it is implemented, everybody is already in agreement. On the other hand, we have observed that while Americans make decisions quickly, implementation, involving standard operating procedures and acquainting the rest of the organization with an innovation, may take six months. So in the long run, there may not necessarily be any time advantage to one style over the other. Perhaps the Japanese would remind us politely that the ringi system achieves ultimate efficiency since agreement is reached before implementation.

Using the go-between system. Another conflict-prevention strategy is the *go-between* system. In this system, a neutral third party hears both sides of a disagreement or conflict. The person in this role works out differences between the two parties in ways that "save face" in the negotiation process. The exact details of how this form of negotiation works is highly culturally dependent, but its existence as a concept is important to learn. The group-harmony value of saving face in Japanese culture is illustrated by the word *wa,* or promoting group harmony. Also, the exchange of gifts, *oceiba,* and *ochugan,* favors, leads to trust and obligation. In fact, all of these interactions are supposed to take place in *kuuki,* a human atmosphere or a feeling of commonality.[14]

Another way to deal effectively with conflict is to understand deeply held cultural values and to engage those values in an appropriate way. An excellent way to visualize solution-focus in reducing conflict is to see what happens when individuals from different cultures come to work in the same organization. Consider, for example, the comparison of Japanese, American, and Yugoslavian (former) cultures presented in table 10.2. When issues of merit, promotion, and work responsibility are brought up, it is not difficult to see why cultural differences intervene in many organizational settings.[15]

Furthermore, organizational conflict can be said to have its roots in methods of decision making. Ed Stewart applies decision-making strategies within organizations to intercultural differences. His matrix assumes four types of decision-making styles relevant for our discussion. In reality, the four major categories of decision-making styles are on a continuum: technical, logical, bureaucratic group, social-collective. For some decisions one style might be more appropriate than the other. Conflict comes when people do not understand the other person's use of style or they misuse a style. For example, a technical decision style, made with relevant skills and techniques appropriate to that decision, usually involves different approaches than a social-collective decision-making style, in which a person applies intuition, emotions, and holistic themes to the problem. The conflict emerges if one thinks the other style is wrong or irrelevant for the kind of problem. It is easy to see how the two could be missing each other in their communication. Each

Interfacing with Cultural Values: The Workplace as a Case Extension of Cultural Values

Table 10.2 Organizational Culture Values

Japan	United States	Former Yugoslavia
lifelong employment	short-term employment	lifelong employment by state
slow evaluation and promotion	rapid evaluation and promotion	no evaluation/limited promotion
nonspecific job assignment	specialized career path	shifting job path
implicit control	explicit control	negotiated control
consensual decision making	individual decision making	intergroup decision making
collective responsibility	individual responsibility	individual and collaborative responsibility
collective concern	individual concern	diverse collective concern

Source: Cushman and King 1985.

expects a different set of approaches to the process of resolving conflicts, but each misses the other person's diverse decision-making style.[16]

Also, Lea Stewart reminds us that conflict arises because of the clash between decision makers in an organization and the technical people in the organization, for instance, between management and scientists. Her analysis points to certain conflict when rules are made by nonprofessionals, without regard to front-line needs. Many times different goals as well as procedures are in conflict.[17]

Decision-making styles also can lie at the root of many of our conflicts (see table 10.3). Kume compares the communication function in decision making across cultural differences. For example, the locus of the decision for American style is the individual; that is, the leader is expected to take on much responsibility. However, for Japanese the locus of the decision is in a group-collective format. These cultural procedures and styles can be very frustrating, as the following examples from Kume indicate.[18]

He first presents statements from Northern American managers' about working with Japanese:

> Usually in American companies we have one strong man. There is a definite line of decision making, but it is not clear in the Japanese decision-making process. You are never exactly sure of whose decision it was.
>
> Everybody's involved in everything. Everything is put on the table. Nothing is hidden. You may not understand the production aspects, but you listen and you learn certain things.

Communication Function for Decision Making	American Styles	Attendant American Cultural Factors	Japanese Styles	Attendant Japanese Cultural Factors
1. Locus of decision	individual leader has capacity to direct and take personal responsibility	individualism independence control of events	group leader has capacity to facilitate and take shared responsibility	collectivism interdependence group orientation
2. Initiation and coordination	top-down use of expert's information less frequent discussion	power competition self-reliance doing (get things done)	bottom (or middle) up prior consultation frequent discussion	subservience cooperation harmony being-in-becoming
3. Temporal orientation	planning ahead quick decision slow implementation	future-oriented linear thinking sense of urgency individualism	adjusting to changing circumstances slow decision immediate implementation	present oriented circular thinking gradual buildup group loyalty
4. Mode of reaching decision	individual decision majority decision split decision	choice among alternatives equal opportunity to express "matters of procedures"	consensus	acceptance of a given option conformity "tentativeness"
5. Decision criterion	"rational" practical empiricism	analytical materialistic	"intuitive" group harmony	holistic spiritual commitment
6. Communication style	direct confrontation	cognitive dichotomy	indirect agreement	affective "feeling around"

Source: Kume 1985.

In most American companies, company policy is set by executives. And in this company I see that policy can come from me and many other employees. I think it is good and more appropriate for our company.

American meetings are generally more rapid—discussion, response, discussion, while Japanese meetings seem to go on and on.

Kume also presents examples of Japanese managers responding in some positive and some negative ways, too:

I really think American people work very individually. The quality control people in manufacturing departments seldom hold meetings. They don't think it necessary to hold cross-departmental meetings.

There may be a time when it is better to age a little bit. I think it is better not to make a snap judgment or a quick decision, but to think about it a little bit and get someone else involved.

Americans take it for granted that 2 or 3 percent of the total number of products will be defective, but the Japanese managers really try to make sure that not a single product will be defective. Of course, the Japanese way will take much more time.

So whether it is American or Japanese, Asian or Latin American, Middle Eastern or European cultures, the scenario can be the same. There are differences in communication style, organizational style, value differences, and methods of decision making that can lead to frustration or promise. Our understanding of those differences marks a major milestone in successful intercultural communication where organizational cultures are involved.

Practicing Relational Empathy

Relational empathy skills and active listening form the basis for beginning the conflict management process. Empathy and especially listening involve the process of interpreting spoken messages through our communication filters, such as emotions, attitudes, and values. Unaltered, these become an obvious source of conflict. Listening involves a number of skills that usually need to be developed and managed. Studies in the U.S. indicate anywhere from 45 to 55 percent of a person's time is spent listening each day. Reasons that people are not good listeners follow.

1. *Assuming listening is hearing.* Listening is not the same as hearing. Most people have the ability to hear, a natural gift from birth. It is a fallacy, however, to assume that because we can hear, we also practice good listening skills. Billions of dollars are lost in industry every year because of poor listening and communication habits. For instance, one international manufacturing executive lost several thousand dollars one day when he discovered that the machinists did not listen to instructions on making new valves.

2. *Prejudging messages.* Sometimes we anticipate what the other person is going to say, mentally filling our minds with what we assume to be a completed message. Such prejudging is a silent interruption at best.

3. *Filtering messages.* Another fault in listening is taking out message information that we find disagreeable or threatening. One tendency is to distort such messages. Another tendency is to take out the disquieting message altogether, screening it entirely from what we heard.

A Case Study of Conflict

Kristina and Delores are two preprofessionals who are planning to work together and join a management team of six people. Their friendship was being subtly eroded through a number of small conflicts, until one week Kristina became furious with Delores. When Delores asked Kristina to come over to resolve the conflict, Kristina again erupted in anger. The wounds from the entire series of incidents surrounding this conflict took nearly a year to resolve and Delores and Kristina needed counseling and intervention by trained experts to help them overcome their hostility. Several empathy and listening principles came to light as they were asked the following questions.

1. *Assuming viewpoints were universally understood.* Generally, a person is better off to assume others do not share the same point of view and to actively listen for areas of agreement or points of difference. At least do not assume complete overlap of information. For instance, a major part of Kristina and Delores' breakdown was the assumption that they knew exactly what was in the other's mind. Delores particularly was not accustomed to clarifying her feelings with words.

2. *Interruption.* Allowing the other person to finish completely is a basic listening skill. Kristina and Delores, for example, not only prejudged the other's thoughts, they also consistently interrupted each other.

3. *Lack of positive feedback.* Good listening depends upon each person's providing encouraging, positive listening cues. In Kristina's case, she habitually looked down or put her head in her hands when Delores expressed ways to resolve their conflict.

4. *Failure to ask for information.* Active listening involves follow-up comments that ask for clarification or generally for more information. That shows the other person you are interested in the topic. Each one never asked such examples as, "Delores, the main point is clear, but I didn't get all your reasons," or "Kristina, here is an area where I feel lost; could you summarize the implications?"

5. *Presenting ego threat.* Both Kristina and Delores constantly attacked the other person. Even in the guise of honest communication, they blamed, accused, or attacked. Part of it was their competition with each other. Part was their demanding of each other.

6. *Lack of paraphrase.* A great technique in active listening is to paraphrase what the person has just said. This gentle repetition clarifies understanding and strengthens the relationship emotionally, since the other person perceives that you really are being attentive to his or her needs. Neither participant had practiced paraphrase.

---

4. *Difference in thought and talk speed.* Most people think at about 450 words per minute. Most people speak at about 150 to 175 words per minute. With such a large gap between talk and thought speed, listeners can wander off into mental excursions while another person is talking. Because of the ease of distraction, many people miss significant amounts of information from the person with whom they are interacting.

Developing Skills in Reducing Conflict

Some of the following suggestions come from Dr. Clyde Austin, noted intercultural researcher and therapist. These simple and direct techniques have been useful to many skilled communicators.

1. *Avoid emotional presentations.* Adding emotion to your message usually does not bring the ultimate benefit of conflict resolution. Crying, pouting, using silence, and anger are common emotional strategies. Unfortunately, these emotions cloud communication.

2. *Deal with one issue at a time.* Too many of us bring up an issue and then raise unresolved questions from the past. Bringing up more than one issue at a time obscures the question for now. It is better to resolve one issue at a time.

3. *Do not insist on your own way.* This suggestion comes from the Corinthian letter in the New Testament and has been labeled "steamrollering" by some authors. Some people charge into an issue and intend to get exactly what they want by manipulating any way they can. Solution-focused individuals clearly state their position, but they are not domineering and do not use power to achieve those results. Rather, they use reason and perseverance and are willing to cooperate if they do not get their way.

4. *Be clear and direct.* Say what you mean. You are not being ugly or harsh to speak what you really think.

5. *Openly admit error.* When you are wrong, say so. Without vengeance, conflict-resolvers are willing to seek for truth, not merely defend their positions.

6. *Have a coping outlook.* Assertive persons not only focus on clear analysis of a problem, but they are eager to move toward resolution of problems. They do not get stuck on problems only. In this sense, they are copers, looking for methods to resolve problems.

7. *Make "I" statements.* This technique of making "I" statements refers to owning your feelings. Rather than accusing another person ("You really don't care about me"), it is better to take responsibility for the feelings that are engendered by the other person's actions. In this case, you might say, "When you do this, I'm left with a feeling that you do not care as much as I thought you did." The value of this strategy is that it takes the pressure off the other person to defend himself. If he feels responsible for the problem, there is a tendency to see this situation as an attack. If you take the responsibility for your own feelings, then the condition can become one of objective discussion, not one of blame resulting in personal defense. Of course in certain cultures "I" statements, no matter how well intended or skillfully applied, sound arrogant and offensive. In these cases, cultural rules should override this suggestion.

8. *Develop a positive communication climate.* A major improvement to one's intercultural and interpersonal communication is to try to develop a healthy communication climate. Such a dyadic system can be improved by being supportive, nonjudgmental, spontaneous, and open-minded.

This chapter deals with communication competencies associated with conflict applied to intercultural communication. Intercultural conflict through competency-based communication concepts is improved by developing self-disclosure and thus becoming more transparent and open. The advantages of self-disclosure center around self-awareness as well as the possibility for greater trust, liking, and mental health. Other concepts involve applying an understanding of hierarchical communication (by understanding tendencies to control or manipulate, to dominate or be submissive), formality in relationships, communication in the workplace, acceptance, empathetic communication, and communication avoidance.

Management directed toward a solution-focus of intercultural conflict includes using an interpersonal balance model to facilitate liking, applying leadership systems to thinking and applications, using rhetorical styles and devices in emphasizing cultural values, and participating in building a third culture for sharing listening and relational empathy.

Exercises

1. Observe a business meeting. What variables from this chapter do you observe in the participants' communication? Give examples. Are differences rooted in culture observable?

2. Do a field study in a public setting. Compare communication effectiveness between friends with noncommunication between strangers.

3. Analyze news reports of some international conflict. What intercultural skills could have been employed?

Endnotes

1. Sidney Jourard, *The Transparent Self* (Princeton, N.J.: Van Nostrand Reinhold, 1964).

2. William B. Gudykunst, Stella Ting-Toomey, and E. Chua, *Culture and Interpersonal Communication* (Newbury Park, Calif.: Sage, 1988).

3. Christine M. Meyer and Philip Salem, "Reciprocal Self-Disclosure in Intercultural Friendships" (paper presented to the Southern States Communication Association, San Antonio, Texas, April 1992).

4. William B. Gudykunst, "An Exploratory Comparison of Close Intracultural and Intercultural Friendships," *Communication Quarterly* 33 (1985): 270–83.

5. Fathi Yousef and Nancy Briggs, "The Multinational Business Organization: A Schema for the Training of Overseas Personnel in Communication," *International and Intercultural Communication Annual* 2 (1975): 74–85.

6. Larry Sarbaugh, *Intercultural Communication* (Rochelle Park, N.J.: Hayden, 1979).

7. Jean Marie Ackermann, "Skill Training for Foreign Assignment: The Reluctant U.S. Case," in *Intercultural Communication: A Reader,* 2d ed., ed. Larry A. Samovar and Richard E. Porter (Belmont, Calif.: Wadsworth, 1976).

8. Yousef and Briggs, 1975 (see note 5).

9. Benjamin J. Broome, "Building Shared Meaning: Implications of a Relational Approach to Empathy for Teaching Intercultural Communication," *Communication Education* 40 (1991): 235–49.

10. Fritz Heider, *The Psychology of Interpersonal Relations* (New York: Wiley, 1958).

11. Robert E. Quinn and Michael R. McGrath, "The Transformation of Organizational Cultures: A Competing Values Perspective," *Organizational Culture,* ed. Peter J. Frost (Beverly Hills, Calif.: Sage, 1985).

12. Lawrence B. Nadler, Margorie Keeshan Nadler, and Benjamin J. Broome, "Culture and the Management of Conflict Situations," in *Communication, Culture, and Organizational Processes,* ed. William B. Gudykunst, Lea P. Stewart, and Stella Ting-Toomey (Newbury Park Calif.: Sage, 1985).

13. Stella Ting-Toomey, "Toward a Theory of Conflict and Culture," in *Communication, Culture, and Organizational Processes,* ed. William B. Gudykunst, Lea P. Stewart, and Stella Ting-Toomey (Newbury Park, Calif.: Sage, 1985).

14. Donald P. Cushman and Sarah Sanderson King, "National and Organizational Cultures in Conflict Resolution: Japan, the United States, and Yugoslavia," in *Communication, Culture, and Organizational Processes,* ed. William B. Gudykunst, Lea P. Stewart, and Stella Ting-Toomey (Newbury Park, Calif.: Sage, 1985).

15. Ibid., 1985.

16. Edward Stewart, *Outline of International Communication,* (Washington, D.C.: The BCIU Institute, American University, 1973).

17. Lea P. Stewart, "Subjective Culture and Organizational Decision Making," in *Communication, Culture, and Organizational Processes,* ed. William B. Gudykunst, Lea P. Stewart, and Stella Ting-Toomey (Newbury Park, Calif.: Sage, 1985).

18. Teruyuki Kume, "Managerial Attitudes Toward Decision-Making: North America and Japan," in *Communication, Culture, and Organizational Processes,* ed. William B. Gudykunst, Lea P. Stewart, and Stella Ting-Toomey (Newbury Park, Calif.: Sage, 1985); Donald P. Cushman and Sarah Sanderson King, "National and Organizational Cultures in Conflict Resolution: Japan, the United States, and Yugoslavia," in *Communication, Culture, and Organizational Processes,* ed. William B. Gudykunst, Lea P. Stewart, and Stella Ting-Toomey (Newbury Park, Calif.: Sage, 1985).

Part Five

Sources of Social Influence

on Intercultural

Communication

Chapter 11

Social Influence of Network

Cultures and Information Flow

OBJECTIVES   *After completing this chapter, you should be able to*

1. Determine how similarity/homophily influences information flow and acceptance in intercultural contacts

2. Delineate basic dimensions of homophily

3. Identify elements of intercultural credibility

4. Apply strategies to manage credibility for influence in intercultural interactions

5. Develop a model describing opinion leadership influence

6. Assess opinion leadership influence in network cultures

7. Identify information roles in social networks and their influence

One way to understand intercultural communication is to examine the interpersonal networks through which messages flow. The resulting "networking cultures" as we will term them represent distinct human information pathways through which information flows, relationships form, and influence occurs in interpersonal relationships. These webs of information pathways and their resulting influence lead us to believe these network cultures are powerful factors in considering culture and its impact on communication. Three important reasons for these information groups are the foundation for this chapter: similarity or homophily, credibility, and opinion leadership.

The Homophily Principle: The Influence of Communicator Similarity in Network Cultures

Many interpersonal relationships begin because we discover similarities that draw us toward another person. Sometimes they end because we find differences that repel us. This propensity greatly affects our intercultural relationships, for we hang mental labels on others of "similar" or "different" and often act in a manner consistent with our evaluation.

Imagine for a moment an ambassador from Saudi Arabia talking with an ambassador from Sweden; a British agricultural extension representative attempting to persuade a Boran herdsman from Kenya; a middle-class Anglo selling furniture to urban ethnic group members; or an Anglo school teacher persuading a Mexican American community to adopt youth recreation programs. Each of these situations involves potential circumstances where understanding how information flows through personal networks is important.

A fundamental focus of our model in this text is how perceived differences can prevent clarity and foster mutual suspicion, distrust, and ambivalence. This perception of difference is a primary assumption about intercultural communication: the need to recognize differences and to adapt through communication. The term referring to differences between two people is *heterophily.* The degree of similarity is called *homophily.* The tendency to communicate with those similar to us is called the *homophily principle.* Furthermore, clusters of individuals in information sharing networks form around similarity as one dimension of communication relationship development.

Dimensions of Homophily

Actually, homophily or similarity between people is defined in terms of several factors. These dimensions are analogous to internal measures on a similarity-difference continuum. No wonder this concept is important to intercultural communication, for it explains a fundamental social perception system that explains what happens to information between people.

Physical homophily. In general, persons who have similar physical characteristics judge one another as similar. This feeling applies not only to generalized appearance, but also to looks, size, and even clothing. The problem of cultural stereotyping is partly related to this perceived factor. For instance, a North American and a Saudi see each other approaching in a hallway. Based solely on appearance, they may come to the mutual, though silent, conclusion, "This person is different from me." In turn, that heterophily perception may precipitate little more than a greeting—or worse, hostility. Many people close their thinking at the point of appearance only.

According to the homophily principle, we tend to interact with other individuals similar in social characteristics. © Owen Franken/Stock Boston.

Background homophily.   We also judge others on our perceptions of age, education, residence, and other demographic features, ratings of similarity that we call background homophily. In many diversity culture studies, the gap between the higher and lower social classes is well known. In these cases information typically passes within a social class. In other words, homophily was so predominant that information did not "spill over" to outside groups differing in background homophily.[1]

Attitude homophily.   Attitude homophily includes similarity of personal attitudes and opinions. These similarities are attractive to forming and maintaining friendships, and as Shuter implies, integral in intercultural relationship formation.[2]

Value homophily.   Another element of homophily is a perception of similarity in morality, sexual norms, ways of treating people, and other general values. Value homophily, sometimes referred to as morality homophily, requires an assessment of long-enduring judgments of good and bad conceptions. As an illustration, consider cultural values in Sweden's antispanking law, which prohibits parents from spanking their children. The reasons advanced for this law included norms of antiviolence and arguments that spanking would lead to child beating and abuse. Various microcultures disagreed, claiming that it stripped parents of their natural rights to correct their children by what they consider tried and proven methods. At its root, this clash focuses on values of protection on one hand and values of physical punishment as a means to a greater end on the other hand.

Personality homophily.   In addition to these other dimensions of homophily, people also perceive similarity or dissimilarity of personality. Research studies indicate that we attribute greater feelings of friendship and attraction to people we perceive as similar to us. Also, friends are more similar in personality than non-friends, according to studies comparing friendship pairs.[3]

These factors make it plain to see how we might perceive cultural differences thus affecting and initiating intercultural communication. These are bold areas of assessing differences between people.

Many times we obtain information from interpersonal networking cultures with daily reference group relationships—friends, family, work associates. The homophily principle explains the theory behind the influence and why we develop the networks we do. As a result of similarity, information is received more readily and persuasion occurs more frequently, as many of the following concepts from Rogers' prolific research indicates.[4]

The Homophily Principle and Intercultural Communication

Homophily information sharing. The consequence of homophily is best described in the homophily principle, which is to say that we share information with similar persons. Consequently, communication is generally more effective than heterophilous communication. A number of examples reflect the homophily principle: political voting choices are usually discussed among people of similar age and education; farmers talk with other farmers perceived to have attitude and value homophily; Chicago inner-city dwellers talk about family planning with other inner-city dwellers of similar social status, age, marital status, and family size; Indian villagers discuss social questions with other villagers of similar caste, education, and farm size. In general, information is usually shared within background homophily social strata.[5] In study after study, the model presented in figure 11.1 seems to capture the usual flow of information highlighting homophily in network cultures.

Homophily and persuasion. Research indicates that homophily can facilitate persuasion. In wide ranging studies, from laboratories to field studies with farm practices, a significant body of literature supports the contention that homophily not only acts to open information between people, but it serves in social influence. As homophily increases, there is a corresponding increase in information acceptance, thus depicting one part of networking cultures indicated in figure 11.2.

This principle is further illustrated in a classic scientific research effort in which researchers followed the prescribing of a new drug in a New England community among physicians practicing in the community. Not only did they discover the predominance of clique groups (figure 11.3), or what we are calling networking cultures, but also the extreme similarity among group members in age, ethnicity, religion, father's occupation, and specialty. Furthermore, adoption of the new drug followed lines of clique group membership, so that clique groups, marked by their homophily, tended to adopt around the same time.[6] These classic studies have been followed by recent network theory development which confirms how information and influence are primary outcomes of networking cultures.[7]

Optimal heterophily. There is a range of tolerable difference in information relationships called *optimal heterophily*. This concept clearly recognizes a simple fact: if two people are perfectly homophilous, then one would know little more information

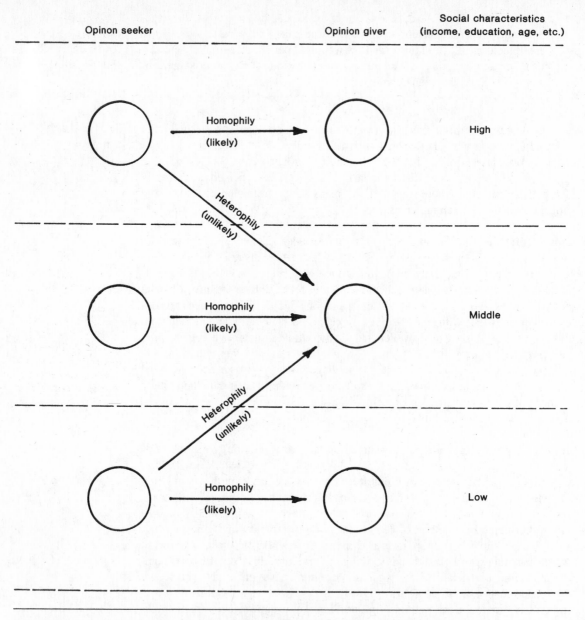

Figure 11.1

Homophily principle: people communicate and share information with individuals similar in social characteristics.

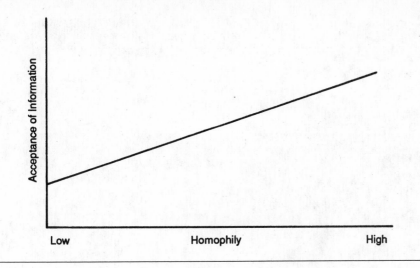

Figure 11.2

Acceptance of information increases as homophily increases.

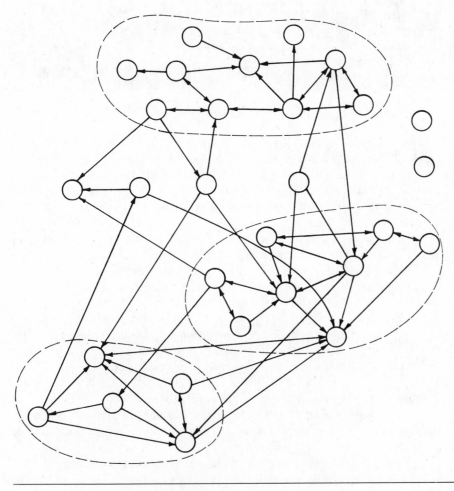

Figure 11.3

Illustration of new drug diffusion among New England physicians. The study showed who talked with whom on social occasions. Clique groups tended to adopt simultaneously.

In traditional towns and villages, information tends to flow horizontally and informally among people with homophilous social characteristics, illustrated by this Moroccon town. © Dave Bartruff/Corbis.

than the other. That makes good friendship, but neither knows more than the other. Problem! Solution? Seek a person heterophilous in knowledge, but homophilous enough in social characteristics to feel socially comfortable. For instance, suppose an Ethiopian villager was deciding upon a new type of seed for seasonal planting on the farm. Depending upon motivation, the farmer would need information from someone more knowledgeable than he and yet someone with whom he could identify. A scientist might be too heterophilous and a close relative too homophilous. Ideally, the farmer could discover someone with homophily in some characteristics but heterophily in knowledge. This situation calls for optimal heterophily.

So how do similarity and networking cultures affect me? I don't live in a village—or in another country. These principles are described for two reasons. First, social networks in many parts of the world are major social forces. It is difficult to fully comprehend the dynamics of many cultures without understanding this closeness and interpersonal bonding. The sense of bonding is particularly strong in collectivist cultures, according to Ting-Toomey. In fact, perceptions of similarity form a major axis upon which social identity is built.[8] Being identified with a significant group has enormous implications for self-worth. Even in individualistic cultures, many find strength in the homogeneity among the group membership. For this reason, we can better understand the network dynamics of unity among peer groups and friendship groups.

Second, similarity theory explains our tendency to cluster around in-groups and to avoid out-groups. In-groups hold attraction and the promise of self-worth. The comfort zone reflected here is common within cultures. As long as we remain in a cocoon of network similarity, we lose the power inherent in difference. We learn, grow, and develop when interaction includes some differences. The opposite breeds ethnocentrism, negative stereotypes, and bias. That is not to mention the possibility of incomplete or inaccurate data. The studies of groupthink remind us of the political, social, and economic disasters resulting from intolerance of difference.

One method for measuring homophily is the use of a scale, primarily focusing on interpersonal dimensions of perceived homophily.[9] This scale, shown in table 11.1, has high reliability and has demonstrated across samples of high school, college, and adult populations, though mostly in the United States. By asking respondents for their attitudes toward a target individual, the higher the number (after appropriate reversal from 1 to 7 and 7 to 1 for opposite worded items) the greater the perceived homophily.

Measuring Homophily

In addition to similarity-dissimilarity (homophily-heterophily), intercultural information is influenced by the perceived credibility of another person. To be effective, as A and B develop a successful third culture C between them, they must each perceive believability or else motivation to use competence and communication adjustment may be missing.

Intercultural Credibility and Network Cultures

As a result of several efforts similar to the presentation by Helen Sohns indicated in the cultural insight, villagers had a greater sense of trust from the birth attendants in this traditional setting and found them calling upon her much more frequently and readily. The villagers not only perceived trust, but expertness and a certain oneness with this nurse, or, as she went on to state, "They do not regard me as a rival now, but as a colleague."

This case identifies a common question when people are speaking or listening. How can I reduce my uncertainty or anxiety about this person? There is a dynamic perception on the part of listeners causing them to interpersonally believe or disbelieve, trust or mistrust, praise or blame. What are those qualities perceived between people? Intercultural credibility alters our relationships and impacts the information roles among networking cultures.

Credibility is a multidimensional perceptual concept.[11] It is also cultural in nature, or as Pennington states " . . . the phenomenon of interpersonal power and influence operates across cultural lines"[12] The first dimension of intercultural credibility we will examine in this section is competence.

Intercultural Competence

Competence indicates that the influential people in a network culture have knowledge, insight, credentials, qualification, information, or expertise. It refers to the ability to conduct a task well and have others believe in your ability to conduct tasks. We might examine competence in two ways.

1. *Competence by power.* Sometimes individuals are competent because of power. Power itself is frequently related to (1) role or position (like the chief of a village, a medicine healer, money and status, etc.), (2) the ability to reward

Table 11.1   Scale for Perceived Homophily

With a person in mind, evaluate the similarity or difference between you and the person you have selected using the following evaluation items.

Attitude Dimension

Doesn't think like me:	1 2 3 4 5 6 7	:Thinks like me
*Behaves like me:	1 2 3 4 5 6 7	:Doesn't behave like me
*Similar to me:	1 2 3 4 5 6 7	:Different from me
Unlike me:	1 2 3 4 5 6 7	:Like me

Background Dimension

*From social class similar to mine:	1 2 3 4 5 6 7	From social class different :from mine
Economic situation different from mine:	1 2 3 4 5 6 7	Economic situation like :mine
*Status like mine:	1 2 3 4 5 6 7	:Status different from mine
Background different from mine:	1 2 3 4 5 6 7	:Background similar to mine

Value Dimension

Morals unlike mine:	1 2 3 4 5 6 7	:Morals like mine
Sexual attitudes unlike mine:	1 2 3 4 5 6 7	:Sexual attitudes like mine
*Shares my values	1 2 3 4 5 6 7	:Doesn't share my values
*Treats people as I do:	1 2 3 4 5 6 7	:Doesn't treat people as I do

Appearance Dimension

*Looks similar to me:	1 2 3 4 5 6 7	:Looks different from me
Different size than I am:	1 2 3 4 5 6 7	:Same size I am
*Appearance like mine:	1 2 3 4 5 6 7	:Appearance unlike mine
Doesn't resemble me:	1 2 3 4 5 6 7	:Resembles me

Source: McCroskey, Richmond, and Daly 1975.
*Scale for these items should be scored in reverse direction, 7 to 1.

Credibility and Persuasion

A few years ago, Helen Sohns, a German nurse, worked among the Mataco Indians at the northernmost part of Argentina's border and described her attempts to introduce better birth delivery techniques. At first, the Indian women eyed her suspiciously, but gradually, after a series of special lessons for birth attendants, her credibility as a trusted source increased. She particularly credited the following message, presented during her lessons, for some of her increased credibility:

When you make bread, you need flour; when your husband makes a chair, he needs wood (most men here are carpenters). In the same way, woman in whose body a baby is growing needs enough food to form the baby's body. If she does not have enough food, the baby will be weak, and her own body will suffer and get weak. Have you noticed how the women's teeth go bad after having a baby? That is because the baby takes what it needs to form its bones, and the mother's body suffers. Now, your custom is that a woman who is expecting a baby must eat very little during the last three months so that the baby will be small. It is true that we do not want an enormously big baby that will cause difficulty in delivery, but we do want a strong baby. There are some foods that make a person fat, such as bread, noodles, sugar, semolina, rice, etc. It is right that an expectant mother should not eat too much of these. But there are other foods which give a lot of strength and do not make a person fat, such as meat, fish, eggs, milk, fruit, and vegetables. A pregnant woman should eat plenty of these, so that the baby will be strong without being fat.

Source: Helen Sohns.[10]

---

or punish, or (3) power because of some kind of hero or celebrity status. This type of competence is illustrated in statements of transplanted Jews who were influenced by competent rabbis in their new home: We do not want only to hear orders from far away people, even if they are very wise and know everything. Our rabbis know that the best way is to gather all of us in the synagogue and to tell us about it and to explain it to us. Otherwise, we do not listen. . . .

In our place, they (old leaders) were really very important and honored as they knew everything about our tradition, how to arrange things, the right ways to behave. But here it changes, it is otherwise. . . . They do not always understand this, and they cannot help us in getting our way here. That is why I became interested in the new (political) organizations and frequent these meetings. The organizers here are really important people and know how to advise you, and so some of us are going there.[13]

2. *Competence by information.* Those who hold relevant or significant information also hold influence and persuasive ability. What is defined as relevant and significant, of course, is culturally dependent.

Intercultural Trust

Trust, honesty, unselfishness, virtuousness, and character—these also create feelings of high credibility. During the cold war years of the 1950s, for example, the credibility gap between the United States and the former Soviet Union was a trust gap. Neither side could be certain that the other would not trigger a nuclear war. The tensions became so great that steps were taken to ease the tension that threatened a world holocaust. According to analyses by Windt, for the Russians to be successful in gaining their concessions, Khrushchev needed to alter America's perception of his being a "communist devil" to one of his being a trustworthy source. During his visit to the United States in September of 1959, Khrushchev attempted to create credibility by appearing trustworthy. For instance, in the Camp David talks with President Eisenhower, he modified his position and thus gave Americans "one piece of evidence that Khrushchev was not as unreasonable as he had been portrayed" for he "contributed to a modification of our perceptions of him. He conveyed the shadow, if not the substance, of a reasonable politician, a man prepared to negotiate." In contrast to a demagogue like Hitler, bent on world destruction, Khrushchev was entirely different. A preacher of peace and understanding, he looked more like a businessman than a politician. One reporter likened him to "any prosperous, hard-working, penny-pinching farmer who has reached the chairmanship of the local school board by sheer weight of his own toilsome success with the field." Furthermore, he had a sense of humor that he displayed publicly and often turned on himself. His wife, Nina Petrovna, added to his image. No Mata Hari she, but rather a kind and gentle-looking matron who moved another American reporter to write: "There was the feeling that anyone who had the good sense to marry her, stay married to her, and bring her over here couldn't be all villain, no matter what he was doing during Stalin's regime."[14] In this way, Khrushchev skillfully replaced the devil image with that of a trusted politician, or as Windt continued, "His agile and human responses to situations conveyed to the American people a leader who broke the mold of their stereotyped dictator."

In other historical examples, President Jimmy Carter's successful peace negotiations during the Camp David talks in 1978 between Prime Minister Begin of Israel and President Sadat of Egypt stressed trust and sincerity. Carter's respect for both leaders, his high expectations, and his encouraging an atmosphere of ultimate trust lead to the historic settlement. It is unlikely that such success would have occurred had President Carter held ethnocentric attitudes, mistrust, or lack of respect toward either of the other men. In sharp contrast, the Beijing massacre of June 1989 revealed little or no trust, only coercive power. The deathly aroma of powder-burned, lifeless bodies testifies to the ill effects of credibility gone sour.

The first Rodney King trial of 1992 in which four Los Angeles police officers were tried and acquitted for beating black motorist Rodney King, lead to extraordinary riots in Los Angeles. The lack of trust in particular and low credibility overall in the judicial system was a major factor in this situation.

Intercultural Similarity

According to Tuppen, another factor of credibility is similarity, or a perception of oneness or commonality. People judge other people by their value systems, group memberships, likability, and personal goals and quickly form attitudes based solely on those characteristics.[15] One of the goals in intercultural communication is to give your cocommunicator the perception of wanting the same things, or in other words, to establish coorientation. The German nurse's communication, as noted earlier, clearly sought to establish identification with the villagers, as if to say, "We truly want the same things—we have a common goal."

Other historical examples visualize this point, as in the case of Indonesian President Achmed Sukarno's speech to the United Nations in 1970, in which he clearly allied himself with a prevailing theme at that time of rule by the will of the people in the third world.

"Today, it is President Sukarno who addresses you. But more than that, though, it is a man. Sukarno, an Indonesian, a husband, a father, a member of the human family. I speak to you on behalf of my people, those ninety-two million people of a distant and wide archipelago, those ninety-two million who have lived a life of struggle and sacrifice, those ninety-two million people who have built a State upon the ruins of an empire."[16] One of the crucial mistakes of third world leaders may well be their failure to establish a perceived similarity between themselves and their people. In not coorienting themselves with their people, leaders of nations can suffer dire consequences, as Prosser wrote in this same volume.

In a perceptive research article dealing with political communicator credibility, Larry Winn called attention to a fact of political ethos that applies to intercultural credibility. Blending historical forces, Gallup Poll findings, and a factor analysis of the Carter-Ford presidential debates of 1976, Winn concluded that credibility depends upon rhythms of history. Apparently, for a given people, political communicator credibility depends on cycles of history, which in turn dictates their demand for certain dimensions of political ethos. For instance, Winn's factor analysis revealed four major factors in the Carter-Ford debates: leadership, consubstantiality, trustworthiness, and dynamism. Ford scored higher on leadership, but Carter scored higher on the consubstantiality dimension, which was defined broadly but similarly to coorientation. Winn anticipated the ultimate victory by Carter, since American history was ripe for a sense of plain-folks commonality in a post-Watergate era. At another time in history, the coorientation of Jimmy Carter may have yielded to a perception of authority and leadership of some other political candidate, which may explain the 1980, 1984, and 1988 Reagan-Bush victories. In 1992 and 1996 the Clinton victories may indicate the curve has turned again toward the coorientation dimension.

The point of Winn's study for our discussion is that history repeats norms significant to communicator credibility. During one period of a culture's history, coorientation may indeed be the most important factor in establishing credibility. Another era may demand high leadership or power, depending on historical rhythms. This insight suggests that we sensitize ourselves to culturally preferred and culturally diverse avenues of credibility.[17]

Intercultural Charisma

Another element of intercultural communicator credibility is *charisma*. Charisma is a type of leadership based on (1) a leader's extraordinary claim to remedy a distressful situation, and (2) an acceptance of this leadership. To put it another way, when people believe that a person has special gifts or powers to lead them out of a crisis, charismatic leadership can take root, depending on the strength of the leader's claim. For instance, many British citizens believed Winston Churchill to be extraordinarily talented and accepted his charismatic authority to lead England out of World War II. In a sadly tragic direction, Jim Jones led converts to accept his messianic role as cult leader and to believe that he was the only one able to deliver them from various world crises, including nuclear fallout and worldly concerns.

While an in-depth exploration of charismatic leadership is the subject of an extensive work by Max Weber and later writers interpreting Weber, the following are five characteristics of charisma as a part of credibility.

Charisma accrues when followers accept. Each of the factors of credibility is perceptual in some ways, but charisma is especially dependent upon the followers' faith that the charismatic figure can lead them into a promising future.[18] The point of charismatic leadership depending upon a foundation of follower acceptance is illustrated in the story of Fidel Castro's rise to charismatic status, as Fagen indicated:

> The theme of historical blessedness and protection received popular reinforcement from the circumstances surrounding Castro's return to Cuba from Mexico in 1956 with eighty-two men and the avowed purpose of overthrowing Batista. Only Castro and eleven others escaped to the Sierra Maestra, where they launched the guerrilla action which culminated in the downfall of Batista two years later. All the elements of high drama and miraculous escape were attached to the story of the guerrilla band during these two years. At one time, Castro was reported dead, and subsequently, a price of $100,000 was set on his head.[19]

Charisma is contextual. Charismatic leaders arise during times of extraordinary stress. In this way, charisma is contextual, so that a charismatic leader in one situation may be ineffective in another, or as Fagen emphasized, "there are no universal charismatics." There is no "right time" for a charismatic leader to emerge; such leaders arise not because of facilitating conditions but often because of adversity. For example, a man like Churchill could inspire his listeners to visualize victory, despite Germany's devastating air strikes on England during World War II. Each crisis context seems to produce charismatic leaders who believe in their control over the destiny of a particular crisis, much like Churchill, DeGaulle, and Roosevelt during an intense saga of world history.[20]

In her analysis of the well-publicized Jesse Jackson visit to Syria in December 1983 to seek the release of hostage Robert Goodman, Pennington concluded that Jackson's success in influencing the ultimate release in 1984 was partly trust, but largely a context-specific multidimensional charismatic leadership. Pennington associated Jackson's communication style with sincerity, religiosity, morality, and personal trust toward the Syrians, a feature perhaps difficult to duplicate at another historical time. His charismatic style is evident in Pennington's article: "I didn't come here on a mission seeking justice. I didn't come here because America is morally correct. I came on a mission of mercy. I don't argue the rightness or wrongness of Goodman. I am seeking mercy and the lowering of the temperature of war so that peace may come."[21] His ability to raise the context above politicality to morality and spirituality may well have matched a middle eastern cultural view of credibility as personalized and passionate, features more resonant with nonwestern cultures than logical-reductionist arguments or deductions of right and wrong, according to Pennington.

Charisma is missionary.   The charismatic leader is highly motivated toward a mission, which Max Weber described as "new, outside the realm of everyday routine, extraordinary and revolutionary." The leader believes in shaping the destiny and history of his or her people. There is a type of bond, an identification between leader and led, that makes the leader's appeal one of a "secular savior."[22]

Beyond mass perception, the charismatic leader's self-concept is one of master of history, transcending the moral order of things and inspiring the people to maintain their confidence in the leader. Under stressful conditions, such as poverty, war, and despair, it is possible that leaders like Hitler can convince nations of their mission. Charismatic leaders like Ghandi, Churchill, Roosevelt, and Martin Luther King believed in their task and perhaps viewed themselves as extraordinary people able to lead their nations from stress into victory.

Charisma is unstable over time.   A key element in Max Weber's classic work on charisma is that charisma is effervescent—but over time, the charismatic leader usually suffers a demise. Again Fagen interpreting Weber cited several reasons why charisma is short lived. One reason is that the leader's image of infallibility is naturally tarnished because of inevitable failures, leading writers to note a "natural entropy of the hero's charisma." A second reason, according to Weber, is that the charismatic leader, over time, naturally must attend to the affairs of state, a concern that causes the leader to be perceived as bureaucratic. This new image stands contradictory to the charismatic leader's earlier denunciation of the previous regime and thus produces a popularity loss. This circumstance, caused by the need to attend to daily administration, is called the *routinization of charisma.*[23]

Charisma is passed on by social ritual.   Almost every culture has ways of passing on official charisma or charisma of the office. Power is passed on by ceremonies, charms, incantations, and the like. In the Serbian culture, for instance, the mother spits over the head of her baby in a religious initiation ceremony as a method of passing on blessings and a good spirit. Many cultures practice "laying on" hands as a way of passing on special powers. Coronations of kings and inauguration ceremonies of heads of states illustrate formalized ways that cultures imbue recipients with impersonal charisma as Thomas Dow notes.

A final element in intercultural credibility is dynamism, which refers to enthusiasm and personal involvement. Dynamism is often described in terms appraising a communicator's aggressiveness, empathic nature, boldness, activity, and energy.

Intercultural Dynamism

Dynamism certainly intersects with charisma, since a charismatic leader is often dynamic. The key ingredients for dynamism involve verbal and nonverbal elements. The inflammatory rhetoric of terrorism, for instance, is marked by dynamic qualities both in rhetoric and in terrorist action. Campus protests are often remembered for their dynamic qualities. African rhetoric and preaching is highly dynamic and stylized in its performance.[24]

We must recognize that the mix of competence, trust, similarity, charisma, and dynamism depend on their relative importance in a group or culture. Many intercultural situations demand a strong dynamic quality, for many cultures do not

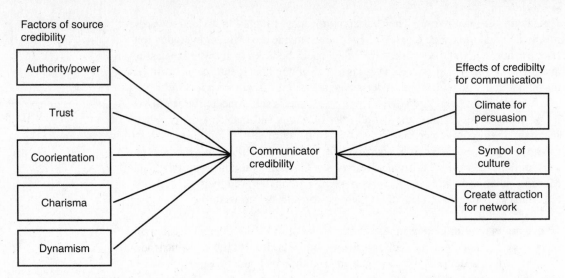

Factors of source credibility

Authority/power

Trust

Coorientation

Charisma

Dynamism

Communicator credibility

Effects of credibilty for communication

Climate for persuasion

Symbol of culture

Create attraction for network

Communicator credibility
and its effects.

share European and North American emphasis upon scientific proof and logic. In fact, persuasion in parts of Africa and Latin America occurs in significant measure through emotional appeal and dynamic delivery, not syllogisms and cold logic.

The Effects of Intercultural Credibility

1. *Persuasion.* The first effect of credibility in the intercultural situation is its effect on persuasion. Writers as far back as Aristotle confirm that communicators perceived as highly credible are more persuasive than communicators with low credibility.

2. *Cultural identity.* Communicator credibility symbolizes a culture and identity. This quality makes credibility an important ingredient in networking cultures.

3. *Attraction.* A final effect of credibility is the ability of credible persons to attract and influence others. The very fact that people are in a group network testifies to friendship and the mutual believability of peers.

Opinion Leadership and Network Cultures

Several years ago, while conducting fieldwork in Africa, I learned an important lesson about opinion leadership. One purpose of this trip was to speak with large numbers of villagers and to collect data for my dissertation. Upon entering a village where few foreign outsiders had traversed for a while, I went directly to the chief's hut—though not without the fanfare of a couple of dozen children and about half a dozen dogs. Although the chief was meeting with the other elders of that village, my arrival seemed no bother, and they welcomed me. After a visit of some forty-five minutes, in which I explained the purpose of my visit and engaged in conversation of several current topics, the chief suddenly asked me, to my surprise, if I wanted them to ring the gong. Being too embarrassed to question what the gong was, I simply said yes. With such affirmation, the chief and other lead-

Opinion leadership
lends interpersonal
influence in a culture
of information flow.
© Bob Daemmrich/
Stock Boston.

ers went to the front of the chief's hut and rang a large bell, after which all the village family heads gathered within a matter of minutes. Unfortunately, I was speechless by the process, so that the few words I spoke were probably not worth the trouble it had taken the villagers to gather. However, the remainder of my stay in that village was filled with warm receptions from many households.

This incident solidifies a number of elements of a larger concern—and a principle of intercultural communication often discussed in the literature as opinion leadership. My going to the chief and village leaders tapped an interpersonal network that legitimized my work in that village. Within any cultural system, individuals develop informational and social networks.

Opinion Leaders as Information Roles in Network Cultures

In one sense, every person we meet has some influence on our decisions, but all people do not exert equal amounts of influence. Those individuals, however, who have a greater influence on the opinions of others are called opinion leaders.

By definition, opinion leadership is not necessarily large-scale community leadership. Rather, people influence people informally where respect and communication exists. There is a web of interpersonal relationships from villages to modern cities.

The discovery of opinion leadership in the interpersonal network sense emerged from an unlikely set of studies. For almost the first half of this century, people assumed that the mass media were all powerful, able to sway passive audiences, shaping them into a malleable culture moved by the whims of those who controlled the mass media. Second World War propaganda in Nazi Germany, Orson Welles's "War of the Worlds" broadcast in 1938, and the influence of Madison Avenue advertising in electronic and print media created a perception of mass media power. This theory of mass media was called the *hypodermic needle theory* and conveyed an image of a message being injected into the minds of passive audience members.

However, researchers using this model overlooked the important information roles interpersonal networks play. When the book *The People's Choice* by Lazarsfeld, Berelson, and Gaudet first documented the influence of communication on voters' choices during the 1940 presidential election, they were convinced their study would demonstrate mass media influence contributing to voters' decisions in elections. To their surprise, they discovered that fewer voter choices were influenced directly by the media than by interpersonal sources. When these interpersonal sources appeared to influence three or more people, they were called opinion leaders.

In another now classic study, Steinfatt, Gantz, Seibold, and Miller highlighted the importance of interpersonal sources of communication in serious news events, such as assassinations.[25] They compared several cities for news sources and reported the predominance of interpersonal communication sources for the following events:

Event	*Percent Hearing from Interpersonal Sources*
1. John F. Kennedy assassination	
a. San Jose, California, sample	50 percent
b. Iowa City, Iowa, sample	55 percent
c. Dallas, Texas, sample	57 percent
2. George Wallace assassination attempt	70 percent

Not only do these figures accentuate the importance of interpersonal communication sources in news events, but they illustrate the prominent role of interpersonal communication networks.

Starosta underscored the highly interpersonal nature of information sources within Ceylon. "These disquieting conclusions are replicated in my own field study of three villages in central Ceylon, where many villagers relied almost exclusively on the words of neighbors, shopkeepers, and "others in the market" for their information. . . . The radio set or the newspaper is always to some degree an intruder. The villager who would have a prescribed ritualistic response for his dealings with the village headman might be overwhelmed by the tremendous volume of ideas that would flow from the media to the degree where he would set up defenses against the influx of impersonal and alien stimuli."[26] This relative value of interpersonal networking has been documented in numerous studies across dozens of other cultures.

Not all interpersonal communication is with opinion leaders, but all relationships with opinion leaders are interpersonal. Because this bond is unique, subtle, and influential, it represents a significant intercultural communication role relationship.

Communication Characteristics of Opinion Leaders

By noting the communication qualities associated with opinion leadership in networks, we do not mean to suggest that the concept is static or one-way from leader-to-follower. The relationship is subtle and dynamic. Influence goes two ways. When

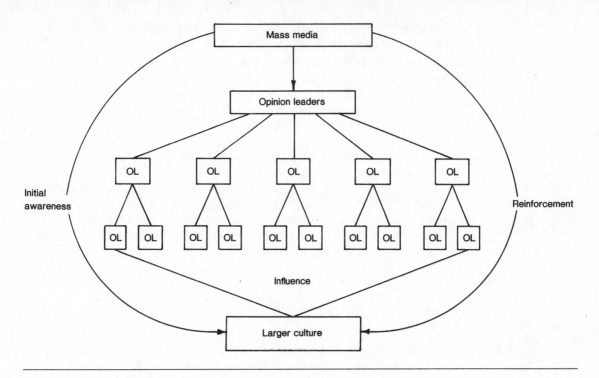

Figure 11.4

Multistep flow of information.

we isolate, for purposes of analysis, the apparent leadership qualities of individuals within networking cultures, some evident communication characteristics emerge.

Information competency.   Opinion leaders have interest, accuracy, and familiarity with the issues. They are information rich and are exposed to relevant mass media and interpersonal sources including other opinion leaders to gain information access.[27] Their relationship to interpersonal communication sources is pictured in figure 11.4 which illustrates a multistep flow of information.[28]

Interpersonal communication competency.   In addition to their information sufficiency, opinion leaders practice interpersonal communication competency. One way is their ability to pass on quality advice. Decisions concerning grazing domains among herdsmen in Kenya, for instance, are made through respected leaders who pass on advice, decisions, and information through dialogue. A second way they are communication competent is their high quantity of contact.

Personal openness and accessibility.   A third quality of communication is their openness. Driskill and Dodd found opinion leaders scored higher on a communication openness index and concluded that communication access is a vital part of understanding the opinion leadership relationship.[29]

Range of opinion leadership: monomorphic and polymorphic.   In some cultures, opinion leadership is *monomorphic,* meaning that a person is an opinion leader in a specialized topic. Monomorphic opinion leaders are influential in a limited field, while *polymorphic* leadership works with more than one topic.[30]

Researchers seem to agree that monomorphic styles appear more in technical information cultures, while polymorphic styles are associated with less technically information concerned cultures. Studies have found also that polymorphic opinion leaders are more likely to be "super OL's" who influence a larger network of people than monomorphic opinion leaders who typically work within very small networks.[31]

Overall, opinion leaders function as sources of information and evaluation. Persuasive efforts are likely to be more effective when the message is focused toward opinion leaders, who in turn influence, or at least pass on information, among those homogeneous groupings of people with whom they typically interact (figure 11.5).

Figure 11.5

Opinion-leadership communication as part of a social network. Opinion leaders pass information on to those they influence, and opinion leaders influence one another within a cultural communication network.

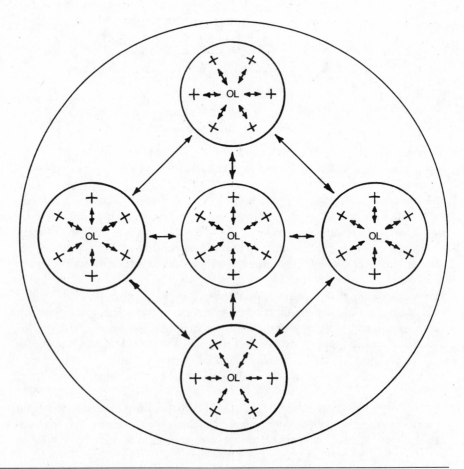

Table 11.2	Comparison of Opinion Leadership Assessment Techniques	

Technique	Concept	Example
1. Sociometric choice	Ask respondents to whom they go for information and advice about a particular topic.	A respondent says: "I go to person A for information about a new type of seed."
2. Self-report	Ask respondent if anyone has sought his or her advice over a certain period of time.	Person A responds: "Yes, three people have asked me about this new type of seed."
3. Key informant report	Ask a person of the culture in question to tell you who is influential on specific questions.	The informant indicates: "Well, most people would probably go to Person A, since he really understands new things about farming."

Over a period of years, three techniques have proved useful for assessing opinion leadership: the sociometric choice technique, the self-report technique, and the key informant report. From all indications, while these three techniques generally produce similar results, they are presented in rank order in table 11.2 which summarizes the methods.[32]

Measuring Opinion Leadership

Sociometric choice technique. With the sociometric choice technique, the researcher asks the respondent to whom that person would go for information or advice or both about a particular topic. The exact nature of the specific question depends upon the culture, the topic under consideration, and so on. Typically, however, the sociometric choice technique asks respondents for their choice of a person in specific categories, some of which are noted in the following.

1. *Value relationship.* Asking the respondents which people they value for the way they do their work. *Example:* "Which two farmers do you consider good farmers?"

2. *Communication-task relationship.* Asking the respondents to whom they would most likely go for advice regarding a decision. *Example:* "To whom would you likely go for advice on adopting a new farm program?"

3. *Communication-social relationship.* Asking the respondents with whom they like to socialize. *Example:* "With which two farmers do you most frequently visit?"

4. *Liking relationship.* Asking the respondents which people they like the most. *Example:* "Which farmers do you like the most?"

Self-report technique. The self-report technique is largely a matter of asking respondents if anyone has asked information of them over a certain period of time. For instance, a typical question might ask if anyone has specifically asked for advice on certain topics within the last month. If a respondent reports that he or she has had as many as three or more requests for information, then there is a likelihood that the respondent is an opinion leader.

Key informant report.   A third method of locating opinion leaders is to ask a key informant of the culture for that person's analysis of people to whom others go for information and advice concerning topics under consideration. This method extends ethnomethodology by working closely with informants who typify the culture in question. These informants are more than "guides," for they should be able to discuss a number of factors about the culture and serve as translators (when necessary); many times they provide excellent case studies.

Interpersonal Relationships and Information Roles as Sources in Network Cultures

Homophily, credibility, and opinion leadership are major reasons why informal networking cultures evolve. Homophily heightens attraction and information sharing; credibility opens believability and influence; opinion leaders facilitate information flow and influence while also networking with still other opinion leaders. The term networking culture in this text refers to a *communication network* formed by the flow of information between individuals in a system. As Weimann defines it, a communication network is stable over time, predictive of behavior, and is a major part of a culture's social structure. The basic concept is to ask "Who talks with whom?" When these associations are determined the result is an interconnected group of individuals exhibiting a patterned flow of information between them.[33]

First, however, it is important to understand the structure of a network. When an entire organization or system is the unit of analysis, communication flow between members of the system results in a *sociogram*. A sociogram shows who talks with whom. The smaller groups of friends or associates are cliques. A *clique* is a subgroup within the larger system whose members interact more often with each other than with other members of the network.

Second, the individuals within a communication network are *nodes* who may or may not hold role and communication functions, such as opinion leadership. A *link* is the communication tie between nodes (on the individual level of analysis) or between cliques, organizations, and cultures (on a group level of analysis). Examples of links are illustrated in figures 11.6 and 11.7 by the lines between people inside and outside the cliques.

Third, members play certain information roles. *Gatekeepers* let information pass into a clique. *Opinion leaders* evaluate information and are sought out for their advice. *Liaisons* link two or more cliques but themselves are not members of any one clique. *Bridges* are members of one clique who link information to another clique. *Cosmopolites* link the entire network or system to other outside networks. *Isolates* have no links. *Dyadic isolates* link with each other but have no other contact. Weimann's research cited above describes how the *intragroup* flow of information is orchestrated by the centrally positioned people, such as gatekeepers and opinion leaders. The *intergroup* flow of information is carried out by people outside the cliques, such as liaisons or cosmopolites.

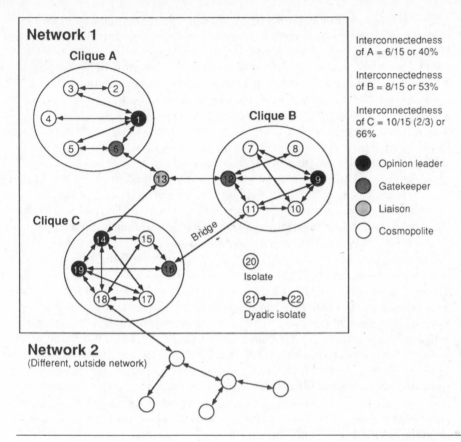

Network 1

Clique A

Clique B

Clique C

Bridge

Network 2
(Different, outside network)

Interconnectedness
of A = 6/15 or 40%

Interconnectedness
of B = 8/15 or 53%

Interconnectedness
of C = 10/15 (2/3) or
66%

● Opinion leader

● Gatekeeper

● Liaison

○ Cosmopolite

20 Isolate

21 ← → 22
Dyadic isolate

Figure 11.6

Sample network
analysis.

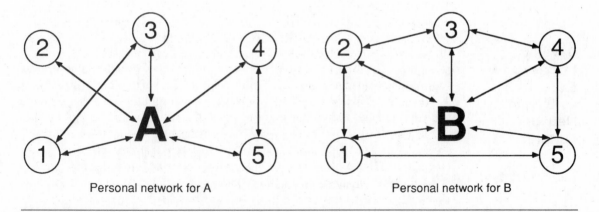

Personal network for A

Personal network for B

Figure 11.7

Personal network interconnectedness or integration.

Fourth, we can examine the overall nature of these cliques and networks. For instance, if members of a clique interact frequently, the clique is highly interconnected. The *index of interconnectedness* refers to the amount of member interaction within a unit, such as a clique. The formula is the *actual* links in a group divided by the potential links. Potential links are derived from the formula, where N is the number of people in the group being evaluated and that number is multiplied by that number minus one and the entire result is divided by 2. In figure 11.6 the first clique in the network has a lower interconnectedness index than the second or the third. The actual links (6) divided by potential links or $6 \div 15 = 40\%$. Cliques B and C have 53 percent and 66 percent respectively.[34]

Finally, we can focus more exclusively on any one individual within a clique and analyze that person's ties to the group. In the material presented previously, the clique group was the unit of analysis for interconnectedness and identifying the roles within the network culture. Now, we examine communication not looking in on the group, but by looking out from any one group member's view as to how many people are connected with that one individual. Thus, a *personal network* analyzes the communication among individuals linked to a focal person. In figure 11.7, persons A and B are each linked with the same number of people: each is linked to persons 1 through 5. However, there is a difference in the two personal networks. A's personal network of 5 are not connected with each other to the extent that B's personal network of 5 are connected with each other. When a personal network has overlapping, interrelated, interconnected people with each other as well as with the target individual, it is also said to be an *interconnected personal network*. (This term is used to avoid confusion, but some researchers use the terms interlocking versus radial and high versus low communication proximity to describe this phenomenon.) Links serving multiple purposes with one tie are called multiple ties, as when 1 and 2 are simultaneously friends or fellow workers.[35]

Overall, high interconnectedness usually results in a faster flow of information within the group. This is because information is heard more rapidly and accurately within the group. Also, acceptance of innovations is expected to occur more frequently.[36]

Developing Intercultural Skills Concerning Network Cultures

1. *De-emphasize backgrounds in cases of wide economic disparity in background.* Too often, a person may unconsciously view wealth and power as a solution to many problems, rather than specializing in developing healthy intercultural relationships. It may be better to value attitude relationships, where you can build friendships in the absence of appearance and background homophily.

2. *Seek a common ground.* If one person values material possessions, for example, a second person who finds these values extreme may feel little commonality. Build common ground by emphasizing areas of similarity.

3. *Respect differing values.* Inevitably, values between persons of different cultures clash. Despite these differences, you can build a "homophily" of respect and of tolerance for difference. Encourage communication about those differences and strive to build bridges of affection and empathy.

4. *Try to understand different views of knowledge.* Some people view knowledge as personal only, while other people perceive knowledge and attitudes as valid for everyone.[37] Differences in knowledge and attitudes between two people should not be viewed as I am right and you are wrong, but as differences to be shared. Rather than assume knowledge and attitude heterophily, suspend judgment and invite dialogue.

5. *Develop sensitivity to values.* By remaining alert to others' needs and values, you can turn heterophily into productive interaction. Heterophily gaps can serve to fill areas where you find yourself not very knowledgeable, but you must initiate the discussion.

6. *Find cultural models.* Understanding culturally preferred models can help us grasp a role standard. For example, observing highly credible communicators within a culture can help us discover if the culture relies more on emotion or logic, wisdom or science.

7. *Do not misuse authority.* Many visitors to a host country, for example, feel compelled to share knowledge. Unfortunately, some cultures take this behavior to mean that the visitor is acting without humility. In Japan, a U.S. naval officer stopped to assist a Japanese man whose motorcycle needed emergency repair. The officer acted judiciously, offering indirect advice, asking for permission to try an "experiment" on the motor. The reason for this indirect advice to the distressed motorcycle owner stemmed from the culture's value of not embarrassing people by causing them to feel that they do not know how to do something. A quiet humility was appropriate—the cycle was repaired, and a friendship was established.

8. *Discover how to be trustworthy.* Studies among North Americans show that self-disclosure, friendship, and trust interact. The more trust we reveal, the more likely the chances of establishing and maintaining friendship, as long as we do not come across too strong early in a friendship. Similarly, intercultural relationships rely on trust—and in some cases, the trust extends far beyond our own cultural expectations. For instance, trust in some cultures results from offering hospitality or showing wisdom and insight. Other cultures withhold trust unless there is some proof of loyalty, or in some cases, courage. Developing credibility in the context of intercultural relationships begins by probing ways to be trusted.

9. *Show personal concern for others.* Coorientation is important and translates into a genuine concern for others. Build common ground interculturally; focus on similarities, not differences. Practice empathy.

10. *Be natural but flexible.* Sometimes, being natural can be offensive to other cultures. Then again, a person cannot be radically opposite of his or her basic nature. Be yourself, but talk and act as consistently as you can with the culture. Patience, humility, empathy, and willingness to try are characteristics that may help you maintain naturalness with yourself but flexibility in meeting people from other cultures. Couple with that a willingness to learn and a respect for others, and you will have overcome many beginning pitfalls.

11. *Facilitate a heightened sense of respect for yourself and foster interpersonal relationships by personally adopting some opinion leader qualities, such as gregariousness, amiability, and empathy, as well as knowledge about the topic of concern.* When you interact with other people, for instance, if you "cut them off" or in some way show disrespect, it is unlikely that such people will continue a long-enduring friendship with you. Look for rapport building efforts that often begin with a keen interest and a lot of listening.

12. *Know when and how to involve opinion leaders in message facilitation.* Opinion leaders can add credibility to a message in a way that often reduces the "emotional blinders" and suspicions that sometimes prevent adequate attention to a topic of potential interest. When someone you respect asks you to listen to something, you are more likely to do so than if an impersonal source invites your attention.

13. *Be aware of links, cliques, and networks.* Information travels fast, especially among people who are closely connected. Realizing that people represent their information networks helps us to understand why our interpersonal communication is not the only voice they hear.

This Chapter in Perspective

The concept of homophily implies similarities in social characteristics. Heterophily implies differences, while optimal heterophily indicates a tolerable range of heterophily, where two people are socially homophilous but heterophilous on competence and information. Appearance homophily refers to similarity of dress, looks, and so on. Background homophily refers to similarity of residence, education, social status, race, and so on. Attitude homophily refers to perceived similarities on topics, while value homophily involves outlook and long-enduring judgments of good and bad. Personality homophily emphasizes the similarity of personality between two people. The chapter includes the influence of homophily in communication, such as in persuasion. A scale to measure homophily is presented, also.

This chapter indicates the nature of intercultural communicator credibility and its effects in intercultural situations. Competence (with its several dimensions), trust, coorientation, charisma, and dynamism are foundational concepts. Their effects are found in their contribution to perceived communicator credibility, which in turn produces a climate for persuasion, a symbol of a culture, and source for cultural identity. Obviously, these factors and their effects do not work independently—they work in concert. However, any one factor may be dominant, depending upon cultural expectations and specific crises facing a culture or a nation.

Opinion leaders are information rich people in role relationships with others similar to them in a communication network. They have high interest and competence in the subject, are accessible, have access to relevant information, and are similar to the people they influence. An opinion leader in one particular group probably will not be an opinion leader in another group, unless the needs and conditions of the groups are similar. Functionally, opinion leaders open channels of information. They also reinforce group norms and individual opinions and provide a source of social support.

Some opinion leaders serve a communication information role for only one topic area (monomorphic opinion leadership). Other opinion leaders function as information sources across a variety of topics and are called polymorphic leaders.

Opinion leaders are vital parts of social networks. And social networks, with their accompanying communication roles, influence our interpersonal communication; for in part, we interact not with individuals but with their social networks.

The chapter concludes with an analysis of an integration of interpersonal relationships as information roles and as the foundation for network cultures. By understanding such roles as gatekeeper, bridge, liaison, link, isolate, clique, interconnectedness, as well as opinion leaders, we are in a better position to visualize the social influence in cultures that is associated with these powerful sources of information and persuasion: network cultures.

Exercises

1. Ask some of your friends to complete the interpersonal homophily scale with regard to a person mutually known and somewhat respected. Now have them complete the same scale for someone in the news from a foreign country. What differences do you observe between the two?

2. Ask an international student to discuss with you the nature of interpersonal relationships in his or her country. In what ways does the homophily principle operate the same as in the United States? In what ways is it different?

3. Observe interethnic, intercultural, and intracultural communication in a public place. Do you see some ways in which homophily operates in these situations? How? In what ways does heterophily operate? Why?

4. Ask your friends what they admire most about specific national leaders. Then ask them what they like least about the same national leaders. How does this list compare with the factors mentioned in this chapter?

5. Examine newspaper articles about various cultural leaders both in the United States and abroad. What features are emphasized in these articles? How do these emphases match the five credibility factors found in this chapter?

6. When a highly credible leader takes an unpopular stand on some major issue, list what people around you say about this leader. Does the leader's credibility seem to rise or fall? What kinds of messages change credibility?

7. List examples of charismatic leaders whose routinization of administrative details leads to their unpopularity. What could such leaders do to retard this demise? Ask people in your class to whom they go for information concerning some topic of significance. Who are the opinion leaders? What characteristics do they seem to have? Do they offer opinion leadership on a number of topics? Why or why not?

8. Spend some time in an organization, asking who talks with whom about various topics. Why do patterns of informal communication emerge? What are the interpersonal networks and relationships in the organization?

Endnotes

1. Everett M. Rogers, *Diffusion of Innovations,* 4th ed. (New York: Free Press, 1995).

2. Robert Shuter, "The Centrality of Culture," *The Southern Communication Journal* 55 (1990): 237–49.

3. Ellen Berscheid and Elaine Walster, *Interpersonal Attraction,* 2d ed. (Reading, Mass.: Addison-Wesley, 1978).

4. Rogers, 1995 (see note 1).

5. Everett M. Rogers and D. K. Bhowmik, "Homophily-Heterophily: Relational Concepts for Communication Research," *Public Opinion Quarterly* 34 (1971): 523–37; Carley H. Dodd, "Homophily and Heterophily in Diffusion of Innovations: A Cross-Cultural Analysis in an African Setting" (paper presented at the Speech Communication Association Convention, New York, November 1973). In these studies researchers began to identify the friendships, values, as well as background homophily elements such as same village, religious membership, and so on that researchers continue to affirm in studies today. See also Rogers, 1995 (see note 1).

6. Herbert Menzel and Elihu Katz, "Social Relations and Innovation in the Medical Profession: The Epidemiology of a New Drug," *Public Opinion Quarterly* 19 (1955): 337–52.

7. Rogers, 1995 (see note 1); Gabriel Weimann, "Social Networks and Communication," in *Handbook of International and Intercultural Communication,* ed. Molefi Kete Asante and William B. Gudykunst (Newbury Park, Calif.: Sage, 1989).

8. Stella Ting-Toomey, "Identity and Interpersonal Bonding," in *Handbook of International and Intercultural Communication,* ed. Molefi Kete Asante and William B. Gudykunst (Newbury Park: Calif.: Sage, 1989).

9. James C. McCroskey, Virginia P. Richmond, and John A. Daly, "The Development of a Measure of Perceived Homophily in Interpersonal Communication," *Human Communication Research* 1 (1975): 323–32.

10. Helen Sohns, "Training Mataco Indian Birth Attendants," *Missiology* 3 (1975): 314.

11. Christopher Tuppen, "Dimensions of Communicator Credibility: An Oblique Solution," *Speech Monographs* 41 (1974): 253–66.

12. Dorothy Pennington, "Interpersonal Power and Influence in Intercultural Communication," in *Handbook of International and Intercultural Communication,* ed. Molefi Kete Asante and William B. Gudykunst (Newbury Park, Calif.: Sage, 1989), 261.

13. S. N. Eisenstadt, "Communication Processes among Immigrants in Israel," in *Communication and Culture,* ed. Alfred G. Smith (New York: Holt, Rinehart, and Winston, 1966), 581, 584.

14. Theodore Otto Windt, "The Rhetoric of Peaceful Coexistence: Khrushchev in America, 1959," in *Intercommunication among Nations and Peoples,* ed. Michael H. Prosser (New York: Harper and Row, 1973).

15. Tuppen, 1974 (see note 11).

16. Michael H. Prosser, ed., *Intercommunication among Nations and Peoples* (New York: Harper and Row, 1973), 165.

17. Larry James Winn, "Jimmy Carter and the American Political Image," (paper presented at the Southern Speech Communication Association, Atlanta, April 1978).

18. Thomas E. Dow, "The Theory of Charisma," in *Intercommunication among Nations and Peoples,* ed. Michael H. Prosser (New York: Harper and Row, 1973).

19. Richard R. Fagen, "Charismatic Authority and the Leadership of Fidel Castro," in *Intercommunication among Nations and Peoples,* ed. Michael H. Prosser (New York: Harper and Row, 1973), 223.

20. Dow, 1973 (see note 18).

21. Pennington, 1989 (see note 12).

22. Dow, 1973 (see note 18).

23. Fagen, 1973, p. 215 (see note 19).

24. Molefi Kete Asante, "The Tradition of Advocacy in the Yoruba Courts," *The Southern Communication Journal* 55 (1990): 250–59.

25. Thomas M. Steinfatt, Walter Gantz, David R. Siebold, and Larry Miller, "News Diffusion of the George Wallace Shooting: The Apparent Lack of Interpersonal Communication as an Artifact of Delayed Measurement," *Quarterly Journal of Speech* 59 (1973): 401–12.

26. William J. Starosta, "Toward the Use of Traditional Entertainment Forms to Stimulate Social Change," *Quarterly Journal of Speech* 60 (1974): 306–12.

27. Rogers, 1995 (see note 1).

28. Elihu Katz, "The Diffusion of New Ideas and Practices," in *The Science of Human Communication,* ed. Wilbur Schramm (New York: Basic Books, 1963).

29. Gerald Driskill and Carley H. Dodd, "Opinion Leadership, Personal World View, and Communication Style in an Organizational Culture" (paper presented to the Speech Communication Association, Chicago, November 1988).

30. Everett M. Rogers with Lynne Svenning, *Modernization among Peasants: The Impact of Communication* (New York: Holt, Rinehart and Winston, 1969).

31. Felipe Korzenny and Richard Farace, "Communication Networks and Social Change in Developing Countries," *International and Intercultural Communication Annual* 4 (1977): 69–94; Dodd, 1973 (see note 5); Driskill and Dodd, 1988 (see note 29); Virginia Richmond, "Monomorphic and Polymorphic Opinion Leadership within a Relatively Closed Communication System," *Human Communication Research* 6 (1980): 111–16.

32. Many of these techniques and approaches have been so well developed that we must acknowledge the continued work of Everett Rogers, 1995 (see note 27) in years of refinement of these and many other concepts related to the interpersonal aspects of diffusion and social influence in groups and cultures.

33. Gabriel Weimann, "Social Networks and Communication," in *Handbook of International and Intercultural Communication,* ed. Molefi Kete Asante and William B. Gudykunst (Newbury Park, Calif.: Sage, 1989). See also Everett M. Rogers and D. Lawrence Kincaid, *Communication Networks: Toward a Paradigm for Research* (New York: Free Press, 1981); Rogers 1995 (see note 27).

34. Formula was first noted in Everett M. Rogers, *Diffusion of Innovations,* 2d ed. (New York: Free Press, 1983).

35. Gabriel Weimann, "Social Networks and Communication," in *Handbook of International and Intercultural Communication,* ed. Molefi Kete Asante and William B. Gudykunst (Newbury Park, Calif.: Sage, 1989).

36. Rogers, 1995 (see note 27).

37. Brent D. Ruben, "Human Communication and Cross-Cultural Effectiveness," *International and Intercultural Communication Annual* 4 (1977): 95–105.

Chapter 12

Media as a Source of Influence on Intercultural Communication

OBJECTIVES   *After completing this chapter, you should be able to*

1. Identify ways in which the mass media influence cultural change

2. List the effects of mass media on cultural thought

3. Demonstrate the relationship between mass media and cultural learning, consumerism, and ethnic stereotyping

4. Indicate and discuss how to use strategy involving media to adapt to a cultural audience

5. Identify trends of mass communication changes in international contexts

The mass media's role in intercultural communication is complex, ranging from association with national development to various reasons related to social influence. This chapter surveys the role of the mass media in influencing culture and individuals. Tracing media influence begins with the role media play in creating social influence and persuasion within culture.

Mass communication has enormous effects on culture today. Over the years of work researching this area, scholars developed models in the 1930s and 1940s of an all-powerful mass media (the metaphor of a hypodermic needle was used, see figure 12.1) to limited effects of media to mediating effects and back again to direct effects. As the culture has changed, so media have changed to directly match and play a powerful role in many topics. The complex outcomes of media effects have now been well documented by scholars. Beyond effects on individuals, researchers and media critics have begun to identify how media is shaping cultures throughout the globe. More than merely homogenizing the globe, media are believed to create changes in economics, values, tastes, language, families, and institutions.[1]

Media and Persuasion

With the internet, satellite, and cellular technology, and rapid video and film distribution, we see a world that is saturated with media, though dominated by western media and its gatekeepers and carriers. People have a choice, it is argued, but media create a new world of information and change never contemplated just a few short years ago.

From the 1940s forward, researchers have probed a number of other elements that interrelate jointly with media to explain persuasion and change. Media effects are thought of as dependent on a complex set of variables. Gandy and Matabane state that we must account for the variables that intervene in the theoretical path between exposure and effect, including:

1. Interpersonal networks;
2. Cultural norms, values, and world view;
3. Demographic categories (such as age, education, occupation, ethnicity, and so on) and group memberships;

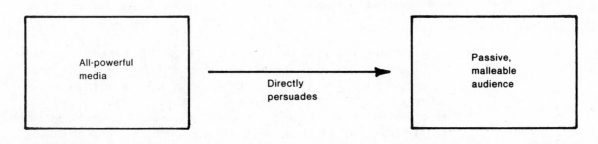

Figure 12.1

Hypodermic needle theory of mass media influence. This early theory was replaced by a model of mediating variables of mass media influence.

4. Motivation, needs, and salient means of gratifying those needs;

5. Personality characteristics.

We must agree that not all mass media effects are directly influential. But the evidence is closing down very few areas that do not hold the major influence potential of media over choices individuals within a culture must face.[2]

Media create awareness. The mass media serve an *awareness* function, creating interest in an event or an idea through direct information about its existence. News, sports, economic developments, political changes, and consumer innovation are but a few of the areas touched by media awareness.

Media set agendas. Mass media develop an *agenda;* that is, they call attention to what is salient. When news commentators say, "And that's the news," the subtle implication is that they have explained what is important and thereby call attention to that event exclusively. For the next few days, people then discuss that agenda. Unfortunately, such "agenda-setting" often omits cocultures who feel marginalized by the agenda omissions for their particular concerns. This marginalization has been true especially for developing nations who experience less access to world media sources.

Media accelerate change. The mass media serve as *accelerators for change,* creating a climate in which change can more easily occur. In instances like the historic Solidarity Movement in Poland there was worldwide media attention, which likely speeded world-opinion change. The atrocities of war in Bosnia and Croatia brought instant world attention to various plights.

Media influence interpersonal sources of information. The mass media often work in concert with and through *interpersonal sources,* depending upon the saliency, immediacy, and timing of the event. Special programs in India and Latin America, such as Telescuela, have enjoyed success in agricultural innovations when radio messages are listened to by an assembly of village family heads and leaders. Following the program a village worker leads a discussion, and the villagers return home, often to implement new ideas for productivity. It seems apparent from such examples that the mass media and interpersonal contacts have a simultaneous influence. As we read in an earlier chapter, mass media often influence opinion leaders who in turn influence a number of people in the culture including other opinion leaders.

Media stimulate rumors. The short nature of many electronic news broadcasts or advertisements means that, by necessity, some details are omitted. This screening sometimes leaves ambiguity or vagueness, features that can heighten the possibility of rumor formation. An old rumor that the Wendy's restaurant chain was mixing worms with its hamburgers was traced to a media story on worm farming in the United States which was construed to be part of the Wendy's operation.

Media as addiction. Scholars are learning that media is like a commodity or a substance. For a minority of individuals in the U.S. media can become obsessive-compulsion. A national study of 2,200 adolescents reported a 5 percent rate of obsessive qualities toward movies and music videos. Although the rate is 5 percent, the acting out level among this minority of media addicted teens was unusually high: 4 times higher alcohol use rate, 3 times higher drug use, 5 times higher sexual promiscuity rate, and generally valueless and proneness to violence. Many countries like Singapore have outlawed certain kinds of video games, believing them to be addictive. Therapists from several countries are reporting clinical depression, lowered performance, and other negative mental health outcomes in a growing number of patients.[3]

Media as source of violence.   The media can predispose some adults and children toward *violence*. As indicated, violence, as one type of what therapists call acting out behavior, is an outcome of several factors. There are two basic theories about media and violence. One is that media can intensify some people already predisposed to violence, something like turning up the heat for those so prone to respond. A second theory argues for direct cultural persuasion with the increased exposure in many parts of the world. In the U.S. children experience over 15,000 hours of violence by age 17. Critics and educators suggest that media have robbed children of innocence and that media have become the direct causes of increases in adolescent crime and violence.

Unintended effects of media.   As this heading suggests the media create effects not necessarily deliberately envisioned by creators of the media programming in question. The mass media have an unintended influence that is sometimes subtle, sometimes obvious, but nevertheless real according to author Aronson.[4] Historical evidence is compelling. The 1977 showing of Alex Haley's "Roots" on ABC television to over 130 million viewers, the largest television audience at that time to watch any one program in the United States, captured attention and inspired African Americans to take an increased pride in their heritage. The number of people in the United States to trace their genealogy increased, indicated by the genealogical inquiries after that showing. In 1978, NBC showed "Holocaust," a dramatization documenting the Nazis' execution of millions of Jews. When the same program was telecast in West Germany, it was credited with providing the motivation for the passage of a law stiffening Nazi prosecution. The 1974 showing of the NBC television movie "Cry Rape," in which a rape victim went through more trouble in trying to press charges than the horror of the rape itself, may account for the decreased number of rapes reported to the police in the weeks that followed.

Contemporary evidence is equally compelling to consider untended effects. What the examples in the previous paragraph suggest is that media presentations that are not intentionally trying to persuade us or even inform us may actually have a greater effect than some media messages with such intents. Perhaps the emotional appeal coupled with the vivid imagery of the cinema and television productions make a subtle impact on our conscious and subconscious minds. Thus, the media may be unwittingly influencing us in beliefs about things we see portrayed on the screen. If McDonald's restaurants advertise at intervals during a children's program that portrays violence, the child may unwittingly associate the positive image of Ronald McDonald with the violence. The reporter who selectively reports riots, murders, earthquakes, and international wars may inadvertently convey to viewers that all people behave violently and that the world is a pretty bad place.

Media shapes thought and logic of individuals in cultures. © Spencer Grant/ Stock Boston.

Media as a Shaper of Cultural Thought Processes

It seems strange to consider the mass media as actually changing the way people think. Yet that is the assertion of the influential work by Marshall McLuhan.[5] He described the mass media as an institution of culture and an influential shaper of culture. His catch phrase, "The Medium is the Message," or massage, as McLuhan so tersely put it, has become almost legend. The clear implication is that a medium dominates our perceptions of an event, since it is precisely through some medium that we become aware of many events in our world. To put it loosely, we become the recipients of those scenes that the director selects, the reporter pens, and the gatekeeper for the news service allows to go through the wire. Should error exist, listeners have no way to check reality since the medium has, in a sense, become the reality.

However, media and culture intertwine, more on the cultural and cognitive level. We have taken some liberties with McLuhan's notions and have adapted and extended his idea that cultures might be examined in stages. Let us posit a relationship about how people in a culture think and communicate. This connection is illustrated in figure 12.2. This relationship is called the *linear-nonlinear* nature of culture. Type I is a culture we might term nonlinear. The thought framework (or how people think) in this society is configurational (nonlinear), which implies that it has multiple themes that are expressed in oral terms. Because of its configurational orientation, type I culture involves the simultaneous bombardment and processing of a variety of stimuli—so these people think in images, not just in words. Time orientation is less important than people and events, and time is not segmented.

Type II is a culture that has transformed auditory and oral communication into visual communication by means of written symbols, organized into linear thought patterns. This culture has beginnings and endings to its events, unitary themes throughout any one episode being described. It is object-centered rather than people- or event-centered, and it is empirical in its use of evidence. Furthermore,

Cultural level:	Type I	Type II	Type III
Thought framework:	Nonlinear	Linear	Nonlinear-linear

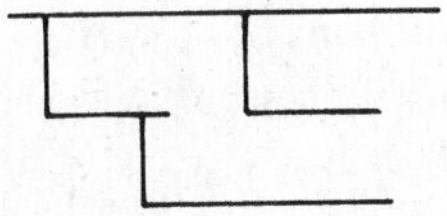

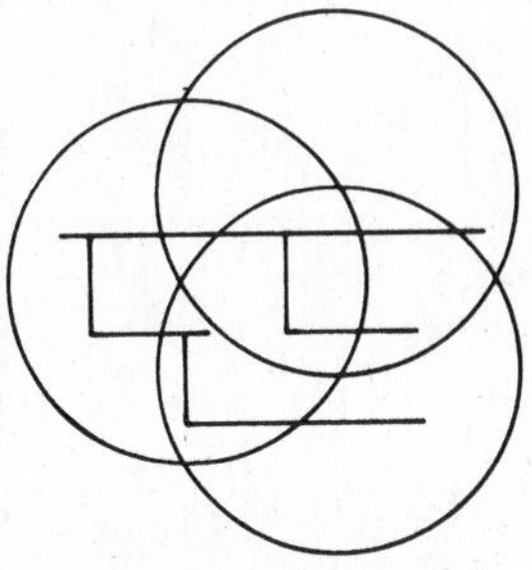

Communication behavior:			
	1. Does not necessarily have one theme.	1. Organized with beginning and ending points and subpoints.	1. Main central theme with numerous subthemes.
	2. Auditory in nature.	2. Consistently has one theme.	2. **Definite time frame with precise beginning and end.**
	3. Evidence stems from traditional wisdom themes and traditional authority.	3. Both visual and auditory, but superimposes visual thought pattern (spatial) on auditory communication.	3. Potentially numerous themes portrayed simultaneously.
	4. Heightened by nonverbal communication.	4. Usually occurs in relatively short amount of time.	4. Primarily visual.
	5. Lends itself to relationships and personal interaction (active communication).	5. Well suited for print media.	5. Evidence stems from experience, societal norms, and cultural themes.
	6. Event oriented (i.e., men returning home from the hunt, discussion ensues).	6. Evidence stems from logic and empiricism.	6. Passive in nature; little or no cultural themes.
	7. Events happen; little plot or planned movement occurs.	7. Object oriented (material technology heralded; machine is more important than person).	7. Events portrayed, objects viewed with wishful thinking.

Figure 12.2

The linear-nonlinear nature of culture through media: Type I, II, and III cultures.

its speech patterns superimpose a visual (usually outlined) structure upon the auditory speech process. That is, these people think from left to right (or right to left in some cultures) in a linear fashion.

Type III is an electronic culture that is simultaneously configurational and linear. Events can be portrayed with several themes running simultaneously, although evidence is based on experiences of receivers who remain passive while viewing events through the media of the culture. Television and film illustrate communication in a type III culture where linear and nonlinear sensory stimuli are focused on the viewer simultaneously. Often, a single, organized theme undergirds the nonlinear collage of filmed scenes.

Media and Cultural Learning

The mass media also indirect or directly affect teaching and promotion of social models. For instance, the negative stereotypes of African Americans, Hispanics, and Asians on television have harmed the images of those minorities. Efforts have been underway for years to eradicate sexism and negative male and female stereotypes from television and books. The opponents of media stereotyping generally object to the role models that the mass media, particularly television, inculcate by teaching through example. According to a news story released in June of 1993 by George Gerbner and associates at the Annenberg School of Communication, after a ten-year study, these minority stereotypes and media usage of minorities have changed little. The exception is African Americans, who appear in the media 13 percent more now than ten years ago.

The media can inadvertently perpetuate stereotypes regarding childbirth, old age, adolescent behavior, sexuality, religion, war, parenthood, and a number of other topics. Serious news programs can help to erase misunderstandings on top-

Media sets an agenda for information and for cultural learning. © Joe Schuyler/Stock Boston.

ics vulnerable to stereotypical perpetuation, but entertainment in movies, the theater, and television may inadvertently foster perceptual error. Fortunately, socially conscious network efforts are attempting to eliminate media stereotyping.

One television-specific application of social learning theory is the *cultivation hypothesis.* Developed by George Gerbner and associates, this principle states that the more a person is exposed to a construction of reality, the more it is believed. For instance, can recurring patterns of violence with women and minorities as victims cultivate a belief that violence against them is okay? Through repeated exposure, television cultivates an indirect, cumulative set of beliefs and ideals. Not all experts agree, but few deny the power of myths conditioned or reinforced by television.[6]

Another theory of mass media effects holds that the mass media solve needs and stimulate individual motivation to acquire solutions to needs. That is, the mass media content can solve audience needs, and sometimes the attention to the medium itself can be gratifying, as, for example, science fiction or mystery stories that provide escapism and emotional release. In fact, it can be argued that the mass media create a motivation to buy new technology and other consumer products; unfortunately, a person or culture experiencing an economically deprived state can feel a great deal of frustration when media are used this way.

Media as the Creator of Consumer and Entertainment Needs

The media, according to *uses and gratification theory,* may satisfy different social and emotional needs at different times in different ways. In fact, the media sometimes share in a division of labor. For instance, a person may want a radio on at work for entertainment, a newspaper for information, and a television for entertainment in the evening. A person who has interpersonal difficulties or problems with self-awareness may turn to various mass media sources.[7] One is tempted to wonder, for instance, if some television talk shows and soap operas are not means of vicariously working out one's own problems or perhaps escaping from them. The rise in recent years of a number of magazines dealing with personal insight and self-help testify to audience needs met by media.

Some evidence suggests that media satisfaction may be connected to a culture's overall satisfaction with its vital information.[8] Ultimately, we may discover that media consumption and satisfaction link with a culture's stress among its members.

Media and Ethnic Identification

As indicated above, for much mass media, only minor change has occurred in the last decade in portraying minorities and various marginalized groups. However, there is a more hopeful side according to media experts Gandy and Matabane. They conclude that media exposure can also facilitate and potentially influence ethnic identification in somewhat positive ways. First, media influence the very names or labels ethnic groups adopt. Second, similarity and identity operate simultaneously. For instance, African American viewing levels for programs with African American characters are higher than Anglo viewing. Further, African Americans evaluate the characters more positively than Anglos and are more likely to *identify* with them. Exposure ranging from "Roots" to "Cosby" to coverage of Jesse Jackson's campaign leads to a stimulus of sorts for

African Americans to find and reinforce positive identity.[9] This same point was articulated by Samuel Betances, himself a biracial sociologist and former talk-show host in Chicago.[10]

Media and International Communication

The international use of media has opened exciting new vistas of a global village. Television, satellite dishes, VCRs, computers and internet, faxes, and cellular technology open new borders around the world. Ironically, however, the technical sophistication of media scope and quality also functions to create several problems.

First, technical innovation, McPhail argues, fractures the mass audience. We are living in a self-help generation, and media have become the way each one can participate in information to foster one's specialized interests. The result is fracture, not uniformity within countries.[11]

Second, media communication has become a vehicle for globally relevant media events. This feature testifies to the overwhelming success of media, which allows the world to visualize simultaneously the same event: the Olympics, crises, famine, war, peace talks. This success in sending global information has been viewed as having a negative result—the same media that inform globally also dominate globally. This concern is so pervasive that it is called *Dallasization* of the world. McPhail continues by saying that corporations pay handsomely for the exporting of media messages and entertainment, and the networks commit upwards of $125 million for future marketing rights of events such as the Olympics.

Third, some observers see media as a support system for one culture to dominate another culture—a uneven process called *hegemony*. This idea implies that mass media colonize the thinking and values of a society. Even the global media events noted previously imply that the dominant elite have control.[12]

Developing nations, often the first ones to feel these effects, are not without blame. There is a thirst for media programming not quenched by local media systems. The result? They import foreign entertainment and programming. Once the system is created, the hungry rhinoceros has to be fed, and he has a big appetite, as Rogers put it. Cost limitations for domestic television production mean the hungry rhinoceros is fed with "Dynasty," "Diff'rent Strokes," and "Dallas."[13]

Rogers laments these developments. They promote little development of the local cultures and create antidevelopment consequences such as *consumerism* and *overurbanization*. Incorrect attributions and stereotypes can be added to the list. Also, the information gap between developed and developing countries continues to widen—at least it is unbalanced.[14]

Developing Skills in Understanding Media and Culture

Developing skills in understanding media as culture involves a set of cognitive skills. By looking for examples of how media and culture interrelate, you can understand the importance of media in the intercultural climate.

1. *Stay tuned to current events.* Knowledge of current events can assist all of your intercultural communication relationships.

2. *Try to be conscious of ways in which the media may have personally affected your perceptions of some group.* The media can portray positive stereotypes

or negative stereotypes. Understanding the source of your personal feelings can be enlightening.

3. *Be aware of the positive value of the media.* The mass media can open us to new ideas, current events, and explanations of certain dynamics that we previously did not know. These positive learning effects can improve our understanding of culture.

4. *Use media as a tool for understanding one view of culture.* Media sources can highlight for us a culture's agenda—things that are considered important for that culture. For example, you might be surprised by how much you can learn about certain American values by browsing through a sales catalog. However, media sources also envision and produce erroneous stereotypes.

This Chapter in Perspective

This chapter reminds readers of the important influence of media in shaping culture and individuals within a culture. Exploring these theories should assist in understanding social influence and the potential communication accommodation that shapes thoughts and action. This chapter initially focuses on the ways in which the mass media create persuasion—and ultimately cultural change. While some scholars argue for the momentous impact of the mass media, others ponder the harmful effects of rapid changes attributed to media systems. Too, observers question the validity of a mass media system that often does not reach the illiterate masses because it favors programming that serves primarily elite, urban populations.

This chapter identifies a number of media and technology effects on culture. Typically, the mass media serve to make people aware of new information and to reinforce previously held opinions. While a large body of research shows that the media serve as influential initiators of information, another body of literature demonstrates that mass media influence is mediated by a large number of factors, including culture and personal influence. This section also highlights an increasing concern about the mass media as a shaper of culture—an institution and a process that influences culture and yet is also sensitive to culture's reciprocal influence. Finally, this section calls attention to some unintentional, yet pervasive, media effects, as well as to the ways in which the media gratify audience needs, offer ethnic identity, and set an agenda for future international communication changes.

Exercises

1. Clip a number of newspaper articles dealing with current events. The same day watch the evening news on one of the national networks. How are the same stories treated? What effect do you think the treatment of each story has, in the long run, on your culture?

2. Try to pick out some item of news or some current rumor that is traceable to a mass medium and then ask twenty people or so three questions: (1) From whom or from what source did you first hear this information (that is, the

news, rumor, etc.)? (2) If from a person, was this person a stranger, an acquaintance, a family member, or a close friend? (3) When did you *first* hear or discover the information? You can ask more questions if you want to, but these simple questions can provide abundant information about the comparison of mass media messages to interpersonal sources. How are the two the same? How do they differ?

3. Some claim that regionalism will overtake the place of the monolithic, centralized mass society in a process called demassification. Some authors predict that demassification will result in the death of the mass media as we know them. Do you agree or disagree? Why?

Endnotes

1. Many books and articles offer critical evidence of the pervasive effects of media and technology communication on culture. The limited effects and intervening effects models of the 1960s and 1970s have been replaced by a technology system and media message mileau that is believed to create powerful changes around the world. See Philip Patterson, *Redeeming the Time: The Christian Walk in a Hurried World* (Joplin, Mo.: College Press Publishing Company, 1995); Michael Medved, *Hollywood vs America* (New York: Perennial, 1992); and other publications by Medved who is a media critic and author.

2. Joseph T. Klapper, *The Effects of Mass Communication* (New York: Free Press, 1960); Thomas E. Patterson and Robert D. McClure, "Political Campaigns: TV Power Is a Myth," *Psychology Today* 10 (1976): 61–64f.; Larry Caillouet, "Comparative Media Effectiveness in an Evangelistic Campaign," (Ph.D. dissertation, University of Illinois, Urbana, 1978); Carley H. Dodd, "Sources of Communication in the Adoption and Rejection of Swine Flu Inoculation among the Elderly" (paper presented to the Southern Speech Communication Association, Biloxi, Mississippi, April 1979); Oscar H. Gandy, Jr. and Paula W. Matabane, "Television and Social Perceptions Among African Americans and Hispanics," in *Handbook of International and Intercultural Communication,* ed. Molefi Kete Asante and William B. Gudykunst (Newbury Park, Calif.: Sage, 1989); David Lewis, Carley Dodd, and Darryl Tippens, *Shattering the Silence* (Nashville: Christian Communications, 1989); David Lewis, Carley Dodd, and Darryl Tippens, *Dying to Tell: The Hidden Meaning of Adolescent Substance Abuse* (Abilene, Tex.: Abilene Christian University Press, 1992); Everett M. Rogers, *Diffusion of Innovations,* 4th ed. (New York: Free Press, 1995); Philip Patterson, 1995 (see note 1); Michael Medved, 1995 (see note 1).

3. David Lewis and Carley Dodd, "Hooked on Hollywood: National Survey Report of Adolescent Media Behavior," (presented to National Youth and Family Conference, Abilene, Texas, February, 1996).

4. Eliot Aronson, *The Social Animal,* 3d ed. (San Francisco: W.H. Freeman, 1980).

5. Marshall McLuhan, *The Medium is the Message* (New York: Bantum, 1967).

6. Gandy and Matabane, 1989 (see note 2).

7. Elihu Katz, Jay Blumer, and Michael Gurevitch, "Utilization of Mass Communication by the Individual," in *Inter/Media,* ed. Gary Gumpert and Robert Cathcart (New York: Oxford University Press, 1979).

8. Philip Palmgreen and J. D. Rayburn, "A Comparison of Gratification Models of Media Satisfaction," *Communication Monographs* 52 (1985): 334–46.

9. Gandy and Matabane, 1989 (see note 2).

10. Samuel Betances, "The Media and Multicultural Societies," in *Intercultural Skills for Multicultural Societies,* ed. Carley Dodd and Frank Montalvo (Washington, D.C.: SIETAR, 1987).

11. Thomas L. McPhail, "Inquiry in Intercultural Communication," in *Handbook of International and Intercultural Communication,* ed. Molefi Kete Asante and William B. Gudykunst (Newbury Park, Calif.: Sage, 1989).

12. Peter Yaple and Felipe Korzenny, "Electronic Mass Media Effects Across Cultures," in *Handbook of International and Intercultural Communication,* ed. Molefi Kete Asante and William B. Gudykunst (Newbury Park, Calif.: Wadsworth, 1976); Gandy and Matabane, 1989 (see note 2).

13. Everett M. Rogers, "Inquiry in Development Communication," in *Handbook of International and Intercultural Communication,* ed. Molefi Kete Asante and William B. Gudykunst (Newbury, Calif.: Sage, 1989).

14. Kaarle Nordenstreng and Wolfgang Kleinwachter, "The New International Information and Communication Order," in *Handbook of International and Intercultural Communication,* ed. Molefi Kete Asante and William B. Gudykunst (Newbury Park, Calif.: Sage, 1989).

Chapter 13

Intercultural Communication, Innovation, and Creating Planned Change

OBJECTIVES   *After completing this chapter, you should be able to*

1. Identify variables that influence the rapid spread of information among cultural members

2. Describe the decision-making process of individuals when confronted with information needs

3. Categorize early and late adopters of innovations by their personality characteristics

4. Develop strategies for effective intercultural efforts at social change and development

5. Summarize the factors that predispose a person or culture toward innovativeness

6. Understand factors related to group and organizational innovativeness

What would you do if you were asked to introduce a YMCA program in a predominantly Hispanic community? How would you involve elderly people in a community nutrition program? Working with a medical team as an intercultural communication specialist, how could you invite highland Indians in Ecuador to engage in different eating habits to correct a culture-wide nutritional deficiency? Suppose you were interested in a summer field trip to Guatemala to help in a reforestation project where woodland mountainsides have been stripped for firewood. What process of communication would initiate and sustain a reforestation effort among villagers? If you were working at a summer camp, how would you involve surrounding communities in a program of volunteerism to help you with large projects at the camp?

The principles stated throughout this book will assist you in being effective interpersonally and with groups. This chapter provides an answer to the question: How do you develop strategy for innovation and intercultural change? Two theory positions are stated. One is diffusion theory and its suggestions for strategic change, and the other is a summary of organizational development and change.

A few years ago, the Kenyan government offered herdsmen new land with low-interest loans near a new beef producing location. The spread of this information, the decisions that were made, and the consequences that resulted are typical categories that social change researchers would investigate. Of course, the emphasis throughout this discussion of diffusion and social change is intercultural communication. In this case, the process of social influence is concentrated on.

How Diffusion and Innovation Studies Emerged

The study of diffusion is traditionally linked with social and economic development in societies. For example, the stone axes among the Yir Yoront of Australia were symbols for masculinity and authority. Their replacement by steel axes led to the demise of that culture. Since values were undermined, prostitution, drunkenness, and other social breakdowns became rampant, and the culture lost its traditional structure. Early studies from 1940 to 1980 largely focused on change as a one-way process.[1]

Now, numerous research studies have used communication and cultural variables to analyze the social change process. The trend is to focus on how systems and people can be joint participants in exploring change. The early days of dominant development programs communicating change have given way to alternative paradigms involving participation, sharing knowledge, and equality among people.[2]

From that body of research come several important concepts of how information (particularly innovations) flows. This information flow affects people in cultures. This is called *diffusion theory.*[3]

Components of Diffusion and Innovation Processes

The basic components in the theory of diffusion and social change are: (1) the *innovation,* (2) which is communicated through certain *channels* (3) over *time* (4) among members of a *social system* (5) with certain *effects.* These categories stand as a type of model, highlighting major components. Everett Rogers and his various co-authors prolifically synthesized much of the diffusion research and theory, as an earlier footnote explains. Close to three thousand diffusion studies have been conducted with a number of aspects of diffusion applied to numerous intercultural situations.

Diffusion theory concentrates on how innovations are diffused in a culture. © Spencer Grant/Stock Boston.

The innovation as a cultural message. An innovation is an idea or product perceived as new. Since perception is a subjective measure of the innovation that does not make it objectively new or acceptable, then an innovation has two components: (1) an *idea* component and (2) an *object* component, which is the physical referent of the idea. All innovations contain the first component, but not all innovations have a physical referent. For instance, adoption of improved farming methods is easily observable. Other innovations, however, such as political ideology, rumors, and new events, may not be as directly observable. Like any other persuasive message, an intercultural innovation message contains inherently motivating features.

The following five characteristics of innovations can make innovation messages innately motivating:

1. *Relative advantage* is the degree to which the innovation appears better than its predecessor. For instance, a government development officer must show how a village water system has advantages over the old method of carrying water from the river.

2. *Compatibility* represents the degree to which the innovation is congruent with existing beliefs, attitudes, values, experiences, and needs of the receiver. In intercultural efforts to persuade nationals to use a certain crop fertilizer, one obstacle sometimes facing change agents is cultural attitude and world view

toward the earth. Among certain Central American Indians, for instance, the adding of fertilizer is considered sacrilegious. Consequently, a successful field worker must outline persuasive messages that demonstrate the cultural compatibility of the innovation. One solution for Central American Indians has been to describe the fertilizer as food for the earth.

3. *Complexity* is the extent to which the innovation appears difficult to understand and to use. As you might expect, simplicity is linked to adoption.

4. *Trialability* is the degree to which an innovation can be sampled or tried on a small-scale basis. For that reason, free samples constitute one reliable strategy for marketing new products in the United States.

5. *Observability* is the degree to which an innovation can be viewed and scrutinized before actual adoption. For instance, if a target population can see a comparison of a fertilized crop and an unfertilized crop, chances for adopting fertilizers are heightened.

These five factors must be carefully considered in message development for planned social change.[4]

The time it takes for a message to spread throughout a social system is an important and distinct consideration in the diffusion process. However, personal choices depend not only on available information but also on the characteristics of the people making those choices.

Decision Making and Choice About Innovations

When we face an especially important decision about a purchase, for example, or about engaging in some behavior, we almost always go through a period of awareness of the possibilities, talk with others if it is a major decision, and then continue a mental debate until a decision is made. Intercultural communication concerning some innovation also causes people to engage in a decision-making process. Figure 13.1 presents a model to depict this process. In the *knowledge stage,* the individual becomes aware of the innovation and gains some understanding about it. The *persuasion stage* marks the person's evaluation of the innovation. During the *decision stage,* an individual may run a small-scale trial of the innovation. A potential adopter must mentally debate, choosing to adopt or reject the innovation. In some cases, a small-scale trial may constitute an important part of the decision to adopt. Many times, marketing firms apply this principle as they distribute free samples of everything from soap in the mail to sandwiches at the grocery store. After decision comes *implementation,* which involves adoption of the innovation into the existing system. At the *confirmation stage,* the person seeks reinforcement for the innovation decision that has been made. The alternatives, of course, are continuance or discontinuance of the decision. The dotted lines in the figure indicate that these stages may be short-circuited, compressed, and even reversed.

The model underscores how different information sources can best serve as resources at different points along this time continuum. Media impact the decision-making process mostly at the knowledge and confirmation stages. Personal influence is highest at the persuasion stage, while people rely on self-influence at the decision stage.[5]

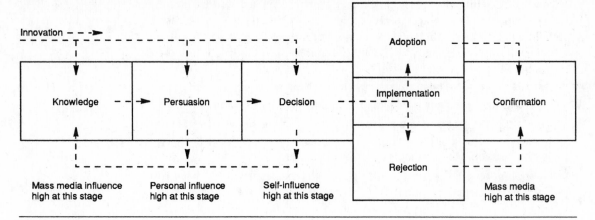

Figure 13.1

Innovation-decision process and channels of influence at various stages.

Whenever individuals choose an innovation, some people adopt early, late, or not at all. The measure of time of adoption, called innovativeness, can be plotted mathematically. An average plotting across a number of studies results in a bell-shaped curve, illustrated in figure 13.2. The curve's significance lies in dividing the curve into mathematical segments (called standard deviations), which allow us to *categorize* people across these consistent units. Immediately, we observe that an entire sample can be divided into those who are early and those who are late, simply by splitting the sample in half at the average time of adoption. The question that remains is whether some kind of systematic difference lies between the early people and the late people. The answer, from previous research studies, is yes. In fact, investigations have taken the question a step further by analyzing not just the early and late adopters but also the percentages that fall under this bell-shaped curve within the early group and the late group. Furthermore, researchers like Rogers have been able to detect personality differences among these categories.

1. *Innovators* make up the first 2.5 percent of the population who adopt under the bell curve. Their most salient characteristic is that they are *venturesome*. They are eager to try new ideas and usually can afford to take risks. For one thing, they are often deviant from their social system, meaning that they do not necessarily follow the norms of the locale where they live. In fact, other more normative members of the social system may think them very unusual. In addition, innovators are open to irrational adoption and consequently are subject to making many mistakes. Perhaps their irrationality is one reason why the majority of their social system do not necessarily look upon them with favor.

2. *Early adopters* compose the next 13.5 percent of the population who adopt an innovation. This group is best characterized by the word *respect*. As a whole, they are more innovative than the majority of the social system, but not so much as to be deviant. They are usually more local than innovators and adhere closely to community norms. In a sense, they are not too far ahead of other peo-

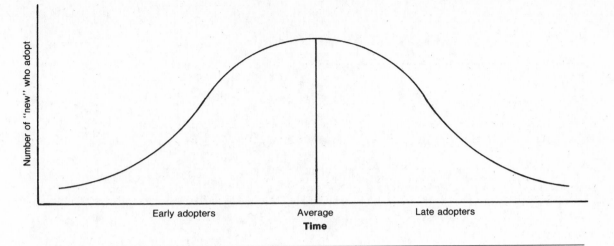

Figure 13.2

This bell-shaped curve shows the theoretical adoption of an innovation over time by the members of a social system. The curve develops when the number of new people adopting the innovation are plotted against time.

ple in the culture, as the innovators are, but they are knowledgeable enough and respected enough to be a type of role model. The early adopter category is especially important in that it contains the highest number of opinion leaders.

3. The *early majority* are the 34 percent of the population who adopt an innovation just before the average person of the social system. Not many leaders stem from their ranks, but they serve as an important legitimizing link in the diffusion process. A key word for this category is *deliberate.*

4. The *late majority* are the 34 percent who adopt just after the average member of the social system. For the most part, adopters in this group are cautious, since they approach innovations with healthy skepticism. They may well see the value of an innovation but do not move to adopt it until public opinion favors the innovation or until peer group pressure is strong enough to motivate their adoption.

5. The *final adopters* are the final 16 percent of the population who are the last to adopt an innovation or who may never adopt at all. They are highly traditional, usually basing decisions on those of previous generations. Often quite suspicious of innovations, innovators, and change agents, this group is oriented toward local issues, and members of this group may function as negative opinion leaders.

Factors Associated with Individual Innovativeness and Change in a Culture

People choose innovations not only because of the qualities outlined earlier, but also because of a cluster of factors they experience within their culture. Why do some people adopt earlier than others in their social system? Why are some social systems resistant while others are open to change? These kinds of questions have led to research exploring *innovativeness.*

This Masai tribal man has adopted social change by putting a film canister in place of a traditional ear decoration. (Photo by Mike Moore, Kenya.)

Sources of innovativeness or factors related to why people might adopt an innovation more quickly are as follows.

1. *Communication sources.* Orientation outside the social system, media exposure, and interpersonal communication contribute to innovativeness.

2. *Attitudes toward change.* Some individuals who are initially responsive to change in one set of innovations are often receptive to additional innovations.

3. *Leadership status.* A person who perceives herself or himself as an opinion leader typically adopts early.

4. *Social and demographic variables.* Education, literacy, and previous experience predispose individuals to early adoption.

5. *Personality characteristics.* Cosmopolitanism, venturesomeness, empathy, desire to achieve, and levels of aspiration also contribute to early adoption.

6. *Economic factors.* Size of organization, high income, and loan ability are some of the economic factors that can intensify innovativeness.

7. *World view.* A personal or cultural outlook toward fate, family, or spiritual fortunes can restrain innovativeness.

4. The organization de-emphasizes rules and procedures in members' performing their roles. Extreme formalization reduces innovativeness.

5. Organizational members experience high social interconnectedness. Interconnectedness is the degree to which people have a number of social communication networks. New ideas flow more rapidly, contributing to innovativeness.[8]

Strategies for Group Innovation and Change

Many plans and methodologies have proven helpful in introducing change in organizations. The diffusion approach, discussed in the first part of this chapter, offers valuable insights to the problems of organizational change. The strategies listed here for consideration with planned, organizational change are especially useful for organizational innovativeness.[9]

Get close to the market. Staying close to the customer has been a traditional phrase of organizational researchers as long as a decade ago. Now, in his book *Liberation Management,* Tom Peters emphasizes that change is market oriented: "*The* innovation issue is learning that in a fashionable world we *must* create organizations that attempt, at least, to survive by getting close to the market, putting zanies in charge, and staying small enough to shift focus fast."[10]

The presence and communication of innovative information. When organizations consistently emphasize development and innovation, members are obviously more inclined to accept change. Even if no norm for innovation is already established, decision makers can focus on and diffuse information about new processes. An up-to-date data base can stimulate the creativity of organizational members. The key is the communication and availability of new data.

Social network method. The social network methodology emphasizes the need to make contact with gatekeepers, opinion leaders, and liaisons in the informal communication networks that exist within the organization, as described in an earlier chapter. These are key people who are sufficiently influential in not only providing information to potential users, but in urging their acceptance of innovations.

Outside pressure. Obviously, organizations change in response to strikes, boycotts, demonstrations, pressure group demands, and legislation. Also, outside professional consultants can bring about change. The intervention strategy of consultancy can not only provide new data assessing needs for change, but the interventionist can often convince key leaders and top management of the structural, procedural, and economic methods that enhance performance.

Change in top leaders. Organizations change when the top management exercises personal and corporate change. During the economic recession of the 1980s, Lee Iacocca, president of Chrysler Corporation, accepted only a dollar a year for his otherwise extremely high salary. He then asked the auto union working with Chrysler to make a wage concession, which was accepted. As a result, Chrysler went from virtual bankruptcy to become a highly competitive automobile manufacturer in just a few short years and even paid off its federal loan early (which by obtaining presented the federal government with an innovative change).

Job expectation technique.   The job expectation technique (JET) is used to clarify job expectations among managers, peers, and subordinates. The method allows individuals to write their job descriptions. Relevant management team members also contribute to the job description. By using this team-building approach, job productivity increases, role conflict and ambiguity are decreased, and quality-directed job effort results.

Management by objectives.   Management by objectives (MBO) creates a system in which management and subordinates participate in setting goals for the subordinate. This method increases participatory style and communication and clarifies job expectations for a prescribed time period. The most common goals are set for six months or a year, after which evaluation is made and recommendations for the future are suggested.

Job enrichment.   The job enrichment technique attempts to make the work more satisfying. The assumption here is that challenging and more satisfying jobs create more motivation. Job enrichment can include changes of title, structure, implementation, responsibilities, and growth potential in a job category.

Team building.   The team-building strategy involves providing team members with an opportunity to discuss possibilities for change. Because team members discuss their ideas for improvement and make implementation suggestions, they tend to work more cohesively. Also, the ideas are generally useful, although not every idea can be implemented. The Japanese model of *quality circles,* a similar concept, has richly paid off for their corporate cultures and is being adopted by other nations.

Organizational development.   Organizational development (OD) attempts to increase organizational effectiveness by connecting individual desires for growth with organizational goals. OD is not so much technique in itself as it is a name for a total set of change strategies for the entire system over time. The heart of the planning really involves creating a support climate discussed earlier in this text whereby individuals are encouraged to develop creativity. By encouraging communication encounters among all levels of team management and employees, individual goals and organizational goals can be linked.[11]

Terms related to OD include first order change and second order change. First order change offers changes in externals, such as colors, dress, new machines, and even procedure. Second order change implies changing the mission and purpose, the fundamental ways of thinking and doing, values, and world view. Most agree that second order change is more difficult but makes the biggest difference in the long run. First order change is necessary, but we should not be under the illusion that these changes necessarily cause a shift in fundamental outlooks and beliefs.

Changing the root metaphor.   An excellent way of creating second order change is to change a group's root metaphor. Leaders in organizational theory and organizational change, such as Karl Weick, remind us that people operate on key assumptions that stem from their personal metaphors or the organization's most important metaphors about the organization. For instance, if the metaphor about a company is "family" then we could expect significant behaviors arising from that metaphor, assuming an individual accepts it and there are no intervening conditions preventing its potential actions. To change the root metaphor is to change fundamental assumptions about the way people look at their jobs, co-workers, and the organization as a whole.

The following are principles for a person seeking to engage in intercultural persuasion and social change. Although the list is not exhaustive, it does point to relevant considerations for the practitioner.

1. *Tailor a message to fit cultural values and past experiences.* Some years ago, a large drug-manufacturing firm in the United States developed a new headache pill to be taken without water. However, subsequent marketing revealed that the pill was unsuccessful. For a while, the manufacturers were baffled about the failure until finally they discovered that Americans simply had little faith in any headache medicine taken without water. Americans are more comfortable taking pills with water. These examples illustrate why a study of cultural values and a perusal of past experiences is vital to an understanding of effective change.

2. *Consider need before an innovation's introduction.* After an unsuccessful introduction of irrigation among the Papago Indians, Dobyns (1951) concluded that introduction of change will be successful to the degree that those who are affected by the change are brought into its planning and execution and thus made to feel that the innovation is their own.

Margaret Mead once said, "change can be best introduced, not through centralized planning, but after a study of local needs"[12] Those local needs must involve indigenous planning.

3. *As a communication planner, concentrate on opinion leaders.* One failure in intercultural communication may well stem from a preoccupation with innovators in a culture rather than opinion leaders. Characteristics of opinion leaders have already been documented. The key method is to discover respected members of a social system and work with those members. Numerous intercultural failures in social change occur from faulty planning and a disregard for cultural opinion leaders.

4. *Close the heterophily gap.* A *change agent* is a professional who works for adoption of an innovation within a social system. Usually, this person is heterophilous from most people with whom he or she is trying to bring about change. However, this person can close that heterophily gap by working with opinion leaders. Heterophily should be less of a barrier to opinion leaders than to their followers. In this way, information is introduced to the social system, and its dissemination is maximized.

Developing Skills in Planning for Innovation and Cultural Change

5. *Anticipate and prevent undesirable social consequences of innovation adoption if possible.* The phenomenon of overadoption is not altogether uncommon. For example, after the introduction and diffusion of the weedkiller 2, 4-D, some farmers were so impressed with the results that they used it on their cornfields to excess and ultimate waste.

6. *Perform demographic analysis of the target culture.* Understanding significant demographic variables and their importance can enhance a change movement. For instance, dominant involvement with youth in a culture that advocates decision making among and respect for older cultural members can result in a youth movement with little future potential or leadership. Targeting the message toward specific demographic categories has several additional advantages:

   a. The message is more easily tailored to fit existing conditions of various age groups, professions, and so on.

   b. The message has a chance of being spread by word of mouth among homogenous groups distinguished by their demography.

   c. The message can be aimed at "influentials" and informally respected persons in a village or other unit.

7. *Understand the use of the mass media.* Communication theory indicates that the mass media serve primarily to alert villagers to innovations, to reinforce villagers who already have adopted, and to develop a climate for change. Studies show, however, that the mass media do not influence adoption as directly as demographic, interpersonal, and cultural factors. Thus, the message must take on a grass roots, interpersonal dimension. If the media are used, the communication planner must understand their strengths and limitations. For instance, a strategy using a knowledge of demographic factors and interpersonal communication factors in conjunction with the mass media would be more effective than any one of these factors acting alone.

8. *Build bridges not walls.* The first people to adopt an innovation frequently are persons culturally disengaged from mainstream cultural life. Consequently, their rapid acceptance may produce a credibility gap for subsequent adopters who belong to the cultural mainstream. Therefore, work toward introducing the innovation to informal opinion leaders and to decision makers. Such a strategy need not ignore innovators, but direct contact with opinion leaders does provide a legitimizing effect that lends credence to the message. Consequently, opinion leaders' influence, through their existing communication networks, accelerates message flow and impact.

9. *Don't seek the cultural recluse.* This suggestion is related to the previous point. More rapid growth and acceptance occurs among people who are culturally involved in terms of group membership, attention to the mass media, and favorable attitudes toward others in their villages. Therefore, try to choose adopter prospects carefully, avoiding the disgruntled, disengaged, and reclusive individual. The cultural recluse may temporarily join the change agent's efforts but ultimately prevent long-range cultural penetration.

10. *Direct efforts toward members of existing homogeneous units.* People organize themselves into units that approach similarity in viewpoint, lifestyle, and

so on. While the most obvious units are the tribe, clan, and village, do not overlook nuclear and extended family units and friendship relations. Data reported earlier in this chapter revealed that the more accelerated adoption rate was accompanied by consultation with friends. Inviting sociological networks of friendship units or other salient units to jointly hear an innovation message is one useful strategy.

11. *Practice empathy.* Numerous studies show that empathy is highly linked with change agent success. Listen rather than dominate.

12. *Realize that some innovations may be harmful.* You may believe that some message or idea is necessary or important—not every culture agrees. If you are not wanted or are uninvited, then your effort may be futile. Cooperation is important. Remember that some innovations do not fit in a culture. Develop enough insight so that you do not give steel axes to a culture where such an innovation could bring harm.

This Chapter in Perspective

The theory of diffusion and social change provides insight into a grass roots movement of ideas from person to person within a culture. For instance, various characteristics describe early and late adopters of innovations. Understanding the decision-making process helps us to appreciate different sources of information at various stages of the decision process. This chapter also addresses the question of how individuals perceive innovations in terms of their relative advantage, compatibility, complexity, trialability, and observability. The variables that predispose a person or culture to innovativeness and social change are also examined. Finally, strategy considerations offer practical suggestions for intercultural communication efforts in persuasion.

Planners and communications-development people need to weigh the ethics of social change in their deliberations and to consider genuine needs and a systems approach. Change planners must invite all the input possible in making policies and implementing them. Inviting cultural members to help in the formulation and planning stages can ensure highly ethical decisions and principles. Organizational innovation and change is summarized here and is a function of several factors noted in the chapter.

Exercises

1. Make an appointment to visit some organization that works on community development and social change. It may be some social or governmental organization in your town or city. During the meeting, ask how programs are developed, instituted, and communicated to the target populations. Find out what works well for this organization and what does not work well. How do their insights compare with the principles reported in this chapter? How could the principles in this chapter assist community agencies in communication?

2. Find current magazine articles, newspaper articles, and interviews dealing with some new idea or new technology. Gather as much factual reporting as you can from these sources and then compare what various people are saying about the innovation. Do people who seem more interested in the innovation do or say anything different from people who seem opposed to the innovation? Why or why not? Try to sketch a profile, from reading these interviews and articles, that characterizes early and late adopters of this innovation.

3. Choose some new idea or technology, perhaps the same one you chose for exercise 2. Interview five people, and ask each one to define what they like best and least about the innovation. Ask them what characteristics could be presented about the innovation that would motivate people toward persuasion. Do these characteristics add to the list of innovation characteristics given earlier in this chapter? What is it about persuasive messages that makes them compelling?

Endnotes

1. Everett M. Rogers, *Diffusion of Innovations,* 4th ed. (New York: Free Press, 1995). Rogers has been prolific in this area of communication studies with numerous publications. The most well known is the *Diffusion of Innovations* series first begun in 1960 and now in its fourth edition. Rogers and his colleagues have developed outstanding principles and theoretical positions about the nature of innovation and change. The author acknowledges the tremendous contributions and gratefully shares them with his readers in various adapted forms, having tested many of these concepts in field research myself.

2. Everett M. Rogers, "Inquiry in Development Communication," in *Handbook of International and Intercultural Communication,* ed. Molefi Kete Asante and William B. Gudykunst (Newbury Park, Calif.: Sage, 1989).

3. The topics of social change communication efforts are varied, ranging from agricultural practices to family planning. Scholars continue to try to explain the social change process, including the nature of the innovation, Everett M. Rogers, *Communication Strategies for Family Planning* (New York: Free Press, 1973); the nature of the interpersonal relationships involved, Felipe Korzenny and Richard Farace, "Communication Networks and Social Change in Developing Countries," *International and Intercultural Communication Annual* 4 (1977): 69–94; the nature of intercultural contact and attitude change, William B. Gudykunst, "Intercultural Contact and Attitude Change: A Review of Literature and Suggestions for Future Research," *International and Intercultural Communication Annual* 4 (1977): 1–16; news diffusion, Bradley S. Greenberg, "Diffusion of News in the Kennedy Assassination," *Public Opinion Quarterly* 28 (1964): 225–32; and other variables. For the rhetorical nature of social change, see William J. Starosta, "Toward the Use of Traditional Entertainment Forms to Stimulate Social Change," *Quarterly Journal of Speech* 60 (1974): 306–12; William J. Starosta, "Critical Review of Recent Literature," *International and Intercultural Communication Annual* 2 (1975): 108–15; William J. Starosta, "The Village Worker as Rhetorician: An Adaption of Diffusion Theory," *Central States Speech Journal* 27 (1976): 144–50.

4. Rogers, 1995 (see note 1).

5. Rogers, 1995 (see note 1); Carley H. Dodd, "Sources of Communication in the Adoption and Rejection of Swine Flu Inoculation among the Elderly" (paper presented to the Southern Speech Communication Association, Biloxi, Mississippi, April 1979).

6. W. H. Schmidt, *Organizational Frontiers and Human Values* (Belmont, Calif.: Wadsworth, 1970); W. H. Schmidt, "Communication, Change, and Innovation: A Selective View of Current Theory and

Monochronic-Polychronic Scale
Charles Phipps J.D.

Please answer the following questions using this scale:

Strongly agree(SA) Agree(A) Neutral(N) Disagree(D) Strongly disagree(SD)

1. I usually feel frustrated after I choose to do a number of tasks when I could have chosen to do one at a time.   SA A N D SD

*2. When I talk with my friends in a group setting, I feel comfortable trying to hold two or three conversations at a time.   SA A N D SD

*3. When I work on a project around the house, it doesn't bother me to stop in the middle of one job to pick up on another job that needs to be done.   SA A N D SD

4. I like to finish one task before going on to another task.   SA A N D SD

*5. At work or school, it wouldn't bother me to meet at the same time with several different people who all had different matters to discuss.   SA A N D SD

6. I tend to concentrate on one idea before moving on to another task.   SA A N D SD

7. The easiest way for me to function is to organize my day to day activities with a schedule.   SA A N D SD

*8. If I were a teacher and had several students wishing to talk with me about assigned homework, I would meet with the whole group rather than one student at a time.   SA A N D SD

*9. I like doing several tasks at one time.   SA A N D SD

10. I am frustrated when I have to start on a task without first finishing a previous one.   SA A N D SD

*11. In trying to solve problems, I find it stimulating to think about several different problems at the same time.   SA A N D SD

12. I am mildly irritated when someone in a meeting wants to bring up a personal topic that is unrelated to the purpose of the meeting.   SA A N D SD

13. In school I prefer studying one subject to completion before going on to the next subject.   SA A N D SD

14. I'm hesitant to focus my attention on only one thing, because I may miss something equally important.   SA A N D SD

15. I usually need to pay attention to only one task at a time to finish it.   SA A N D SD

Scoring: Add the scores with SA = 1, A = 2, N = 3, D = 4, SD = 5. Reverse score (SA = 5, A = 4 etc.) for items marked with *. Scores of 30 and below indicated monochronic style; scores of 42 and above indicated polychronic style (reliability = .73).

Ethnocentrism
Kregg Hood Ed.D.

1.	Visitors to America will naturally want to adopt our customs as soon as possible.	SA	A	N	D	SD
2.	Generally speaking, the way we do things in my home town is the best way to do things in most other places as well.	SA	A	N	D	SD
3.	Foreigners have a responsibility to learn our customs when they come to the United States.	SA	A	N	D	SD
4.	Most people in the world really wish they could become American citizens.	SA	A	N	D	SD
5.	In reality members of other cultures cannot adequately copy the characteristics of American culture.	SA	A	N	D	SD
6.	It is wrong for visitors to our country to refuse to adapt to our customs when they come here.	SA	A	N	D	SD
7.	The ceremonies in Africa that initiate a boy into manhood are barbaric.	SA	A	N	D	SD
8.	Western cultures are more civilized than African cultures.	SA	A	N	D	SD
9.	The rapid influx of immigrants into the USA will eventually ruin our country.	SA	A	N	D	SD
10.	American usage of time in business is better than in Africa or South America.	SA	A	N	D	SD
11.	The Asian practice of honoring the elderly is interesting but not very practical.	SA	A	N	D	SD
12.	It would be better if English were spoken as a universal language.	SA	A	N	D	SD
13.	No country has done more for the advancement of civilization than the USA.	SA	A	N	D	SD
14.	It is unwise to trust a foreigner until you know him better.	SA	A	N	D	SD
15.	South Americans are usually poor because they are lazy.	SA	A	N	D	SD
16.	The native dress of an African tribesman looks silly.	SA	A	N	D	SD
17.	Americans tend to be smarter than the people from most other countries.	SA	A	N	D	SD

This scale used with potential expatriates, generally surfaces extreme ethnocentrism.

Scoring: Add the scores with SA = 5, A = 4, N = 3, D = 2, SD = 1. Scores of 35 and below indicated low ethnocentrism, scores of 45 and above indicated high ethnocentrism. Norms: mean = 40, s.d. = 5; Reliability = .82.